D0961845

American
SAVAGE

ALSO BY DAN SAVAGE

Savage Love: Straight Answers from America's Most Popular Sex Columnist

The Kid: What Happened After My Boyfriend and I Decided to Go Get Pregnant

Skipping Towards Gomorrah: The Seven Deadly Sins and the Pursuit of Happiness in America

The Commitment: Love, Sex, Marriage, and My Family

It Gets Better: Coming Out, Overcoming Bullying, and Creating a Life Worth Living (ed.)

DAN SAVAGE

American SAVAGE

INSIGHTS, SLIGHTS,
and FIGHTS
on
FAITH, SEX, LOVE,
and POLITICS

DUTTON

DUTTON
Published by the Penguin Group
Penguin Group (USA) Inc., 375 Hudson Street,
New York, New York 10014, USA

USA | Canada | UK | Ireland | Australia | New Zealand | India | South Africa | China
Penguin Books Ltd, Registered Offices: 80 Strand, London WC2R 0RL, England
For more information about the Penguin Group visit penguin.com.

Sections of "At a Loss" first appeared as "Our Man of Perpetual Sorrow" on *This American Life* (May 1,
2009). "Crazy, Mad, Salacious" first appeared in slightly different form as "My Other Dog's a German
Shepherd" on *This American Life* (March 16, 2007). "The Straight Pride Parade" first appeared in different form as "Happy Heteroween" in *The Stranger* (October 29, 2009). "On Being Different" first appeared
in slightly different form as the foreword to *On Being Different: What It Means to Be a Homosexual* by
Merle Miller, Penguin Classics edition, 2012. "Extended Stay" first appeared in slightly different form
as "In Defense of Dignity" in *The Stranger* (October 9, 2008). Sections of "It's Happened Again" first
appeared in *The Stranger* (November 4, 1999).

Additional permissions appear on page 299.

REGISTERED TRADEMARK—MARCA REGISTRADA

LIBRARY OF CONGRESS CATALOGING-IN-PUBLICATION DATA
Savage, Dan.
American Savage : insights, slights, and fights on faith, sex, love, and politics / by Dan Savage.
pages cm
ISBN 978-0-525-95410-1 (hardcover)
1. Savage, Dan. 2. Gay men—United States—Biography. 3. Gays—United States. I. Title.
HQ75.8.S28A3 2013
306.76'62092—dc23
[B]
2013001374

Printed in the United States of America
1 3 5 7 9 10 8 6 4 2

Designed by Nancy Resnick

While the author has made every effort to provide accurate telephone numbers, Internet addresses,
and other contact information at the time of publication, neither the publisher nor the author assumes
any responsibility for errors or for changes that occur after publication. Further, the publisher does
not have any control over and does not assume any responsibility for author or third-party websites or
their content.

*Penguin is committed to publishing works of quality and integrity.
In that spirit, we are proud to offer this book to our readers;
however, the story, the experiences, and the words
are the author's alone.*

For my father, who lives in a red state, watches Fox News, and votes Republican—but loves me and mine just the same.

And if my ways are not as theirs
Let them mind their own affairs.
Their deeds I judge and much condemn,
Yet when did I make laws for them?

—A. E. Housman

Contents

American SAVAGE

Introduction

This book? The one you're holding in your hands?

I built it. Or wrote it. Or whatever.

Pretty much everything I wanted to say in this book is *in the book*—the one you're holding—but they tell me I have to write an introduction before I can tell people I've finished writing this book. They tell me books like this always have introductions. But here's the thing: Anything I might want to say *here* (in the introduction), I've already said *there* (in the pages that follow).

My editor—to whom I'm very grateful—tells me not to stress out too much about the introduction. Very few people read introductions, as it turns out, so she tells me not to sweat over the introduction too much. It seems that most readers skip the introduction and go straight to the first chapter and start reading the actual book. So it doesn't matter what I say here. I could libel and defame people, reprint my favorite cookie recipes, or try my hand at writing erotica and no one would ever know.

It's freeing, in a way, to think that I could write anything I want to here, on the pulped trees set aside for the introduction, because it's the appearance of having an introduction that matters, not the introduction itself.

This is the first book I've written in a while. It used to be easy to find the time to write a book. "Finding the time to write a book" is *not* to be confused with "actually sitting down and writing a book." Whether writers actually sit down and write is a complicated thing. But finding the time to write used to be pretty simple. Basically, whenever you weren't writing articles or columns, you worked on your next book. But now that all writers everywhere are contractually obligated to blog and tweet all day long, *who has time to work on a book?* Unless you're Glenn Beck or Bill O'Reilly and you can pay someone else—just guessing here—to write your books for you, or you're a high-functioning meth addict who doesn't need to sleep, finding the time to write a book these days is pretty much impossible.

I'm not Glenn Beck or Bill O'Reilly. And I'm not a meth addict. I managed to get this book written without meth or ghostwriters. (I did have an assistant, though, and her name is Ingrid and she's been calling me every day for two weeks yelling, "WRITE THE FUCKING INTRO SO WE CAN BE DONE WITH THE BOOK AND GET PAID ALREADY!")

Did you know that the intro is the last thing someone who's writing a book actually gets around to writing? And by the time a writer sits down to write the intro, he or she—some of my favorite books are by lady writers—is a complete fucking mess. Writing a book is *hard*. Finishing a book is *murder*. I've been up for days. I haven't gotten a decent night's sleep for weeks, let alone eaten anything in which the first two ingredients aren't corn syrup and food coloring. Decent food, human contact, and proper hygiene are always vague and fading memories at this stage of the book-generation process.

Don't get me wrong: *I'm grateful for this gig.* If I weren't writing—columns, blog posts, tweets, and books—I'd be waiting tables somewhere (which I actually enjoy) or working at an office job (which I do not enjoy), instead of working at home most of the time, in my pajamas, surrounded by empty bags of Oreos and sticky bottles of Boylan Black Cherry soda.

Two more pages to fill, Ingrid tells me. I think I'll use this space to reassure Mike Huckabee that I'm okay.

Mike Huckabee, the Fox News host, former governor of Arkansas, and onetime GOP presidential hopeful, worries that I'm unhappy. Mike told Tony Perkins, president of the anti-gay hate group Family Research Council, on his radio show—on Mike's radio show—that I'm "unnecessarily rude, vile, and angry," and he suspects this is the case because I'm "not a happy person." Mike said he sincerely wants me to be happy, and then Tony threatened to sue me, and Mike didn't point out that being sued doesn't make people happy, which leads me to doubt the sincerity of Mike's concern for my personal happiness.

But Mike Huckabee is a man of God—an ordained Baptist minister—so I'm going to take him at his word.

Hey, Mike? I'm happy. I'm fine. Yes, I can sometimes be rude, vile, and angry. But I strive to be just rude, vile, and angry enough to get my point across. And there's a lot out there to be rude, vile, and angry about, Mike, from income inequality to our never-ending health care crisis to candy-corn Oreos. And if I ran around the country calling your love sick, sinful, and perverse, Mike, you'd be angry too.

But you can rest assured that I'm a happy person, Mike.

Have you seen my husband in a Speedo? I'll send you a picture, if you'd like. No gay man with a husband who looks like mine in a Speedo is unhappy. At least not all the time. Sure, I'm unhappy sometimes, but who isn't? But I actually have a lot to be happy about. I have a great job! Giving sex advice, running my mouth on television, getting paid to be rude to vile and angry assholes like your buddy Tony Perkins. I also live in a pretty nice town, close enough to the offices of my newspaper that I can walk to work, and that—having a short commute—turns out to be a big contributing factor to happiness.

"When you look at Americans' day-to-day activity," the author Dan Buettner told NPR, "the top two things we hate the most on a day-to-day basis are, number one: housework and number two: the daily commute in our cars. In fact, if you can cut an hour-long commute each way out of your life, it's the [happiness] equivalent of making up an extra forty thousand dollars a year."

I don't own a car. I don't even know how to drive, and again, I live close enough to my not-at-home office that I can walk to work. So no commute for me. And there are two bars that I love—shout-outs to the bartenders at Liberty and Smith—between my office and my house, so the hour most Americans spend in their cars commuting, I spend at Liberty or Smith imbibing. As for housework: My husband is a stay-at-home dad, and he takes care of most of that. In a Speedo.

Other things that correlate strongly with happiness: friends, marriage, and a cause. I have friends (lots), I'm married (same guy, eighteen years), and there are lots of causes I care passionately about. Carl Jung said that to be happy, human beings need "good physical and mental health," which I've got, and "the faculty for perceiving beauty in art and nature," which I do. And—don't mean to get graphic here but—research has shown that semen is a natural antidepressant, Mike, and there's no shortage of that in my life either.

So, yeah, I'm pretty happy, Mike, don't you worry about me. But I appreciate your concern. It's very Christian of you to worry about my happiness.

Oh, hey, they tell me this is long enough to fill the pages allotted for the intro. So I'm going to get out of the way. Thank you for buying my book. I hope you enjoy it. If you don't, you might want to pick up Neil Steinberg's *You Were Never in Chicago,* Alice Dreger's *One of Us: Conjoined Twins and the Future of Normal,* or Daniel Bergner's *What Do Women Want?* They're all great reads.

1. At a Loss

My dad was in the first class of the ordained permanent diaconate. This sentence may require some unpacking for my non-Catholic readers. So here you go, heathens: Before a man could become a Catholic priest, he would typically spend a year serving as a Catholic deacon. Deacons are to priests as novices are to nuns—or they used to be. In the 1980s, to address a growing shortage of Catholic priests (a shortage that has since gotten worse), the Church created the permanent deaconate. Ordained deacons could do almost everything priests do—pass out wafers, preach sermons, baptize babies—and so my dad was up on the altar of our church every Sunday when I was growing up. Which makes me something of a rarity among Catholics: I am a preacher's kid. (Technically I'm the kid of *two* preachers, as my mother was a Catholic lay minister.)

As the son of a Catholic preacher man—just one of his four children—I attended Catholic grade schools, and yes, I was an altar boy. But, this isn't a story about being sexually abused by a priest. Because I wasn't sexually abused by a priest. Looking back at my childhood, I can identify a couple of close calls—a priest from our parish once took me and another boy skinny-dipping at a Catholic school's indoor pool after hours—but the experiences were creepy, not abusive. In addition to being a Catholic deacon, my father was also a Chicago cop—a cop who loved his children and wore his service revolver wherever he went—and that fact may have given pause to any rapey priests who crossed paths with his children.

I am no longer a practicing Catholic. If I had to apply a religious label to myself, it would be "agnostatheist," an awkward hybrid of agnostic and atheist. I don't believe in a higher power, but I do cross myself on airplanes. I once blew up at a friend who thought he was being funny when he inverted one of the crucifixes in my "ironic" collection of Catholic kitsch. And when I take the Lord's name in vain—when I mutter "Jesus Christ" through clenched teeth as my lead-footed husband passes someone going ninety miles an hour—I am seeking the protection of a higher power.

But I go right back to not believing once my plane safely lands or once Jesus or Joseph Smith or Xenu safely delivers us back to the right-hand lane. Which makes me a hypocrite and an ingrate, I suppose, but not quite an atheist or a believer. Not quite.

I wasn't supposed to turn out this way. I went to the same Catholic grade school my mother and grandmother did; I had the same fourth-grade homeroom teacher—Sister Mary Amadeus—at St. Ignatius as my mother. I was baptized as an infant; I had my first communion at age seven; I was confirmed at age thirteen.

But even at age seven—the age of reason, according to the Catholic Church—I was having trouble reconciling this "loving father in heaven" I'd heard so much about with this "eternal damnation" thing the nuns were constantly threatening us with. But the fatal blow was the realization that I was gay. This realization came at roughly the same time I entered a Catholic high school for boys who were thinking about becoming priests. It was a bit like realizing you're an alcoholic on your first day of work at the Budweiser bottling plant.

Despite all those years of Catholic schooling, my first reaction to the realization that I was gay wasn't, "Holy shit, looks like I'm going to find out what that eternal damnation thing is all about." Instead I thought, "What the Church says about homosexuality—that can't be right. They must be wrong." This intuitive sense that the Church was wrong about homosexuality—this unshakable conviction that the Church was wrong about *me*—led me to wonder what else the Church might be wrong about. Virgin births, maybe? Transubstantiation? Resurrection? Masturbation? It didn't take long to arrive at the biggest doubt of all: the existence of God.

I transferred to a public high school and stopped going to church—except for the odd family wedding, baptism, or funeral. (And they are all odd, aren't they?) For most of my adult life I was likelier to walk into a Planned Parenthood clinic for a Pap smear than to walk into a church.

Then my mother died.

A virus can lie dormant in your body for so long that you can forget you were ever infected. Then something happens that weakens your immune system and the virus seizes its opportunity. For more than two decades the Catholicism I'd contracted at St. Ignatius had lain dormant, manifesting itself only in airplanes and passing lanes. But the seeming immunity I'd long enjoyed was weakened by my mother's death. Because after that sunny, awful day in Tucson, Arizona, when my mother's life ended, I started slipping into Catholic churches.

Not for weddings or funerals, but on totally random days of non-holy non-obligation. Tuesday afternoons, Friday mornings. And I wasn't just going to church. I was going out of my way to go to church. There's a Modernist Catholic chapel near my office in Seattle. The Chapel of St. Ignatius at Seattle University—I think St. Ignatius is stalking me—won a big architectural award (the New York chapter of the American Institute of Architects honored it; a scale model of the chapel is now part of the permanent collection of the Museum of Modern Art in New York), but I think it's ugly. All Modernist Catholic churches look the same to me—like someone slapped a crucifix on the living room wall at the *Brady Bunch* house.

St. James Cathedral in downtown Seattle, which is a much longer walk from my office, looks like a Catholic church should. It looks like St. Ignatius, actually, the parish church attended by four generations of my family. Acres of stained glass, rows of marble columns, crowds of plaster saints. St. James is open for "private contemplation" seven days a week. In the months after my mother's death, I found myself slipping into St. James on more weekdays than I care to recall. The church was usually empty, aside from one or two volunteers straightening up the hymnals and offering envelopes in the backs of the pews—or that's what they were pretending to do. I think they were really there to keep an eye on the homeless people that sometimes come in to get out of the rain. Every once in a while a priest would hurry through, taking care to avoid making eye contact with me or any of the other bums.

When my mother used to call with bad news—a relative I hadn't seen in years diagnosed with cancer, an old friend with a desperately ill grandchild—she would always say, "I know you don't pray, Daniel. Just keep them in your thoughts." My mom knew that thoughts were the best I could do. And for months after my mother's death, sitting in the pews at St. James Cathedral, I stared at a marble statue of the Virgin Mother, trying to keep my mother in my thoughts.

We were close in that cliché way that so many gay men and their mothers are. Today anti-gay bigots argue that being gay is a sinful choice that gay people make because our parades look like so much fun. Psychologists and psychiatrists used to argue that being gay was a choice your mother made for you. Mothers who were too close to their sons, mothers who "smothered" their sons, risked turning them gay. The shrinks got it backward, mistaking one of the consequences of being gay—one of the perks of being gay—for the cause. The kind of relationship I had with my mother didn't make me gay. I had that kind of relationship with my mother because I was gay.

By her own estimation my mother was a good Catholic. She believed that Jesus was her savior and that He died for her sins; she believed in the Resurrection, the Trinity, the Sacraments, the Virgin Birth, the Immaculate Conception. (Don't make the mistake of confusing those last two: Jesus was born to a virgin; his mother Mary was conceived without original sin—those are totes different paranormal phenomena, people.) My mother also believed that sex was sacred, and that people, particularly people who had children, should be married. To each other. But she didn't believe that being a good Catholic meant blind obedience to the old men who ran her church.

You could say that my mother was a good American Catholic. She believed that women should be priests and that priests, male or female, should be allowed to marry. Even each other. And after four pregnancies in four years—and a heart-to-heart with a parish priest who told her that the pope *might* be wrong about birth control and *definitely* wouldn't be paying her children's Catholic school tuition— my mother concluded that birth control was not a sin.

"Catholics have long realized that their own grasp of certain things, especially sex, has a validity that is lost on the celibate male hierarchy," the Roman Catholic author and historian Garry Wills wrote in an essay in *The New York Review of Books*. My mother was one of those American Catholics—a woman with a better grasp of sex than the elderly celibates.

My mother prayed that the leaders of her church would come around during her lifetime, particularly on the issues of celibacy and the ordination of women. Unfortunately, the Church, under the last two popes, moved further away from her. Whenever the current pope, "Benny," as she called him, or the previous pope, "JP2," condemned birth control, attacked gay people, or insisted that women could never be priests, my mother would call me, sigh audibly, and say, "It's like they're trying to make Lutherans of us all."

But she refused to leave the Church. It was her church, too, she insisted, just as much as it was Benny's or JP2's. And popes had been wrong in the past, she'd say. If previous popes were wrong about the movement of the planets, then, by God, the current pope could be wrong about contraception. The little voice in her head said the same thing the little voice in mine did: "That can't be right; they must be wrong." But that voice, a voice that destroyed my faith, somehow strengthened hers.

And my mother's faith was tested.

When I was in high school, the Catholic television network in Chicago featured my family in a special—my dad the deacon, my mom the lay minister, and all four of their confirmed children. (Confirmation is like a bar mitzvah for Catholic kids, only with fewer presents and more modest parties.) One of their sons was even a high school seminarian. We were the perfect Catholic family. We used to joke—just a few years later—about the Catholic television network returning to do a "Where Are They Now?" special. We were still a Catholic family, of course, but we were no longer perfect. My dad had divorced my mother, resigned from the deaconate, remarried, and moved to California. My mother was dating and having sex outside of wedlock. My brother Billy had gotten a vasectomy. A couple of pregnancies were terminated. And I had come out of the closet.

While my mother was a liberal, pill-popping, ordination-of-women-backing Catholic, she nevertheless took it hard when I told her I was gay. Her first impulse was to call a priest. Father Tom, whose last name I won't disclose for reasons that will become clear in a moment, rushed over. Sitting on the front porch, my mother broke down in tears and told Father Tom why she was so upset: "Danny says he's gay."

Father Tom put his hand on my mother's knee and said, "So am I, Judy."

Father Tom told my mother that it was better this way. He knew I had thought about becoming a priest and worried that I might be doing it for the same reason he did: to hide from my sexuality. He had tried that, and it didn't work. Then he had tried to drown his homosexuality in alcohol, as so many Catholic priests of his generation did, and that didn't work either. He assured my mother that it was better for me to live this way—it was better for me to come out, even to her, *especially to her*—than to live the life he had lived.

Whenever someone asks if I was abused by a Catholic priest—and you would be surprised how often gay Catholic adults are asked that question—I always say no, I was never abused by a priest. I was saved by one.

Thanks to Father Tom and my mother's own moral sense, the same moral sense that prompted her to trust her own judgment about contraception, my mother came around on the my-son-is-gay issue pretty fast. And she came out swinging. A rainbow bumper sticker on her car, a PFLAG[1] membership card in her purse, and an ultimatum delivered to the entire extended family: I was still her son; and anyone who had a problem with me had a much bigger problem with her.

The Catholic Church still has a problem with me.

One of the cards in the back of the pews at St. James, tucked in with the hymnals, is addressed to nonpracticing Catholics. WELCOME BACK it reads in large letters across the top.

> Are you a Catholic who's been away from the church? Welcome Back classes are designed to help you return to the sacraments and regular church attendance.

---

1 PFLAG stands for Parents and Friends of Lesbians and Gays.

A return to the sacraments. I sometimes fantasize about "returning" to the sacraments, particularly the sacrament of confession. "Forgive me, father, for I have sinned. It's been twenty-nine years since my last confession. I hope you packed a lunch."

I sit in the pews at St. James because part of me—the part that had me slipping away from work and into church—wishes what I was taught at St. Ignatius was true. I want there to be a heaven. I want my mother to be looking down on me. Though, and I say this both as a gay man and a professional sex-advice columnist, *not all the time*. There are things a mother has a right not to know, my mom used to say, and I did my best to keep those things from her while she was alive.

My mother's death, somehow and unexpectedly, drew me back—not to the faith or to sacraments, but to *church,* to a church, to the pews of St. James Cathedral. I was tempted. I am tempted. I wouldn't have wasted so much time sitting in St. James in the months after my mother's death if I weren't. My husband wouldn't have found numerous WELCOME BACK cards in the back pocket of my jeans that awful spring if I weren't tempted.

But when I feel tempted, when I feel like, maybe I could go through the motions, maybe I could return to the sacraments, maybe I could take what comfort I could from the Church and its rituals, the pope goes to Africa and says that condoms spread AIDS, or an archbishop in Brazil excommunicates a Catholic mother for getting her nine-year-old daughter a life-saving abortion but not the Catholic man who raped and impregnated that woman's nine-year-old daughter.

Or I contemplate how the Church views me and the two people I love most in the world, my husband of eighteen years and our fifteen-year-old son, and I think, no, I can't even go through the motions.

The Church doesn't want me back—not as I am. Every other week there's a story in the news about a Catholic grade school expelling a child who has gay parents or a Catholic parish firing a gay employee—someone they knew to be gay or lesbian when they hired them—for marrying their same-sex partner. When it comes to homosexuality, church leaders are growing ever more, er, rigid.

Gay Catholics are being targeted in ways that straight Catholics are not. While the Church still opposes birth control and abortion, divorce and remarriage, and all non-procreative sex acts (even within marriage), and has become more aggressively political over the last two decades, it can't identify and persecute heterosexual Catholics who trust "their own grasp of certain things." Catholic women have abortions at the same rate as non-Catholic women. Ninety-eight percent of Catholic women use birth control—presumably with Catholic men. Ninety-three percent of Catholics support the use of condoms to prevent disease and HIV transmission. Seventy percent of American Catholics think abortion should be legal. Sixty-seven percent of Catholics believe premarital sex is morally acceptable.

When it comes to the issues of sexual morality, straight Catholics—Catholics like my mother—are telling the celibates that while they may run their church, they may not run, or ruin, their lives.

When a Catholic priest stands on the altar on Sunday and looks out over his congregation—like my father once did—he sees Catholic mothers and fathers sitting with one or two children. He can't see the birth control pills and the abortions that prevented those couples from having more children than they wanted or could provide for. He can't tell just by looking who among his flock has been divorced and remarried—or who, for that matter, masturbates. The Church condemns homosexuality as "intrinsically and gravely disordered." The Church uses the exact same language to condemn masturbation: "Masturbation is an intrinsically and gravely disordered action," reads the Catholic catechism. But there is no effort to turn away the children of divorced and remarried Catholics, or the children of Catholic families that by some miracle only have two children, or to seek out and fire heterosexual church employees who use birth control or masturbate.

The pope, cardinals, archbishops, bishops, and priests know that straight Catholics are using birth control, obtaining abortions, having premarital sex, having sex for pleasure, and masturbating. But they can pretend not to know it because they can't actually see it. All straight Catholics automatically get rounded up to "good Catholics" because their sexual sins can only be guessed at or inferred.

Priests can't do the same when a gay couple walks into a church. A priest can refuse to see—or refuse to do the math on—all the masturbating, birth controlling, divorcing, and remarrying that he knows straight parishioners are getting up to, but he can't *not* see homosexuality. So long as we insist on coming out, so long as we insist on living and loving openly, our "sin" is visible to the naked eye. And Church leaders can't see past our homosexuality; they can barely see our *humanity,* which is hugely ironic, considering how many of those priests in the pulpits of Catholic churches are gay themselves. Father Tom was one of them. I was almost one of them.

Of course I don't think homosexuality is a sin at all. But for the Catholic Church it all comes down to the nature and purpose of sex. Back to the Catholic catechism: "The deliberate use of the sexual faculty, for whatever reason, outside of marriage is essentially contrary to its purpose," as human sexual expression must open to the "gift of life." Birth control, masturbation, homosexuality—any sex act that isn't open to the "gift of life" is wrong. Some well-meaning "liberal" Catholics claim that the Church isn't singling out gay people since all non-procreative sexual activity is wrong regardless of whether it's gay or straight. But only gay people are expected to live lives devoid of intimacy and romantic love. (And, I'm sorry, but you can't claim that supernatural phenomena—miracles—routinely take place and then insist that homosexual acts are closed to the "gift of life." Either God can do anything or he can't, AMIRITE?)

"The natural purpose of sex is procreation," Wills writes, summing up the Church's position, "and any use of it for other purposes is 'unnatural.' But a primary natural purpose does not of necessity exclude ancillary advantages. The purpose of eating is to sustain life, but that does not make all eating that is not necessary to subsistence 'unnatural.' One can eat, beyond the bare minimum to exist, to express fellowship, as one can have sex, beyond the begetting of a child with each act, to express love."

The Catholic Church would like human sexuality to be about one thing—reproduction—but biology tells us differently.

"For *Homo sapiens*, sex is primarily about establishing and maintaining relationships, relationships often characterized by love, or at least affection," writes Christopher Ryan, in *Psychology Today*. "Reproduction is a by-product of human sexual behavior, not its primary purpose.

"The vast majority of species have sex only to reproduce—a function reflected in a very low ratio of sex-acts-to-births," Ryan continues. "Gorillas, for example, have intercourse at most about a dozen times per birth." Humans are different. "We and our chimp and bonobo cousins typically have sex hundreds—if not thousands—of times per birth."

The Church got sex wrong. It is confused about what sex is for, confused about what sex does, confused about why we have it and why we have so much of it—shocking, I realize, considering that the Church is run by people who don't have sex. (Or aren't supposed to have sex.)

Fact is, straight people have more sex—a lot more sex—than they do babies. And gay people have sex for the same reasons straight people do . . . *most of the time.* Gay or straight, we're all having sex for pleasure, for release, and to cement bonds of intimacy. And every once in a while, some of us—even some of us who are gay—have sex in order to make a baby.

The Church has backed itself into a familiar corner. One day the Church will have to admit that it made a mistake. And one day the Church will have to admit that scores of popes, hundreds of theologians, and countless princes of the Church were wrong. Wrong about sex. Wrong about birth control. Wrong about masturbation. Wrong about pleasure. Wrong about homosexuality. One day the Church will have to admit that it got human sexuality wrong, just as it got the movement of the planets wrong.

I'm not holding my breath.

This is typically where Catholics and non-Catholics alike jump in and ask why someone who isn't a Catholic—or isn't a Catholic anymore—cares so much about the Church's teachings on human sexuality. Why concern yourself with the teachings of the Catholic Church when you're not a believer? I could claim that the Catholic Church's teachings concern me only inasmuch as they impact my life. I could point out that the Catholic Church is a political player in the United States, and it backs anti-gay legislation and supports efforts to ban my marriage, adoptions by same-sex couples, and civil rights protections for sexual minorities. I could insist that I don't have the luxury of ignoring the Church.

But I would be lying.

Oh, the Church's teachings do impact my life and the Church actively persecutes gay people and I don't have the luxury of ignoring the Church—all of that is true.

But while I can't see myself going back to the Church—I can't see myself going through the motions of the sacraments, despite their comforting familiarity—some part of me wants the Church to want me back. I want the option of going back. Not because I *believe*—I don't—but because I ache. I ache for my loss.

There are very few tangible remains of my childhood and of my connection to my mother. I have photographs, yes, and I have my memories, and I have some mementoes. But the family home is gone, my mother's possessions dispersed. There's nowhere I can go to feel my mother's presence, no space I can enter that we once physically shared, other than church.

That's why I wound up spending so many afternoons at St. James, the church that reminded me so much of St. Ignatius—St. Ignatius, the church where my mother was baptized, where she took her first communion, where she married, and where her funeral was held. In church I feel her presence, not God's presence, and I can almost feel her looking down on me from the heaven she believed in so passionately.

And if she was right—if there is a heaven and she is looking down on me—I hope she remembers to look away now and then.

Because there are things a mother has a right not to know.

2. It's Never Okay to Cheat (Except When It Is)

I s it ever okay to cheat?"

There's only one answer to the question. Wait—that's not true. There's more than one answer to that question, but there's only one answer an advice columnist is allowed to give. And it goes like this: "No, nope, never, don't even think about it, you scumbag, and don't ask me that question again. Ever. What the fuck is wrong with you?"

To roughly paraphrase the favorite author of hopeless romantics everywhere: It is a truth universally regurgitated (at least by people in my line of work), that a married man in possession of a wife must never be told that cheating is okay. The same goes for a married woman in possession of a husband. No one should ever be told that cheating is okay. Because cheating isn't okay. Ever.[1]

It's not just advice columnists: Licensed therapists and daytime

---

1 For the sake of clarity, and because most of the letters I get about cheating—contemplating cheating, seeking my blessing to cheat, complaining about having been cheated on—are from straight people, I'm not addressing husbands cheating on husbands or wives cheating on wives. This chapter is aimed squarely at straight married people. It's not that married and/or partnered gays and lesbians don't cheat. We can and we do. But gay male couples are much likelier to have hashed out agreements about when "cheating"—sex outside the relationship—is permissible; those agreements are easier to hash out, in part, because threesomes are easier to negotiate when both partners are equally attracted to a potential third. (And can it even be considered cheating if you're cheating at one end of a guy while your husband cheats at the other end of the same guy?) Lesbian couples, for their part, are much likelier to be successfully and effortlessly monogamous. (This presents a real problem for those who argue that monogamy is a defining characteristic of marriage. If marriage should be reserved for those who are good at monogamy, only women should be allowed to marry—and they should only be allowed to marry other women.)

talk show hosts are never allowed to tell married people that cheating is okay. Because cheating isn't okay. Ever.

Except for those times when it *is* okay. Except for those times. And except for those times when cheating isn't just okay, but absolutely, positively, and without question *the right thing to do*.

Except for those times—and some other times—cheating is never okay. Ever.

Okay?

I've been writing Savage Love, my syndicated sex-advice column, for more than twenty years. My typical workday begins with a brisk swim through a deluge of e-mail that arrived overnight from married people trapped in sexless marriages. (When strangers ask me what I do for a living—I spend a fair amount of time in hotel bars—I say, "I get e-mail from sexually frustrated married people, and no, I don't work for AshleyMadison.com.") Some of these sex-starved spouses are in honest, sincere, and pathetic love with their other halves; some have small children; some have chronically ill wives or husbands who depend on them for their health insurance and day-to-day care. Some have faced emotionally crushing sexual rejection at the hands of their spouses for years—some for decades—but they have refused to physically or emotionally abandon the partners who sexually abandoned them long ago. Other e-mail missives are from married people with harmless kinks that their spouses will not or cannot indulge, needs that could be met discreetly and safely by, say, a professional sex worker (a dominatrix, a foot model), instantly alleviating the kinky partner's simmering resentment ("Why won't she do *this* for me?!") and the vanilla partner's exasperation ("Why won't he stop asking me to do *that* for him?!").[2]

---

2 It should be noted that kinky men outnumber kinky women by a factor of a hundred, which is why this example is gendered the way it is.

Frequently these sexually frustrated men and women tell me that they're happy in every other aspect of their married lives. They enjoy their spouses' company, their spouses are good partners and wonderful parents, and they don't want to destroy the lives they've built with their spouses. Many add that they can't see leaving their husbands or wives—or fear being harshly judged by others for leaving them—over something so "trivial" as sex. Some have spouses they can't leave: They're physically disabled or their spouses are; they're financially dependent or their spouses are; they get their health insurance through their spouses or their spouses get their health insurance through them. Many mention having gone five, ten, or fifteen years— sometimes longer—without any sexual intimacy at all. And they usually write to me when they reach the point where they're being driven nearly out of their minds by sexual deprivation. (It's amazing how nontrivial sex becomes when you haven't had any for a decade.)

Then they ask me what to do.

I'm supposed to tell them to remain faithful and to maybe find a couples' counselor. (Or another couples' counselor if they've tried that already, and they've all tried that already.) I'm supposed to tell them to work harder at their marriages. I'm supposed to tell them to drag their spouses to an endocrinologist to have their hormone levels checked. I'm supposed to urge them to drag their spouses to a shrink to rule out depression. And as the advice industry is biased in favor of women—women are our primary customers, you see, as women are likelier to ask for advice (and directions)—I'm supposed to blame the husbands.[3] When the people complaining about sexless marriages are

---

3 My favorite example of a sexist advice columnist: A few years ago, on a quick visit to Toronto, I picked up a copy of the *Toronto Sun*. The tabloid, at the time, ran two advice columns: Dear Abby (written by the original Abby's adult daughter) and Dear Val, by Valerie Gibson, a column I'd never run across before.

The first letter in Dear Val on the Friday I was visiting the city was from a woman who was thinking about divorcing her husband. Four years earlier the woman's husband announced that he was "no longer interested in sex," without giving a reason. "In the last six months I've lost a lot of weight and worked hard on getting fit and suddenly he wants to

male, I'm supposed to tell them that they're to blame. When the people complaining about sexless marriages are female, I'm supposed to tell them that their husbands are to blame.

But that's not what I tell them.

Because if someone truly loves his wife, if someone truly loves her husband, if someone has kids, if someone has already been to a cou-

---

restart our sex life!" The woman resents the fact that her husband "couldn't love me the way I was before" and has decided, now that their kids are grown, to get a divorce. Val's response? "You've worked at getting fit and are at the weight that feels good and you're seeing your life more clearly than you have before," Val wrote. "Consult a divorce lawyer."

Legit advice, I guess, and I've certainly advised people to consult divorce lawyers. But Val didn't mention that the wife might bear some small responsibility for the breakdown of her marital sex life. (I happen to believe that routine physical maintenance—which includes roughly maintaining your body weight—is one way we show our partners that we value them.) Yes, her husband didn't give her a reason for his loss of interest in sex, but what was he supposed to say? "I'd fuck you, honey, but you've put on a lot of weight"? Men are constantly told—by their wives, by Oprah, by Dr. Phil, by other advice columnists—that any discussion of weight is off-limits. The exact same people who urge honesty in all things warn men that they're absolutely, positively not allowed to be honest about *that*. The same people that urge us to own and honor and share our feelings tell men that they're absolutely, positively not allowed to feel *that*.

The next letter in Val's column was from a man who believed his wife had cheated on him—multiple times. Now that his kids were grown, he was contemplating divorce. "She has always denied having affairs but I have quite a lot of evidence to the contrary. I want her to be honest with me so our marriage can continue." Val's advice? The man shouldn't divorce his wife—he shouldn't even confront her with the evidence of her infidelities, as that would put his wife between "a rock and a hard place," leading her "to deny everything." No, Val says, he needs to take a long, hard look at the real culprit: himself!

"If you're convinced of her guilt," Val writes, "you should be asking yourself why she needed to have affairs (assuming your evidence is substantial), what went wrong in your marriage, *and why you didn't satisfy her*." [Emphasis added.]

Val could have said something similar to the wife in the first letter. Something went wrong in her marriage too. She wasn't satisfying her husband either. The first woman's weight gain—there I said it—turned her husband off. And did her husband cheat? Nope, he just lost interest. And now that she's lost some weight, he's interested again—and that's proof, according to Val, that her husband doesn't love her and never did. Divorce him! But when a wife cheats on her husband? Repeatedly? And the husband has evidence that confirms his suspicions? Well, says Val, the husband was clearly doing something wrong. He must have failed to satisfy her in some mysterious, undefined way, and her infidelities are his fault!

It's a wonder that straight men seek relationship advice at all. So many "advice professionals"—from marital counselors to advice columnists to talk show hosts—are like Val: Whatever the problem is, it's *his* fault. Professional advisers know they work for women, and telling women what they want to hear is a good way to protect their jobs. (For another example of this dynamic at work, watch any episode of *Dr. Phil* in which the subject of porn comes up.)

ples' counselor (or three) and an endocrinologist and a shrink, if someone isn't depriving his or her spouse of anything he or she actually values—sex generally, sex with them specifically, time spent exploring kinks their spouses find repulsive—in those cases, I believe it's better to cheat than to leave.

So I sometimes advise people to go ahead and cheat.

Here's an example from my in-box: This man's wife had informed him, ten years and two children into their marriage, that she not only wasn't interested in having sex with him anymore, she was never really that interested in sex with him, or with anyone else, in the first place. And she was done pretending.

"When we met she seemed very into sex," the unlucky guy wrote. "I thought we had a great connection. I'm not a selfish lover, I focused on her pleasure, and I do more than my half of the housework and childcare. She tells me that I'm not doing anything wrong, just that her libido is gone. She says she never really enjoyed sex, and she claims she doesn't miss it. She won't go to counseling. Any conversation about my getting my needs met elsewhere ends in tears. She gets upset when she catches me looking at porn or masturbating because it makes her 'feel guilty,' like she's 'doing something wrong.' It's been five years since I've had sex, and my choices right now boil down to leaving my wife (and my kids, which I don't want to do) and being seen as the bad guy, or cheating on my wife and actually being the bad guy. What the hell do I do?"

The advice I'm supposed to give in cases like this—the advice I'm frequently taken to task for *not* giving—is of the Work Harder on Your Marriage and Do More Around the House variety. If you were doing enough around the house, if you were working hard enough on your marriage, your sex life would be roaring along. Never mind that this guy *has* worked hard on his marriage; never mind that he's already doing his fair share around the house. Most advice professionals write as if they are contractually required to assume that, however hard a sexually spurned husband *claims* to be working at his marriage, he must not be working hard enough; however much he claims to be doing around the house, it's not enough. Because when husbands do everything right—working on that marriage, helping around the house—their wives fuck 'em twice a week at least. Because nothing is more arousing than watching your husband clean the bathroom. (And, yes, I'm taking the letter writer at his word when he says he does his fair share around the house. Some advice columnists do call bullshit on their letter writers, but usually we accept the letter writer's characterization of a given dispute and advise accordingly.[4] Until advice columnists are granted the authority to depose all parties involved in a particular dispute—and I hope that happens soon, *because that would be fucking awesome*—this is a limitation of the medium that we have to live with.)

But let's say this man is doing everything right to no avail. Let's say that his wife truly has no libido and never did. (We won't pause here to consider the dishonesty of pretending to be a sexual person when you're not; and we won't entertain the possibility that the wife is lying when she says she's not interested in sex. It's possible that she is, just not with her husband; it's also possible that she's getting it elsewhere herself. So we're not just giving the husband the benefit of the doubt in this situation—crediting him with doing his fair share of the housework, working on his marriage, and so forth—we're also giving the wife the benefit of some unspoken doubts.) Then what am I supposed

---

4 Advice columnists willing to call bullshit on their letter writers, aside from myself: Carolyn Hax, a writer and columnist for *The Washington Post* and the author of the eponymous advice column; Emily Yoffe, author of *Slate*'s Dear Prudence column; and Cheryl Strayed, the author of Dear Sugar, the advice column at *The Rumpus*. Best example of bullshit-calling by an advice columnist ever: A reader asked Abigail Van Buren—*in 1972*—what she could do to "improve the quality of the neighborhood" after a gay couple moved in down the street. Van Buren's three-word answer: "You could move."

to tell him to do? What's my industry's go-to advice then? I'm supposed to tell him to do the "right" thing and get a divorce. Never mind the love, never mind the kids, never mind the expense, never mind the trauma. If he wants to have sex again—if this particular guy wants to masturbate in peace again!—he has to leave his wife and abandon his children.

What's the one thing I'm not allowed to suggest? The one thing that might actually save this marriage, the one thing that might make it possible for this man to stay married and stay sane: *Get it elsewhere.* If I were to give that advice, and if the letter writer were to follow it, I would also urge him to be discreet (don't humiliate your wife), and to be dishonest (don't make your wife cry by asking permission). But when I tell people who are trapped in sexless-but-otherwise-rewarding marriages to get it elsewhere—and urge them to show consideration by being discreet and compassion by being dishonest—an angry mob gathers under my window to chant, "Cheating is never okay!" (Technically the angry mob gathers in my in-box. And the mob doesn't chant, it types. But still.) Letters pour in from irate readers who insist that cheating never saved a marriage—why, everyone they know who had an affair wound up getting caught and getting divorced.

Sometimes I'll blast an e-mail back at people who write in to make this point. Okay, you say that cheating always ends in divorce because everyone you know who cheated wound up getting caught. But what about the people you know who cheated and didn't get caught? The people who cheated and got away with it probably didn't wind up getting divorced; since they didn't get divorced (which is typically when you find out that a friend or family member has been cheating), you never found out about the cheating. Even if they got caught cheating by their spouses, you wouldn't have found out about the cheating if they managed to work through it and stay together. You follow?

Take, for example, this guy. I'm sure that someone out there—

maybe even someone who has written to me insisting that all cheaters get caught and very soon divorced—knows him:

> I've been married for more than fifteen years. For the first eight or so, everything was great. Lots of mutually GGG sex [GGG is explained in chapter 4], lots of love, lots of openness. Then, my wife's libido failed. We had a lot of discussions about it. Whatever the problem was, she couldn't articulate it. I tried everything—romantic nights out, gifts, thoughtful surprises, not trying to initiate sex for weeks (and months). After a year where we'd had sex just twice, I realized I was with a woman who I loved, and who loved me, but whose libido had died. So, I eventually reached out to someone else. I used Craigslist, and I used it honestly: I explained that I had no intention of leaving my wife, that I was looking for someone in a similar situation. It actually took months to find someone who was not spam, to whom I was attracted, and who had no intention of taking a relationship past fuck-buddy status. We struck up a years-long affair, and it was incredible. Fantasies fulfilled, honest talk, no need for anything other than sex. At the same time, I had a wonderful-yet-sexless marriage. Then, after nearly four years, an interesting thing happened: My wife's libido came back strong. To this day, she cannot explain why it left, or why it came back. But, with the reason for my affair gone, I ended things with my fuck buddy. Years of honest talk with my fuck buddy made this easy for both sides. She understood, and we went our own ways.[5]

---

5 This guy, who had the four-year affair without getting caught, says he pulled it off because he followed these eight rules:
  1. I never told anyone about it. Ever. This is my sole secret.
  2. I chose a partner who wanted exactly what I wanted, and who was not someone I knew socially.

We only hear about cheating—or a four-year affair—when it destroys a marriage. We never hear about cheating—or a four-year affair—when it saves one.

Suggesting that cheating can save a sexless marriage—and we probably shouldn't call it "cheating" in cases where the getting-it-elsewhere spouse isn't actually cheating his wife out of anything she wants, as is the case with the man whose wife is done with sex—is so inconceivable that a recent CNN story offering tips on how to save a "mediocre marriage" suggested divorce before finally, and very tentatively, suggesting that a couple might want to think about the possibility of exploring "ethical non-monogamy," aka cheating with permission (which, again, isn't cheating at all), as an alternative to divorce.

According to CNN—the most trusted name in news—divorce is likelier to "save your marriage" than getting it elsewhere.

Divorce.

Those are just two examples of when this advice columnist thinks it's okay to cheat: One man with a wife who mysteriously (and temporarily) lost her libido and another with a wife who never had much of a libido to begin with, decides she's finished with sex and then engages in emotional blackmail in an effort to get her duped husband to drop the subject. Cheating in both cases? Better than the alternatives, of which there are two: one, the divorces no one involved wanted or two, a couple of marriages poisoned by resentment, both likely to end in

---

3. I never took stupid risks—we only met up when we both had clear time so as not to jeopardize our secret.

4. We didn't film ourselves, as hot as that sounded.

5. We used condoms.

6. I kept my computer clear of any evidence.

7. We never called or texted each other.

8. When it ended, we didn't try to keep in touch.

the divorces that nobody wanted. (Coming up: an example featuring a woman whose husband is done with sex.)

I could give other examples of when it's okay to cheat—men and women whose spouses have Alzheimer's disease and are no longer husbands or wives but nurses and home-health-care aides; men and women who are married to people who don't like sex and do their best to make sure sex is so lousy that their spouses will stop pestering them for it—but here, in the interest of balance, are a few examples of when cheating is *not* okay.

It's not okay to cheat when you've made a monogamous commitment and your partner is doing his or her best to meet your sexual needs, that is, you're getting regular vanilla intercourse; your reasonable kinks are being indulged; you get a pass to watch a little porn and jerk it, if you're the husband; or a pass to read *Fifty Shades of Grey* and vibrate it, if you're the wife. (And, yes, some women do watch porn, just as some men are rumored to have read *Fifty Shades of Grey*.)

It's not okay to cheat on your wife because you're horny *right now* and she happens to have the flu *right now*. It's not okay to cheat on your husband because you finished the last book in the *Fifty Shades of Grey* trilogy last week and he has yet to convert the spare bedroom into a "red room of pain."

Guys: It's not okay to cheat on your wife because she recently had a baby—you did that *with* her, don't forget—and she's just not feeling it at the moment. There are times in our adult married lives when we have to go without for three, six, even twelve months, and a new baby in the house is one of those times.

It's not okay to cheat because you're bored. If you're bored, odds are good that your spouse is too. Before you can justify cheating out of boredom, invite your spouse to go on a sexual adventure with you.

It's also not okay to cheat unsafely. Even if you're not having sex with your spouse anymore, even if there's no way you could pass a sexually transmitted infection to your spouse, sexually transmitted infections are no fun. And coming down with and seeking treatment for an STI—the appearance of symptoms, making doctors' appointments, bringing a prescription home, going on meds for the rest of your life if you're unlucky enough to contract a chronic STI—makes being discreet about cheating difficult, if not impossible.

And, finally, a word to you serial cheaters: It's not okay to make a monogamous commitment that you damn well know you're incapable of keeping. Al Gore invented the Internet so that honest, self-aware, non-monogamous people would have an easier time finding each other, dating each other, and marrying each other, thereby sparing the monogamously predisposed from the heartbreak of marrying a serial cheat. I don't believe "Once a cheater, always a cheater," but I do know there are people who cheat compulsively. They should find and marry each other. ("Cheating compulsively" ≠ "open relationships or polyamorous relationships." People in open or poly relationships aren't cheating.)

All of that said, sometimes people make monogamous commitments that they fully intend to keep; they make commitments that they believe they can keep, and they still wind up cheating. Some, like the two men above, have grounds to cheat and wind up cheating—or wind up considering it—to save their marriages. But some cheat without cause. Some people cheat because they're bored, or drunk, or desperate for some variety (a legitimate and non-gender-specific need that porn and bad BDSM novels can't always meet), and they do something stupid that they regret. Like this woman who wrote to me recently to confess her indiscretion:

> What do you do if you know you're a CPOS [cheating piece of shit]? How do you live with the guilt? Or alternately, how do you tell your partner? Your loving, devoted, honest, hard-working partner that you would never give him up for anything? Except apparently for a quick drunken fuck with a near stranger.

Have I just destroyed my relationship?

Sorry, I'm still drunk and kinda in shock. Never thought I'd be "that person." What the fuck do I do?

It's not like I was raped. If I was sober, this never would have happened. But I never said no, and I let the guy coerce me into doing it. Is there any kind of get-out-of-jail-free card—"Hey honey, I wasn't really raped but I kinda got drunk and made a stupid fucking decision. We cool?" I want to save my relationship, bottom line. I do honestly want to be with my boyfriend, but now I'm terrified he's going to break up with me because I got drunk and made a bad call.

What the fuck do I do from here?

If these cheaters don't get caught—and if they sincerely regret the infidelity and the lesson they took away from it was "I'm never doing that again"—they should resist the urge to unburden themselves to their spouses, resolve never to do it again, and take that secret to the grave. That's your get-out-of-jail-free card.

But what do you do if your spouse does unburden himself or herself after an affair?

My advice: Recognize that monogamy is a struggle. In a terrific piece in *Slate* ("Are Humans Monogamous or Polygamous? Archaeologists, Anthropologists, and Biologists Agree: It's Complicated"), Daniel Engber writes, "According to anthropologists, only 1 in 6 societies enforces monogamy as a rule." Even so, pair bonding is common. "In *The Myth of Monogamy*," Engber continues, "evolutionary psychologists David P. Barash and Judith Eve Lipton say we're not the only pair-bonding species that likes to sleep around. Even among the animals that have long been known as faithful types—nesting birds, etc.—not too many stay exclusive. Most dally. 'There are a few species that are monogamous,' says Barash. 'The fat-tailed dwarf lemur. The Malagasy giant jumping rat. You've got to look in the nooks and crannies to find them, though.' Like so many other animals, human beings aren't really that monogamous. Better to say, we're *monogamish*."

Monogam*ish* is a term I coined to describe marriages like mine. My husband Terry and I are mostly monogamous; we are more monogamous than not, but there are times—certain set and limited circumstances—when it is permissible for us to have sex with others. If we weren't open about this facet of our sex life (which we went public with lest we be busted by some right-wing muckraker for pretending to be monogamous), Terry and I would probably be perceived to be monogamous by our friends, neighbors, and family members. We would be, in the parlance of sex researchers, a socially, but not sexually, monogamous couple.

Social monogamy is easy; all it requires is discretion. Sexual monogamy, however, is a struggle and we should grade people—even people we happen to be married to—on a curve. If you have been with someone for twenty, thirty, or forty years and your spouse only cheats on you once or twice, *your spouse is good at monogamy*. Not bad at it. Good at it. I believe we should place a higher value on marital stability than we place on marital monogamy. Yes, your partner should've thought about your marriage and all it meant to him or her before cheating. But if your partner messed up and got caught—if he or she cheated and you found out—you have to ask yourself: Who do *you* want to be? Hillary Clinton or Jenny Sanford? Robert Pattinson or . . . well, I can't think of another example of a high-profile guy who didn't take his wife or girlfriend back after she cheated on him. But you get my point.

People might have an easier time wrapping their heads around my advice if they knew how common cheating was. Various studies estimate that between 40 to 50 percent of women and 50 to 60 percent of men in long-term relationships have had extramarital affairs.

Whenever a politician gets caught up in a political sex scandal, someone brings up the French. Why can't we be more sophisticated about these sorts of things—you know, like the French? Why can't we turn a blind eye to discreet affairs—you know, like the French? But it's not just the French. When asked about her late husband's "discreet dalliances" in a profile in *The New York Times,* the duchess of Devonshire, one of the famous Mitford sisters, replied, "It was absolutely fixed that we shouldn't divorce or get rid of each other in any way. It's completely different to Americans, who all divorce each other the whole time. Such a bore for everyone, having to say who's going to have the dogs, who's going to have the photograph books." Yes, if not the children, then just think of the dogs, think of the photo books.

I'm not saying that being cheated on by your spouse is not a big deal, or a violation, or a betrayal. It is all of those things. But if more people understood how difficult monogamy is over the long term, and how common cheating is, and if people were encouraged to assess the actual particulars of a particular adulterous incident rather than seeing all cheating as essentially equal (i.e., fucking a complete stranger safely and discreetly, if ill-advisedly, just *once* when she'd had too much to drink on a business trip really isn't equal to her fucking your boss repeatedly in your marital bed), maybe more marriages would survive the nearly inevitable infidelity.

I would argue that as a society we have a responsibility to adjust people's expectations about marriage. Imagine if a newlywed couple's married friends or the spiritual leaders of those marriage encounter weekends told the happy couple this: "If you're with this person for forty or fifty years, and your husband or wife only cheats on you once or twice, you should see your partner as good at being monogamous, not bad at it." But that's not what people are told; they're told the opposite: Any cheating, even just once, negates the marriage and everything else it meant.

Is it any wonder the divorce rate is so high?

Because I don't think that married people should have to live without sex, even if they choose to stay in a sexless marriage. I'm frequently told that I overemphasize the importance of sex. But I think a marriage is about more than sex. I think sex is *less important than marriage.* I believe that there's more than one way to demonstrate your loyalty and commitment. And if your marriage is rendered meaningless the moment your spouse gets naked with someone else—even if it was just that one time on that business trip—then your marriage didn't mean much to begin with.

Cheating is not a bug, as the programmers say; it's a feature. We are socially monogamous—we pair bond; we couple up (not all of us: Some of us are happily single, some of us are happily poly)—but we are not sexually monogamous. Christopher Ryan and Cacilda Jethá, the authors of *Sex at Dawn* (which examines modern premises of marriage and monogamy by studying evidence collected from the fields of human physiology, primate biology, archaeology, and anthropological studies), note that "adultery has been documented in *every* human culture studied, including those in which fornicators are routinely stoned to death. In light of all this bloody retribution, it's hard to see how monogamy comes 'naturally' to our species. . . . Were monogamy an ancient, evolved trait characteristic of our species, as the standard narrative insists, these ubiquitous transgressions would be infrequent and such horrible enforcement unnecessary. No creature needs to be threatened with death to act in accord with its own nature."

If monogamy came naturally, it would be easier. If it were easy, we would do it, easily. But it's not; it's a struggle. Admitting that it's a struggle makes a monogamous commitment more meaningful. The fact that your partner is willing to "forsake all others" only means something if your partner doesn't, on some level, want to forsake all others. And your partner doesn't.

Defenders of "traditional marriage," circa 1750, not 1950, objected to anyone marrying for something so unstable as a *feeling,* Stephanie

Coontz argues in *Marriage, a History: From Obedience to Intimacy, or How Love Conquered Marriage*. Once upon a time, a long, long time ago, no one married for love. You married for property if you were a man; you were married off as property if you were a woman. Couples married to cement alliances. Princes married to unite kingdoms; peasants married to bring small parcels of land together. But marriage wasn't something you did back then. Marriage was something that was done to you: Young, marriage-age adults (or preadolescents) didn't have the power or judgment to craft marriage contracts, negotiate alliances, identify the best acreage in the village. Their families—their fathers or eldest male relatives—did that for them.

Much as the advice business is geared toward the needs of women—or geared toward telling women what they want to hear, which is not always what women need—traditional marriage arrangements were geared toward the needs of men. Historically monogamy wasn't imposed on or expected from men. Traditionally men (and "traditionally married" men) had concubines; men had multiple wives; men had mistresses; men had access to sex workers. It was only in the middle of the twentieth century—as marriage was redefined from an inherently sexist and oppressive institution to something more egalitarian (i.e., women could own property; they weren't property)—that monogamous expectations were imposed on men, with often disastrous results. Men aren't good at it, as anyone who has read a newspaper over the last ten years can attest (Edwards, John; Sanford, Mark; Vitter, David; Petraeus, David, et al.). But rather than extend the same license to women that men have always enjoyed— you can get some on the side, now and then, if you must, but be discreet—we've imposed on men the same limitations that women have always endured. *Cheating is always wrong.*

But no matter how many times we say it—cheating is always wrong!—people still cheat. Because cheating is not a bug; it's a feature. Because we are socially monogamous animals, not sexually monogamous animals. (And not all of us are socially monogamous—see, again, people in open relationships, the openly monogamish, the poly community.) And the pressure to perfectly execute monogamy over the life of a marriage—half a century or more—makes every monogamous relationship "a disaster waiting to happen," according to Meg Barker, the author of *Rewriting the Rules: An Integrative Guide to Love, Sex and Relationships*. "We readily accept someone loving more than one child, sibling or friend without their love for one of them diluting the love for others," Barker notes in a 2012 interview with *The Guardian* on the subject of monogamy, "but when it comes to romantic or sexual love most people cannot accept it happening more than once at a time."

Mixed in with the mail from miserable, sex-deprived readers seeking permission to cheat—which I am, as I've said, likelier to grant than any other advice columnist currently working—are outraged letters from people who insist that men and women who cheat on their spouses can't *really* be in love. This applies, they argue, even in cases where no one is being "cheated" at all (i.e., honest open relationships of whatever stripe). The marriages of cheaters are frauds, they claim—though rarely does anyone suggest that there's something fraudulent about a sexless marriage—and if I had any respect for marriage as an *institution,* I would stop telling people that cheating is ever okay.

But my belief that, in certain circumstances, cheating is okay isn't informed by any disrespect for marriage. Quite the opposite: I have too much respect for marriage to regard it as solely defined by sexual exclusivity. That's setting the bar too low, in my opinion, as marriage is about so much more, as this letter from a reader demonstrates:

> I'm forty-nine and my husband of twenty-one years has
> agreed that I can have sex with someone else since we don't

have sex anymore. We plan on staying together. We are companions and friends. We have shared history and shared burdens. There have been bad times that we got through together—including the loss of our shared sex life. But in a weird way it may be a relief to both of us that the tension about our sex life is over. I'm so grateful that he is sensible about not trying to control my sexuality just because he's no longer sexual due to physical and emotional issues. I have a lover and it makes a huge impact on my life. I'd be a crazzzy woman without it. (I seem to be one of the women for whom menopause has increased my libido.) Sex is considered so important in marriage until one partner can't be sexual anymore and then the other is expected to just give sex up too. It's not that easy.

No, it's not. Giving up sex—which is what most people would've expected this forty-nine-year-old, menopausal-but-still-horny woman to do, and what most advice columnists would've told her to do, either directly ("be faithful to your husband") or indirectly ("see a couples' counselor, do more around the house, have his hormone levels checked, maybe he's depressed, blah blah blah, anything but take a lover!")—is not easy. (Except for asexuals, of course, but can those who never took sex up in the first place really be described as having given sex up?) And when we tell people in sexless marriages that they either have to give up sex or give up their marriage—when we tell them that "cheating" is never okay—we sacrifice perfectly good marriages, marriages like this forty-nine-year-old woman's, on the altar of a perfectly ridiculous, perfectly reductive notion about what marriage is.

Still not convinced? Let's unpack monogamy just a little bit more. At least the lie you're told about it: If you're in love with someone, monogamy comes easy. If you're in love, you won't want to fuck other people. But doesn't that sort of obviate the need for a monogamous commitment in the first place? After all, if being in love means you don't want to fuck anyone else, why are you forced to publicly promise not to fuck anyone else?

The truth is—and most people intuitively understand this truth—that even if you're in love with your partner, and even if your partner is in love with you, you will both be attracted to other people. You'll want to fuck other people. You've committed to refraining from fucking other people. But you will still *want* to fuck other people. And so will your partner. You will feel lust in your heart—and in other organs too—but you will, if you can, keep that commitment, by keeping your heart, and other organs, in check.

We all know this. And yet most people in committed relationships waste a tremendous amount of time scrutinizing their partners for proof that they want to fuck other people. People are angered when they catch their normally discreet—considerately discreet—partner checking out some other person's ass; people flip out when they discover that their partner watched some porn (which can satisfy a desire for variety); people get furiously angry when they see their partner enjoying a little attention from an attractive stranger in a bar or a club.

The ones who really suffer, though, are the fools who believe it. The people who believe that being in love means never having eyes for anyone else. What happens to them when they encounter a stranger in an airport bar or a new coworker who fills them with lust? If they believe that true love means not wanting to fuck anyone else, this desire to fuck someone else—the dude in the airport bar, the new girl at work—must mean they're not in love with their spouse anymore. Conflating love and lust like this, and stigmatizing lust (which forces "good" people to round lust up to love to avoid thinking ill of themselves), creates chaos in the lives of the fools who buy into these romantic and woefully misguided notions of love. Love for your spouse—enduring, solid, reliable love—can coexist with an all-consuming lust for a new person. Telling people they can't both love their spouses and want to fuck the shit out of the hot dude they saw at the airport bar—or have strong feelings of attraction to someone who is a regular presence in their lives—undermines marriages in the guise of strengthening them.

So what's the solution for sexless marriages that are worth saving? Or for good, solid marriages that have lasted decades and only suffered one or two dalliances? Not wide-open relationships, not polyamory for the monogamously inclined, or even for the monogamishly inclined. Not swingers' conventions, not fucking in the streets. Perhaps a little license, a little latitude. An understanding that two people can't be all things to each other sexually all of their adult lives. An understanding that life is long and circumstances change and some things—love, devotion, loyalty—are more important than sex, and that lifelong, perfectly executed sexual exclusivity is not the only measure of love, devotion, and loyalty. And an understanding that making a small accommodation within marriage—or a series of small accommodations—is easier than living in a marriage that has been poisoned by resentment. An understanding that real, imperfect relationships are more important than romantic, idealized, and ultimately impractical notions about lifelong fidelity.

I might have coined the term *monogamish,* but I was only naming something that loving couples throughout history have practiced. It's arguably the more common historical marital arrangement, and not solely to the benefit of those of us with a Y chromosome. The desire to be socially monogamous, if not sexually monogamous, was something that aviation pioneer and feminist icon Amelia Earhart understood way back in the 1930s. In a letter to her then-fiancé, George Putnam, Earhart laid out the terms of their impending marriage: "On our life together I want you to understand I shall not hold you to any medieval code of faithfulness to me nor shall I consider myself bound to you similarly. If we can be honest I think the difficulties which arise may best be avoided should you or I become interested deeply (or in passing) in anyone else. Please let us not interfere with the other's work or play, nor let the world see our private joys or disagreements."

I couldn't have said it better myself.

3. Sex Dread

I magine a driver's-education course that didn't cover steering. Or brakes. Or turn signals. Or what those red octagons on the tops of those metal sticks near all those intersections are supposed to mean exactly. This driver's-ed course is entirely dedicated to the miracle of internal combustion. Now imagine you're fifteen years old and this is your driver's-ed class.

When your instructor isn't drilling you and your fellow students on the inner workings of the internal combustion engine—fuel combines with an oxidizer in a combustion chamber where it explodes and the energy produced by these explosions causes pistons to fire and this miraculous chain of events makes a car move—he's issuing dire warnings about the highly flammable nature of gasoline and wildly overstating your odds of dying in a car accident.

"There's no such thing as 'safe' driving," your instructor warns you at the end of every class. "The only safe driver is the driver who doesn't drive."

Then your sixteenth birthday rolls around and, surprise, you're given a driver's permit and the keys to a car. No one expected that you wouldn't take up driving—not your driver's-ed instructor, not the school administrators who hired him, not the parents who told you to listen to him, not the federal or state agencies that paid his salary. So on your sixteenth birthday you get behind the wheel of a car for the first time.

What happens next?

The odds that you'll get into an accident, perhaps a fatal one, are pretty high. Because you don't know how to drive. You may have taken a driver's-ed course, true, but not one that prepared you to drive a car on actual roads that other people would be driving their own cars on as well. You shouldn't feel too bad about getting into an accident, though—I mean anyone who took a driver's-ed class like the one you took is probably going to kill himself or someone else or a score of people the first time he takes the car out for a spin. And here's the neat part . . .

Well, it's the neat part for your driver's-ed instructor anyway: If you do kill yourself or someone else the first time you drive a car—or the second or third or even the three-hundredth time—your old driver's-ed instructor will cite your death as proof that he was right about driving. He'll show your picture to his current students and describe the accident in gory detail. And he'll tell his students that this wouldn't have happened if only you had listened to him and abstained from driving.

Sex education in America is a lot like a driver's-ed course that covers the internal combustion but not steering or brakes or those red octagons on the tops of those sticks at all those intersections. And while strict "abstinence-only" sex-education programs get all the bad press—and for many years, all the federal funding (to the tune of billions of your tax dollars)—what we think of as "comprehensive" sex-ed programs often aren't much better. Despite what the parents of Taylor Ghimenti, and others like them, believe.

Taylor Ghimenti is a high school student in Fresno County, California, whose parents sued the Clovis Unified School District in the fall of 2012 alleging the district's failure to provide their daughter with a comprehensive sex education. According to the Ghimentis, Taylor was "given no information" about contraception, condoms, or disease prevention in the abstinence-only sex-ed classes at her high school, in direct violation of state law. Instead, they asserted, she was taught—incorrectly—that she could contract HIV, the virus that causes AIDS, from kissing, and told that she should abstain from sex until marriage. If the allegations are proved, what is being taught in the schools of Fresno County isn't sex ed. It's sex dread.

But teenagers lucky enough to receive the kind of "comprehensive" sex education that Taylor's parents are fighting to get into schools in Fresno County—or fighting to get back into schools—often don't get much more than an extended primer on reproductive biology. Like their contemporaries in abstinence-only programs, these students are taught how the human reproductive combustion engine works; they know testes from ovaries, ejaculation from ovulation, and prostate glands from mammary glands. In other words: They learn where babies come from and how to prevent babies from coming.

Reproductive biology is the easy part, though. Everything a young person needs to know about human reproduction can be packed into a single, time-saving, run-on sentence: The nice man puts his erect penis into the nice woman's vagina and moves it back and forth until he ejaculates—lady orgasms are nice, and the clitoris is somehow involved, but only a man's orgasm is strictly necessary—and then the speediest sperm cell, out of the millions of sperm cells in the man's ejaculate, fertilizes one of the woman's eggs (if there's an egg lurking in her lady parts somewhere), and that fertilized egg implants on the wall of her uterus, and nine months later, barring a miscarriage or an abortion or a meteor strike, the woman will give birth to one or more babies—sometimes there are two eggs, sometimes a single egg-and-sperm combo splits and grows into two babies (sometimes three!)—which is why most people use condoms or some other form of contraception when they're having sex—because, you see, most people, including your parents, want to have sex a lot more often than they want to have babies.

Whether reproductive biology is covered in an abstinence-only sex-ed class or a comprehensive sex-ed class—or at the kitchen table after a four-year-old asks his parents where babies come from—it isn't that difficult to impart the basics. About the only thing simpler than reproductive biology is reproduction itself; people, whether they should or not, reproduce constantly, on purpose and by accident.

And studies consistently show that young people who've had abstinence-only sex educations are far likelier to accidentally reproduce than young people who've had comprehensive sex educations. Bristol Palin may be the most famous example. In fact, teenagers who've had abstinence-only sex educations show no delay in "sexual debut," an unbelievably quaint way of saying, "fucked for the very first time." (At some point in our lives we were all sexual debutantes.) But while teenagers who've had abstinence-only sex ed don't wait appreciably longer to become sexually active—certainly not until marriage—they are far less likely to use contraception when they do become sexually active.

Consequently, teenagers who've had abstinence-only sex ed are at greater risk of contracting a sexually transmitted infection or suffering an unplanned pregnancy—and those are the kinds of pregnancies that typically lead to abortion.

While the teen pregnancy rate in the United States has been dropping for years (hitting a six-decade low in 2010, according to research done by the Centers for Disease Control), the United States still has far and away the highest teen pregnancy rates in the industrialized world, and states with abstinence-only sex education have the highest rates of teen pregnancy. The teen pregnancy rate in Mississippi, an abstinence-only state, is nearly four times higher than the teen pregnancy rate in New Hampshire, a comprehensive sex-ed state. (Not only does Mississippi lead the country in teen births, but it takes first, second, and third place in reported cases of gonorrhea, chlamydia, and syphilis, respectively, the overwhelming number of which involve fifteen- to twenty-four-year-olds.) Teenagers who receive comprehensive sex ed are 60 percent less likely to get pregnant or get someone else pregnant than teenagers who have had abstinence-only sex education, according to a study conducted by researchers at the University of Washington. The failure to provide young people with comprehensive sex education drives up the abortion rates in blue states and the rates of single parenthood in red states. A conservative who claims to oppose abortion and single parenthood shouldn't support abstinence-only sex ed, as it only seems to drive up the rates of both.

Despite the growing mountain of evidence that abstinence-only education doesn't work, states continue to pour money into these programs. In 2012 the governor of Tennessee signed into law an abstinence-only education bill that included a provision banning teachers from condoning "gateway sexual activities," such as hugging or holding hands. Tennessee's new law allows parents to sue teachers or "outside parties"—like sex-advice columnists?—who provide their children with any information that contradicts the state's abstinence-only message. And the 2012 Republican Party platform called for abstinence-only sex education in all American schools and condemned teaching about contraception.

Obviously, there are huge differences in outcomes between abstinence-only and comprehensive sex-ed courses—and an outcome like "four times fewer unplanned pregnancies" is the most important measure of success. Yet comprehensive sex-education programs still fall short.

"There is abstinence-only sex education, and there's abstinence-based sex ed," Leslie Kantor, vice president of education for Planned Parenthood Federation of America, told *The New York Times Magazine* in a November 2011 story. "There's almost nothing else left in public schools."

Kantor was quoted in Laurie Abraham's profile of Al Vernacchio, an English teacher at a private high school in Philadelphia who also teaches an elective course called Sexuality and Society. Surveying the sex-ed courses available in most schools in the United States,

Abraham observed, "The approach ranges from abstinence until marriage is the only acceptable choice, contraceptives don't work and premarital sex is physically and emotionally harmful, to abstinence is usually best, but if you must have sex, here are some ways to protect yourself from pregnancy and disease. The latter has been called 'disaster prevention' education by sex educators who wish they could teach more."

"Disaster prevention" sex education . . . or in other words: "You shouldn't have sex because terrible things could happen. But if you do have sex, against our wishes, and despite the terrible things that could happen, then for fuck's sake use a condom." Even comprehensive sex educators are teaching sex dread.

In 2009 researchers at York University in Toronto interviewed twelve hundred teenagers between the ages of thirteen and nineteen about what they learned in their sex-ed classes. Most of the students were deeply frustrated. The teenagers described their sex-ed classes as grim and tedious, focused primarily on sexually transmitted infections and preventing unplanned pregnancies. They learned about condoms, how to protect themselves from STIs, and about a variety of birth control methods, but their sex-ed courses left them feeling unprepared for romantic and sexual relationships. These teenagers told the York University researchers that they wanted—they needed—more information about sexual pleasure, giving and getting, and fewer in-class demonstrations of rolling condoms onto bananas. One highly disturbing finding: Many of the surveyed teenagers emerged from their "comprehensive" sex-ed classes not knowing that "sex was supposed to feel good."

"As fascinated as we all are with spermatogenesis and how egg meets sperm," one of the authors of the study told *The Globe and Mail*, "what's more interesting to everybody, including adolescents, is what do you do with sexual desire, how do you know when to act upon it, what kind of relationship is fulfilling and what should you be looking for to make sure your relationship is healthy and satisfying rather than one that's unhappy, dysfunctional and disappointing."

Al Vernacchio's sex-ed class covers all the basics: reproduction, physical development, sexually transmitted infections, and contraception. But his students are allowed to ask questions, in person or anonymously (there's a box in Vernacchio's classroom where students can leave their written questions), and more importantly, Vernacchio is allowed to answer any question asked by a student. Nothing is off-limits and students drive the conversation. And the one topic his students are most curious about—the topic his class seems to circle back to, again and again—is sexual pleasure. What you do with sexual desire and how you act on it.

Sex-education classes that don't include information about sexual pleasure, or when and how to act on sexual desire, can't be described as "comprehensive." Giving and receiving pleasure is what sex is about. Giving and receiving pleasure is why we have sex most of the time. The average human being has a great deal of sex over the course of his or her life and very few children; most sex is recreational (all of it is if you're gay), and that's not an accident. Human females don't go into heat. We are designed—by evolution—expressly to have sex recreationally. Teaching young people to prevent unplanned pregnancies and to minimize the risk of acquiring STIs is a hugely important task, the first and most important responsibility of all sex educators. But so long as we skip past pleasure, desire, and negotiating a romantic or sexual relationship—less primly: how you talk someone into fucking you—we aren't really teaching young adults about sex.

It's easy to say that pleasure should be included in any comprehensive sex-ed program. But pleasure is difficult to talk about, much less teach, as pleasure is subjective and personal. And when it comes to sex, pleasure is contested; it isn't even acknowledged in most religious traditions as a legitimate reason to have sex.

So I don't want to come down too harshly on sex educators—actual sex educators, not those abstinence-only frauds—who find themselves trapped between the competing demands of curious, hormone-pickled adolescents, naturally conservative parents, nervous school administrators, and skittish school boards.

Like I said, I understand how difficult it is to talk about pleasure. I understand from personal experience. Full confession: I screwed up the sex talk with the one and only child that I was specifically charged with educating about sex. My own.

One day my then-eight-year-old son came into the kitchen and jumped on the counter. He narrowed his eyes and gave me a strange look.

"Two men can't make a baby," D.J. finally said.

That's true, I told him, two men can't make a baby.

"Then you and daddy have sex for no reason," he said.

Most of the sex that goes on out there—gay sex, straight sex, solo sex—is for no reason, or more accurately for a very good reason—for pleasure. And yet almost all parents, myself included, leave pleasure out of "the talk." And if a sex-advice columnist who believes that pleasure needs to be incorporated into sex education leaves pleasure out himself, can you blame sex educators for ducking the issue?

"But if you're not making a baby," my son asked, "why would you want to do it?"

Because it feels good, I told him, because it makes you feel close to another person, because your body is programmed to want and need it.

"But it looks so stupid," D.J. replied.

He was talking about the couples he'd seen kissing on television. (Wait until he stumbles over Internet porn, I thought at the time. He has no idea just how stupid people can look when they're having sex.)

But he was right: Sex does look stupid. We look ridiculous doing it and feel a little ridiculous once we're done. And fifteen minutes later we're ready to do it again.

Because it feels good. Because it's pleasurable.

When we're young we hear about adults "having sex." Mary is having sex; Terry is having sex; Larry is having sex. We're both curious about and repulsed by this having-of-sex business that seems to consume adults. But then, at a certain point during adolescence, hormones kick in and we want to join the sex-having party too.

Sex is a powerful, primal force, and as much as we like to pretend that we're in control of it—as much as we like to pretend we're in complete control of ourselves—we're not. Sex came first. Sex came before Yahweh, Jesus, Allah, Buddha, L. Ron, and Joseph Smith. Before there was marriage, there was sex. Before there was religion, there was sex. Hundreds of millions of years before there were humans, there was sex. And sex will continue long after we're gone.

Humans created religion partly to channel sex, to sanctify and elevate it, to control and regulate it. I don't believe that we should do away with any and all controls; nor do I believe that a particular sexual encounter can't be greater than the sum of its sweaty parts. Sex is a powerful and potentially destructive force; sex can be deeply meaningful. But some of the controls we have placed on human sexual expression are idiotic and unworkable, products of a time when we didn't understand human hair growth—not to mention why the sun came up every day—much less human sexuality.

We have brains, of course, and the ability to make up our own minds, which means we're no more helpless before our sexual desires than we are before the hang-ups pounded into our heads in churches or in our abstinence-only or abstinence-based sex-ed classes. But desire is like breathing: It's a physiological process that we're not entirely in control of. You may have an idea about how sexuality ought to work—how things ought to be—but if your boy junk or girl junk or erotic imagination has some other idea, well, I'm sorry, but you're going to lose the argument nearly every time. You can try to convince yourself that sex is meant to take place solely within the bounds of matrimony, but very few people are virgins on their wedding night and a great many people wind up cheating on their spouse. You can try to convince yourself that you're straight, but if you're emotionally and sexually attracted to members of your own sex, then you're going to have gay sex whether you like it or not. (And you'll like it—trust me.) Fighting your sexuality is like holding your breath: It can be done, yes, but not for long (when it comes to your breath) and not forever (when it comes to your sexuality).

I've been writing a sex-advice column for two decades and my e-mail in-box is stuffed with letters from teenagers. They don't ask me about reproduction. They don't ask me how to get a condom onto a banana or anything else. The questions I get from teenagers are almost entirely about sexual pleasure. They want to know how to find sex partners, they want to know what their sex partners will expect from them, and they want to know what they have a right to expect from their sex partners. They want to know how to tell if they're good at sex or how to get better at sex if they suspect they're bad at it. (Most are relieved when I tell them that no one is any good at sex at first; sex is a skill that takes time, practice, experimentation, and self-discovery to acquire.) They want to know what to do if they're turned on by something odd but relatively harmless (stuffed animals, feet), and what to do if they're turned on by something scary and invariably harmful (actual animals, children).

Teenage girls write every day asking for tips on giving their boyfriends better blow jobs; teenage boys write every day wanting my

advice—a gay man's advice—about helping their girlfriends reach orgasm. (For starters, straight boys, the business end of the clit can be
found on the outside, not the inside, of your girlfriend's body.) Gay,
lesbian, bisexual, and transgender teenagers write with questions
about sexual identity, gender identity, coming out, finding love, and
giving and getting pleasure. Refusing to answer questions about pleasure and performance, sexual identity and sexual anxiety doesn't
make them go away. And if young people don't have a place to take
these kinds of questions—a place where they can get the kinds of answers that can help them create rewarding sex lives for themselves—
they will look to pornography, their misinformed peers, or a random
Google result for answers. Or, worse still, they won't seek out answers
at all.

There are places other than Mr. Vernacchio's classroom and columns like mine where teenagers can get any question answered.
Scarleteen.com—"sex ed for the real world"—is an independent website that provides information and answers about sex to teenagers. It's
a wonderful resource, as is Planned Parenthood's hugely informative
website. But like my column (which is not required reading) and Mr.
Vernacchio's class (which is an elective), teenagers have to find their
way to Scarleteen and the Planned Parenthood website on their own.

Every teenager should be required to take a sex-ed class that im-
parts, yes, a comprehensive body of knowledge about disease, pregnancy, sexual and gender identity, and all relevant health issues. But
an ideal sex-ed course would focus on student questions. Less sex-ed
"disaster prevention," more sex-ed symposium. Students won't leave
this kind of sex-ed class with all the answers, of course. But they will
leave knowing how to ask questions and that they're entitled to ask
questions.

We often tell young people that curiosity about sex is normal and
natural, but the culture sends messages that are louder, less empowering, and more destructive. Girls are told that there's something wrong

with them if they're too interested in or curious about sex, and boys are told that they're supposed to know everything about sex. Girls feign disinterest and boys feign mastery, and the results—at least in the United States (again: highest teen pregnancy rate in the developed world)—have been disastrous. Yet many American adults have convinced themselves that ignorance about sex is both a virtue and a spiritual force field.

No single question asked in a classroom during a comprehensive and free-ranging sex-ed course will be as important as the asking of questions itself. When they have questions later in life, when they're out in the adult world negotiating sex with other adult partners, a person who was empowered to ask questions as a child is likelier to keep asking questions as an adult.

We should think of our sex lives like hostage situations in which we are at once the hostage, the hostage negotiator, and the hostage taker. No one escapes his or her sexuality—just google "Ted Haggard, male escorts" or "David Vitter, female escorts"—but we can learn to live with and take pleasure in our sexualities, while at the same time minimizing the risks for STIs, unplanned pregnancies, and emotional harm (by being considerate of others' feelings and by insisting that others be considerate of ours). But to do that you're going to need to learn to communicate, and communicate honestly, with yourself. And then with your partner or partners. And you can't do that if you're incapable of asking and answering questions.

But, young or old, don't delude yourself. You don't have sex. Sex has you.

Buckle up.

4. The GGG Spot

Maggie Gallagher doesn't think straight people—particularly impressionable young straight people—should take advice from me.

Gallagher is the former president of the National Organization for Marriage (NOM) and currently chairs that rabidly anti-gay organization's board of directors. Gallagher doesn't approve of my column, doesn't like my podcast, didn't care for my show on MTV, and I doubt she'll have nice things to say about my follow-up TV project. But if Gallagher were serious about strengthening the institution of marriage, she would encourage young people, gay and straight, to read my column and listen to my podcast. (Spoiler alert: Gallagher isn't serious about strengthening the institution of marriage.)

Gallagher should get behind one particular piece of advice I regularly give: People in committed romantic relationships should be "GGG" for their partners.

GGG stands for "good, giving, and game," as in, "good in bed," "giving pleasure without expectation of immediate reciprocation," and "game for anything—within reason." GGG is about both partners in a relationship being honest and open with each other about their sexual interests and making a good-faith effort to meet each other's needs. It's popular among straight people: You can find GGG on thousands of straight personal ads at dating websites like OKCupid and Match.com.

(Someone recently sent me a photo of a car in Iowa—*Iowa*—with "I AM GGG" license plates.)

Gallagher disapproves of the GGG concept. Not only that, she thinks I should be disqualified from giving sex-and-relationship advice to heterosexuals for the same reason she thinks I should be disqualified from marriage: I'm a great big gay homosexual.

"Savage, [for] all his experience, does not know what women are like," Gallagher wrote in a post on NOM's blog. "The possibility of taming one's sexual desire for the sake of another, or of a vow, is not in the Savage moral imagination. Libido will have out, and honesty about that is the best policy. He brings, in other words, the best of gay sexual ethics and experience to a straight audience, with potentially disastrous results."

Where to begin?

I know what women are like. I may not know what women *taste* like, as I've never gone down on one. But I know what women *are* like. My mother was a woman; my sister is a woman; my aunts are women; lots of my friends, neighbors, and coworkers are women. Many of my favorite bartenders are women, and like a lot of gay men, I lost my virginity to a woman. (If I'd lost my virginity to a man, the anti-gay haters would insist that I had been "seduced" into homosexuality. If seduction worked the way the haters claim, I would be straight.) And as someone who is and always was attracted to men, as someone who has sex with men, and as someone who is in a successful, long-term relationship with a man, I know what men are like too.

You know who really doesn't know what women are like? Joseph Aloisius Ratzinger, aka Pope Benedict XVI. The eighty-five-year-old pontiff has never had a girlfriend, despite the fact that he didn't become a priest until he was twenty-three years old, and rules a tiny kingdom of male celibates. And yet the pope is *full* of advice for straight couples. No premarital sex, no birth control, no masturbation, no abortion, no oral, no anal, no facials, no pearl necklaces, no cybersex, no phone sex, and on and on. I wasted an hour on Google trying to find any evidence that Gallagher, a practicing Catholic, had ever told the pope to butt the fuck out of straight people's sex lives. But Gallagher has never, so far as I was able to discover, told that fabulously attired old queen in Rome to stick a cassock in it.

As for the "possibility of taming one's sexual desire for the sake of another," that definitely exists in my moral imagination. But so, too, does broadening one's sexual horizons—upping your game, expanding your repertoire—for the sake of another.

In a sex-negative culture, the less sexual partner in a relationship—the partner with a lower libido, the partner with fewer sexual interests—is always seen as more virtuous. The more sexual partner—the partner with a higher libido, the partner with more sexual interests—is always seen as less virtuous. The more sexual partner is expected to round her libido down to her less sexual partner's level; the partner with more sexual interests is expected to go without having his fantasies fulfilled. Should a relationship end due to conflict about sex (frequency, repertoire), the more sexual partner gets the blame.

There are, of course, cases where the more sexual partner is at fault. Some are unrealistic, cruel, selfish, or insensitive (and I regularly call out the unrealistic, cruel, selfish, and insensitive in my column); some are unwilling to compromise. But, in many instances, the less sexual partner is at fault. Needs that could have been met, weren't; small frustrations that didn't need to grow into relationship-threatening resentments, did. Subjecting someone to constant sexual rejection is cruel, selfish, and insensitive. (If you didn't want to fuck your partner, or you're not interested in sex at all, why did you marry your partner?) Expecting your sexually neglected spouse not to fuck around on you—excuse me, not to seek release or intimacy elsewhere—is highly unrealistic in a world with Craigslist, AshleyMadison.com, and good ol' fashioned jack shacks.

But in addition to pushing GGG on my readers, I also push POA on them, or the "price of admission." POAs—or what it costs to ride this ride—are the sacrifices, large and small, "for the sake of another," if I may borrow Maggie's phrase. POAs make long-term relationships possible. And, yes, the price of admission for more sexual partners often involves "taming one's sexual desire." If anal sex is something you enjoy but you're in a monogamous relationship with someone who doesn't enjoy anal sex, then going without anal sex may be the price of admission you have to pay to be with that person. If you're not into monogamy but you fall in love with someone who insists on it, then monogamy may be the price of admission you have to pay to be with that person. No one gets everything he or she wants in life, in love, or in the sack, and while I have given some of my readers permission to cheat, I have urged just as many—more—to tame certain sexual desires, to let some stuff go, to pay the price of admission for the sake of otherwise solid and loving relationships.

But I also urge my less sexual readers to at least try to meet their partner's needs. I don't tell people to do things that leave them sobbing on the bathroom floor for hours afterward. Each of us should, however, be open to expanding our sexual repertoires for the person we love. The more sexual partner shouldn't always be the one who has to pay the price of admission. If you fall in love with someone who's into anal sex, giving anal sex a chance may be the price of admission you have to pay to be with that person. If you're into monogamy but your partner is not, some allowance for outside sexual contact may be the price of admission that you have to pay to be with that person.

I do believe that "libido will have out in the end," but "libido will have out" doesn't translate into "anything and everything goes." Two people in a long-term, committed, loving relationship should be open and honest with each other about their sexual interests, their turn-ons, their libidos—they should communicate with each other—not because that crazy fag with the sex-advice column told them to, but because sexual compatibility and sexual satisfaction are important aspects of a successful long-term relationship.

According to a California State University study on the role of sexual desire and sexual activity in romantic relationships, sexual activity "was related to self-reported satisfaction for both sexes," and "participants who reported higher amounts of sexual desire for their partners were more satisfied, were less likely to think about ending the current relationship, and were less likely to consider beginning a relationship with a new partner than participants who felt lower amounts of desire." In other words: The more sex a person has with his or her partner, the more desire someone feels for his or her partner; and the more people desire their partners, the less likely they are to leave them. The impact of frequent and satisfying sexual activity on men was especially pronounced: "The greater number of sexual episodes involving the partner in which a man engaged, the less anger he felt for that individual and the less often he thought about ending the relationship."

It seems obvious to me that being sexually satisfied by your partner, and satisfying your partner in turn, is particularly important if you're in a sexually exclusive relationship. If you and your partner are each other's sole source of sexual intimacy and release, it might be a good idea to err on the side of more sex, not less, and meeting needs, not frustrating them. And any decent advice columnist would err on the side of advising people to err on the side of more, not less, meeting, not frustrating. Because, again, when people are happy with their spouses, when their needs are being met, they're less likely to cheat, less likely to divorce, and less likely to turn their children's lives upside down. (Think of the children, Maggie.)

Openness and honesty—putting your libido out there—don't automatically translate into everyone getting everything he or she wants. Not all sexual needs *can* be met; not all sexual needs *should* be met. (I wouldn't leave my husband if he announced tomorrow that he was an apotemnophiliac, but I like all four of his limbs too much to chop any one of them off for thrills.) But even if you can't have the sex you fantasize about, even if you have needs your partner can't meet, being heard isn't too much to ask. And, if someone is going to go without, say, anal sex for the rest of his or her life, being given some small measure of credit—along with being given a green light to jerk off to anal porn every once in a while—makes it easier to go without. It makes going without anal sex virtuous, something that reflects well on the going-without-anal partner's character. It's a receipt that says you paid the price of admission.

For some couples an open and honest dialogue about sex leads to something Maggie Gallagher would no doubt regard as a disastrous result: permission for limited outside sexual contact. An example from my column: The husband wanted to be tied up and dominated; the wife, while not disgusted, had no flair for it and no interest in doing it. Gallagher would urge the husband to sacrifice his kinks for the sake of his marriage. They tried that, and it didn't work. The husband grew resentful, the wife annoyed, and they were on the verge of divorce. Yes, over something so seemingly trivial as a sexual kink. (Kinks are only trivial to those who don't have them.) Exasperated, the wife told the husband to go see a professional dominatrix. Which he did. He didn't have to go without; she wasn't being pressured to do something she wasn't interested in. He was happy; she was happy. The wife, who wrote to me, credited this small accommodation—small, if pricey (dominatrices don't come cheap)—with saving her marriage.

Only someone obsessed with sexual fidelity to an unhealthy degree places a higher value on preserving the *ideal* of monogamous marriage over preserving an actual marriage.

These are my sexual ethics, I'm sticking to 'em, and I don't think there's anything particularly gay about them. Openness and honesty, doing your best to meet your partner's needs, your partner doing the same for you, a little flexibility about needs that can't be met, a willingness to make a reasonable accommodation—all of that works as well in straight relationships as it does in gay ones.

Emily Yoffe, who writes the Dear Prudence column for *Slate,* doesn't think very much of my sexual ethics in general or the GGG concept in particular either.

A woman who signed her letter "What's Next?" wrote to Prudie about her long marriage to a discreet cross-dresser. WN's husband didn't disclose to her that he "enjoys wearing bras and panties" until after she had given birth to their first child. "I decided to accept him as he was because I loved him," WN wrote. "[But as] the years went by I found this part of him to be a complete turn-off." Their marriage was sexless, had been for many years, and with their children grown and out of the house, her husband had started painting his toenails bright red and didn't seem to care who noticed. "If he's going to increase his cross-gender desires as we age," WN's letter ended, "I wonder if I can live with him for the rest of our lives. What should I do?"

Prudie advised WN to have a blunt talk with her husband about the state of their marriage—companionate and sexless—and then make up her mind about whether she wanted a future with this man. Then Prudie added . . .

> Your letter is also eloquent counter-testimony to those who say loving partners should try to accommodate each other's sexual kinks. Sure, that's ideal. But it's simply a fact that the partner without the fetish might find the other's a libido-killer, as in your case. It was dishonest, even cruel, for your husband to withhold the revelation that he'd literally like to get into your drawers until the birth of your child.

Prudie was clearly taking a slap at me in that column. (I *am* the advice genre's leading proponent of partners trying "to accommodate each other's kinks," not extinguish them—as if that were even possible.) So it may come as a shock to Prudie to learn that I agree with her. WN's husband *should* be faulted for not disclosing his kinks before marrying her and knocking her up. (In all fairness to Mr. WN, being honest about your kinks was a lot harder thirty years ago than it is today, and the Internet, which made it possible for kinksters to find and date each other, hadn't come along yet.) I firmly believe that all kink cards should be laid faceup on the table early enough that a non-kinky partner can bail if—to use Prudie's excellent expression— the kink in question is a "libido-killer." (I'm simplifying for the sake of argument. Things are rarely as black-and-white as "one partner has a kink; the other doesn't," or "one partner is sexually adventurous; the other is sexually dullsville." Sometimes both partners have kinks, but their respective kinks don't mesh; sometimes a person is genuinely sexually adventurous but not interested in the sexual adventure his or her partner has in mind. A friend who would have no problem with anal sex, which she sees as adventurous, tells me she would have a big problem with her husband wearing her underwear. One taboo [anal] is a big turn-on; the other [cross-dressing] is a big turnoff.)

But vanilla people should resist—and advice professionals like Prudie should encourage their vanilla readers to resist—the impulse to immediately dump a boyfriend or girlfriend who has just disclosed a kink. Too many people round "unfamiliar interest" up to "libido-killer" and dump the kinkster who has done the right thing and disclosed. There are two reasons why that's a bad idea.

First, we all want kinksters to disclose their kinks early in a relationship. But kinksters are unlikely to disclose—early or at all—if disclosure means being immediately dumped. Prudie, if she wants to live in a world where kinksters disclose, should link arms with me and urge her vanilla readers to take a deep breath before deciding that this, that, or the other kink is a libido-killer. Some kinks *are* libido-killers. (It might kill my libido if Terry wanted me to chop off his arms and legs, for instance.) But not every vanilla person whose partner comes out as kinky winds up like Prudie's reader WN (i.e., not every one of them winds up trapped in an unhappy, sexless marriage with an inconsiderate kinky jerk). Something magical can actually happen, in fact, which brings us to reason number two . . .

You'll meet two kinds of people at BDSM clubs, fetish street fairs, and lurking on kink websites like FetLife. People who were always kinky, and people who fell in love with someone who was kinky, didn't immediately dump their kinky partner after he or she disclosed their kinks, and eventually grew to love their partner's kinks just as much as they loved their partners. These people aren't going through the motions; they're kinksters now too—happily partnered kinksters.

The existence of these happy and kinky couples stands as eloquent counter-testimony to those who say that accommodating each other's sexual kinks is a mistake.

While we're on the subject of kinksters and disclosure, I would like to take a moment to codify some dating rules for kinksters and vanillas alike:

Kinky? If you're dating someone you didn't meet via a kink-personals website or social club, you must disclose your kinks early. It's fine to let the other person get to know you first; it's fine to go out on a few dates; it's fine to have vanilla sex a few times. (There's no better way to prove that you can do vanilla and that you enjoy vanilla and that you're good at vanilla.) But you absolutely, positively *must* disclose your kinks before any major commitments are made—before you move in, before you get married, before you scramble your DNA together. Ideally your kink cards should be faceup on the table by three months, and certainly no later than six months. (And here's a bonus tip: Present your kinks like a tragedy, and your partner will react to them like they're tragic. Present them like a *present*—not something weird that your partner *has* to do to be with you, but something fun that your partner *gets* to do with you—and your vanilla partner is more likely to react positively.)

Vanilla? Don't immediately dump the person you're dating—the kinky person you're dating—after he or she discloses. Take some time to think it over. If the kink isn't too extreme, if it's something you could see yourself maybe *trying*, keep dating, keep talking, and keep fucking. Take it slow and don't let your partner pressure you or guilt you into going faster than you're comfortable going. But you should give kink—and your kinky partner—a chance.

One final note for any kinksters out there reading this (before I lay my trump card on the table for Maggie and Emily): Some kinksters conveniently skip past the last two words in the definition of GGG when they're discussing their sexual interests with their vanilla partners. ("Good in bed, giving pleasure without expectation of an immediate return, and game for anything—*within reason*.") Extreme bondage or S&M, snot, shit, and puke, emotionally tricky humiliation play, wanting to see your partner have sex with other people because it turns you on (asking your partner to assume all of the physical risks that go along with that, to say nothing of the emotional risks for a partner who isn't interested in having sex with other people), and so forth—none of that is reasonable. Extreme kinks fall under the FTF exclusion (i.e., "fetish too far"). Into something truly crazy and/or repulsive? Get thee to the Internet, go.

And now, my trump card: Instead of summarizing, I'm going to reproduce the headline:

Science proves it: Dan Savage is right
The sex columnist has urged people to be "game for anything."
New research says that means happier relationships

Debby Herbenick, codirector of the Center for Sexual Health Promotion at Indiana University Bloomington's School of Public Health, a sexual health educator at the Kinsey Institute, and author of five books about sex and love, authored the story that accompanied that particular headline on *Salon*.

> Five years ago, sex columnist Dan Savage suggested that, when it comes to sex, we should all aim to be GGG ("good, giving, and game"). . . . Long embraced by his readers, the GGG approach now has support from a new scientific study published in the *Journal of Sex Research*.

The study Herbenick refers to was conducted by researchers at the University of Arizona and Hanover College. It looked at how being "game for anything—within reason" contributed to intimacy and satisfaction. Well, as Herbenick explains, they didn't actually examine the GGG phenomenon per se; they studied "the nerdier first cousin" of it (Herbenick's words not mine), which they dubbed "sexual transformations," or changes people make for their partner or their relationship.

The study involved ninety-six couples, all heterosexual, who were asked very specific questions about their relationships and their sex lives, the changes they had made to accommodate their partner's sexual desires, and their satisfaction with their sex lives and their relationships. What they found was "women and men reported higher levels of relationship satisfaction when their partners said they'd made more 'sexual transformations' (when their partners had been game for more- or less-frequent sex, trying new sexual activities, etc.)."

Herbenick clarifies that being willing to make "sexual transformations"—being game to try something new—doesn't necessarily translate into being game for anything and everything, nor does it mean going through the motions with a scowl to shut your partner up.

> After all, being "game" for switching up one's sex life isn't about begrudgingly going down on someone or role-playing with a bored look on one's face. Being game is about being willing to give something a whirl, and happily so. It's about bringing your A-game to bed, about not knowing how you'll end up feeling about it but being willing to give it your best shot, with an open mind and heart. . . . As with movies, drinks and food, it's common for people in relationships to have different preferences. One person likes beer and the other digs wine. One likes action flicks and the other favors anything starring Audrey Tautou. One likes vanilla intercourse and the other wants to hold a vibrator to their partner's clitoris while she's upside down in wheelbarrow, wearing a pirate costume.

And this wasn't the only study that seems to prove the GGG concept: Amy Muise, PhD, a lead researcher on a study of communal strength (which extended to the sexual domain of a relationship) in the Department of Psychology at the University of Toronto, sent me an e-mail after their study was published.

> I recently published a paper that you might be interested in. It is on something that I am referring to as sexual communal strength (SCS), and I think it provides support for your ideas about being GGG. One of the conclusions of the paper is that being motivated to meet a partner's sexual needs is good for the self, in that it is associated with higher

sexual desire. People who were higher in SCS (or more GGG) maintained higher desire over the course of time in a long-term relationship, whereas those lower in SCS (less GGG) declined in desire.

If you don't believe me, believe the science: Being GGG strengthens relationships. Not only does the person whose sexual needs are being met experience an increase in desire and affection for his or her partner, the person who is being GGG experiences increased desire too.

Maggie Gallagher's concern is that GGG—the idea of it—is essentially sexist. That it's about me, a gay man, badgering straight women into accommodating the kinks of straight men. While it's true that men are likelier to be kinky, GGG doesn't apply just to kink. It applies to more basic sexual interests and activities. And when I say we should all be GGG for our partners, I do mean *all*—men and women, gay or straight. Women sometimes find it difficult to be assertive about their desires, women are socialized to defer to men, and many women have a difficult time advocating for their own pleasure. When a couple talks about being good, giving, and game, both halves of that couple are engaged in an explicit conversation about meeting each other's needs. Maybe the conversation is initiated by the male half of the couple; maybe it's initiated by the female half. But the conversation is grounded in the assumption that both halves of the couple have needs that the other half should be willing to meet. A conversation about being GGG for each other is empowering—for the male and female halves of opposite-sex couples, and for the kink and vanilla halves of those same couples.

Anyone who wants to strengthen the institution of marriage—anyone who wants to protect existing marriages—should be seconding, not slamming, my advice to be "good, giving, and game." Whether a marriage is open or closed, gay or straight, whether a couple is vanilla or kinky or falls somewhere in between, if both partners are going that extra mile, if both partners are meeting each other's needs—if they're being GGG—the odds that their marriage will last are improved.

Not only do I have science on my side, but I have at least one Lutheran minister. "Underlying all of Savage's principles, abbreviations, and maxims is a pragmatism that strives for stable, livable, and reasonably happy relationships in a world where the old constraints that were meant to facilitate these ends are gone. . . . Who knows how many good relationships have been saved—and how many disastrous marriages have been averted—by heeding a Savage insistence on disclosing the unmet need, tolerating the within-reason quirk, or forgiving the endurable lapse? In ways that his frequent interlocutors on the Christian right wouldn't expect, Savage has probably done more to uphold conventional families than many counselors who are unwilling to engage so frankly with modern sexual mores," Benjamin J. Dueholm, a Lutheran minister, wrote in the March/April 2011 issue of the *Washington Monthly*.

Taking my advice might lead to disastrous results? To the contrary, Maggie. Couples that take my advice are likelier to stay together than couples that take yours.

5. The Choicer Challenge

Okay, who remembers Herman Cain? Anyone?

Herman Cain was the businessman/pizza guy who ran for the Republican presidential nomination way, way back in 2012. And for one brief, shining, credulity-straining moment, Cain was the front-runner for the GOP nomination. Cain's turn as front-runner fell between Michele Bachmann's and Rick Santorum's turns—or maybe it fell between Rick Perry's and Newt Gingrich's turns. (Some facts are too depressing to check.)

Cain's opinions mattered very much during his stint as GOP front-runner, and he was duly asked to opine about absolutely everything from tax policies ("9-9-9!") to the books he'd recently read ("We need a leader, not a reader!") to President Obama's handling of the uprising in Libya ("Um, I do not agree with the way he handled it for the following reason—Nope, that's a different one. . . . I got all this stuff twirling around in my head"). When Cain was asked the inevitable questions about gay marriage and gays in the military, the then-candidate said, "I believe it is a choice."

Joy Behar asked Cain during an appearance on *The View* if he *seriously* believed that some people make an active, conscious choice to be gay.

"You show me the science that says that it is not [a choice]," Cain told Behar.

On a subsequent appearance on CNN's *Piers Morgan Tonight,* Cain reiterated his stand—he told Morgan that he believed being gay is a "personal choice"—which led to this exchange:

> MORGAN: You think people wait—you believe people get to a certain age and say, "I want to be homosexual"?
>
> CAIN: Let me turn it around to you. What does science show? Show me evidence other than opinion and you might cause me to reconsider that. . . . Where is the evidence?

Herman Cain is a choicer.

"Truthers" believe that 9/11 was an inside job, "birthers" believe that Barack Obama was born in Kenya, and "deathers" believe that Osama bin Laden is alive and well and living in the Lincoln Bedroom. And Herman Cain is a "choicer." Like other choicers, Herman believes—despite all evidence to the contrary—that people make an active, conscious decision to be gay, lesbian, or bisexual. Like their truther, birther, and deather brethren, choicers are nutjobs who can't be swayed by the evidence (which they refuse to look at and then claim doesn't exist) or by reason (which they lack any capacity for).

While truthers, birthers, and deathers are uniquely American nutjobs, the United States hasn't cornered the market on the choicer strain of crazy. The leader of British Columbia's Conservative Party, John Cummins, declared in a May 2011 interview on CFAX radio in Victoria that the British Columbia Human Rights Code shouldn't protect gay people because being gay is "a conscious choice."

Cummins's comments get to the heart of what the "choice" argument is all about: Gay people don't deserve civil rights protections or equality under the law because we have a *choice*. Don't want to be discriminated against for being gay? Don't choose to be gay. If you do choose to be gay, well, you can't complain about being discriminated against because you knew what you were getting into when you made that choice, right? And if you want the discrimination to stop—if you want to get married or serve in the armed forces or keep your job—you can just stop being gay.

Since no one has to be gay, the Cain and Cummins line of "reasoning" goes, there's no need to protect gay people from discrimination or to allow gay people to marry or to adopt or to serve openly in the military. But, following that same line of reasoning, no one has to be a Mormon either—or Jewish or Pentecostal or Catholic or Muslim. Religious belief is clearly a choice. It may be a choice your parents made for you, or a choice your grandparents made for you, but it *is* a choice. (What are all those Mormon missionaries doing out there? They're trying to get you to *choose* their religion.) Discriminating against people based on their choice of religious belief is illegal and should be illegal. Arguing that gay people shouldn't complain about discrimination because we can "choose to be straight" is like arguing that Jewish people shouldn't complain about anti-Semitism because they can "choose to be baptized."

I don't want to get into the science of sexual orientation here, because, as a reasonable person, and as someone who can be swayed by evidence, I think Herman and John should be given an opportunity to defend their positions. Both men deserve a chance to prove that they're right about people choosing to be gay. Now it's difficult to find gay people—or scientists—who believe that sexual orientation is a choice;[1] but it's impossible to find a straight person who can recall choosing to be straight. But I try to keep an open mind—I choose to be

---

[1] The scientific evidence that people don't choose to be gay is kept in the same locked filing cabinet with the evidence that climate change is real, the Earth is billions of years old, and life on this planet evolved over hundreds of millions of years. Everyone seems to have a key to this filing cabinet with the exception of conservative politicians, evangelical ministers, talk radio hosts, anti-gay bigots, and the rest of the GOP's base.

"Show me evidence," says Herman Cain. "What does science show?"

There's an entire field of research focused on the science of sexual orientation. There's even a great, big book on the subject published by Oxford University Press that has "science" in the title (*Gay, Straight, and the Reason Why: The Science of Sexual Orientation*), written by British-American neuroscientist Simon LeVay. Since Herman isn't "leading," perhaps he can make time for some "reading." But if Herman only has a moment, these few lines from the Royal College of Psychiatrists sum it up nicely:

an empiricist—so I'm open to the possibility that gayness is a choice that a person can make. What we need is a way for choicers like Herman and John to prove it. And, hey, come to think of it, there *is* a way for choicers to prove that they're right . . .

Choicers like Herman Cain and John Cummins can prove that being gay is a choice *by choosing it themselves.*

Despite almost a century of psychoanalytic and psychological speculation, there is no substantive evidence to support the suggestion that the nature of parenting or early childhood experiences have any role in the formation of a person's fundamental heterosexual or homosexual orientation (Bell and Weinberg, 1978). It would appear that sexual orientation is biological in nature, determined by genetic factors (Mustanski et al, 2005) and/or the early uterine environment (Blanchard et al, 2006). *Sexual orientation is therefore not a choice.* [Emphasis added.]

While there's no evidence that sexual orientation is a choice, there's also no evidence of a single "gay gene," or genetic mutation, that instills a hunger for cock and an appreciation for camp in some men and a taste for pussy and a talent for softball in some women. While homosexual orientation is clearly genetic, no single gene "causes" homosexuality, and nonbiological cultural forces shape the ways in which homosexuality is expressed.

"Even framing it as a search for the 'cause' of homosexuality suggests that being gay is a pathology or unhealthy deviation, in the way someone might speak of the 'cause' of cancer," says Jesse Bering, PhD, science writer and former director of the Institute of Cognition and Culture at Queen's University Belfast. "Contrary to this simplistic disease model, behind *any* sexual orientation is an elaborate orchestra of dynamic factors—genes, hormones, brain development, events in and outside the womb, cultural forces, and so on. To say that there's a single cause to homosexuality is like saying that Symphony No. 5 was caused by Beethoven dipping his pen in ink."

Despite the worrisome implication of a search for a "cause," gays and lesbians used to hope that science would one day discover a "gay gene." If scientists could just locate a little pink gene with a tiny spinning mirrored ball inside—and if you could hear Gloria Gaynor singing "I Will Survive" when you held it up to your ear—*that* would forever shut up the people who argue that homosexuality is a sinful and sick "choice."

Some gays and lesbians worried about what would happen the day *after* scientists discovered that little pink gene. If a single gene *were* responsible for all non-straight people (gays, lesbians, bisexuals, trans people), and if it could be identified, then that same little gay gene could be targeted for elimination. What would stop scientists from genetically engineering us out of existence? *The Twilight of the Golds,* a 1993 play by Jonathan Tolins, explored this fear: A gay man's sister considers terminating a pregnancy when a genetic test reveals that the boy she's carrying will be gay.

As it turns out, homosexuality is multicausal, involving complex interactions between an unknown number of genes as well as the timing and levels of prenatal hormones that are impossible to control for. Homosexuality is, then, far too complicated to be genetically engineered out of existence. Fundamentalist Christians, creationists, and "intelligent design" advocates have a difficult pill to swallow: God, if he did indeed "design" us, seems to have bigot-proofed homosexuality. Without a single "cause"—without that one identifiable gene responsible for homosexuality—eradicating homosexuality is impossible. Genes,

Suck my dick, Herman. You too, John.

I'm serious about this. You guys aren't my type—each of you, in your own special way, is about as far from my type as vagina-free human beings get—but I'm offering to take one (or two) for the team. You guys believe there's a gay/straight switch in our heads that each of us has the power to flip. Okay then. *Flip that fucking switch, guys.* Show us it can be done. Show us how it's done. You guys name the time and

---

hormones, birth order—there are just too many biological variables to control for. Preventing the births of gay, lesbian, and bisexual babies is impossible.

In 2004 Italian scientists researched several hundred families and found that the mothers, maternal aunts, and maternal grandmothers of gay men are more fecund—or, um, "fruitful"—than women who don't have gay male children, grandchildren, or nephews. "These genes work in a sexually antagonistic way," according to Andrea Camperio Ciani, an evolutionary psychologist from the University of Padova who led the study, "that means that when they're represented in a female, they increase fecundity, and when they're represented in a male, they decrease fecundity. It's a trait that benefits one sex at the cost of the other." These findings could help explain the paradox of hereditary homosexuality. In other words, why—if homosexuality is determined by genetic factors and gay people are less likely to reproduce than straight people—has it not been eliminated from the gene pool by now? The answer might be because "the same genes create both homosexuality in men and increased fertility in women [and] losses in offspring that come about from the males would be made up for by the females of the family."

Then in 2012 a groundbreaking study undertaken by the University of California, Santa Barbara, that built on the findings of earlier studies, including this 2004 one, may have finally solved the mystery of why people are gay and just why it offers an evolutionary advantage to both mothers and fathers. The study links homosexuality not just to genetics but to something called epi-markers, essentially data layers that regulate how genes are expressed. These markers are often erased when parents pass on their genetic information to their offspring. But these epi-markers are not erased in homosexuals, specifically when they're passed from mother to son and father to daughter. According to Jason Koebler of *U.S. News & World Report,* who reported on the study, "These epi-marks provide an evolutionary advantage for the parents of homosexuals: They protect fathers of homosexuals from underexposure to testosterone and mothers of homosexuals from overexposure to testosterone while they are in gestation." Follow that? Me neither. But it's the science!

During a hearing about an anti-gay marriage amendment in Minnesota, State Representative Steve Simon asked this question: "How many more gay people does God have to create before we ask ourselves whether or not God actually wants them around?"

To which I would add: Not only does God want us around, he went out of his way to make eliminating us impossible. And not just that: God commanded the first straight couple to "be fruitful and multiply," which anti-gay bigots cite as an argument against tolerating homosexuality. But the more fruitful the straights, the more fruits there are around.

Which proves that God, if he exists and he came up with the human genome in his basement workshop, doesn't just want us around. He has a sense of humor about how he keeps us around.

the place and I will be there with my dick and a camera crew so that we can capture on video the precise moment when a man makes the conscious, personal choice to be gay.

This is a big opportunity for you guys. Not just because I have a nice dick—although there is that—but because my offer will allow you to win this argument once and for all. You can prove that being gay is a choice by *making the choice yourselves*. And then, when you're on *The View,* Herman, or you're on CFAX, or better yet CBC's evening news,

---

One last thing about the whole "being gay is a choice" argument that mystifies me: Why aren't straight people insulted? Yes, it pisses off gay people; the only real "choice" we make is to come out and live with some integrity. But why doesn't the same argument piss off straight people too? It only follows that if homosexuality is a choice, *then so is heterosexuality.*

Herman Cain and John Cummins and Rick Warren and Joel Osteen all seem to believe that straight people can take or leave heterosexuality. Straight? The intimacy you share with your opposite-sex spouse, the love, the connection, the desire, the pleasure you take in each other's bodies—all of that—is something you can choose to walk away from, like an underwater house or a lousy meal. Why don't straight people get angry when they hear another straight person making this sexuality-is-a-choice argument?

Which is not to say that there isn't an element of choice when it comes to sexual *identity.* Straight is assumed, it's the default orientation, and gay, lesbian, and bisexual people have to make an active choice about when and whether to come out. Some gays and lesbians never choose to come out (hey there, Benedict XVI), or they choose to come out to a select few. Some bisexuals round themselves up to gay or down to straight—or "down to gay" and "up to straight," if you prefer—because the "gay" or "straight" label comes closer to their actual sexual expression (i.e., a bisexual woman with a female partner might choose to identify as lesbian, and others avoid identifying as bi on account of the anti-bisexual prejudices held by some gay, lesbian, and straight people). Which brings us to the messy ones.

Some gay people choose to identify not just as straight, but aggressively straight. They're not just straight; they're anti-gay straight. When I hear people say that sexual orientation is a choice, I can't help but wonder if they're speaking from personal experience. I don't mean they chose to be gay, but that they chose to be *straight.* They believe gayness is a choice because they are gay or bisexual men—all choicers seem to be men—who chose not to act on their same-sex desires.

All reputable scientists believe there is a biological basis for homosexuality—and heterosexuality. Straight people are born, not made, just like gay people. Being gay is not a choice I've made; it is not a fit I'm having. It is not a reaction to sexual abuse or a particular parenting style. I am gay; my two brothers—older but very close in age—are straight. If environmental factors made people gay, why aren't my brothers gay? Why isn't my sister a lesbian? Why isn't Terry's brother gay?

And if being gay is a choice, once again, I challenge Herman Cain, John Cummins, Rick Warren, and Joel Osteen to choose it.

All of you guys can suck my dick.

John, and the host snickers when you say that being gay is a choice, you can tell them to roll the tape of you making the choice yourself.

It's time to put your mouths where your mouths are, guys, and prove that being gay is a choice once and for all. Show us how it's done.

Suck my dick.

6. My Son Comes Out

A lot has changed since *The Kid,* my memoir about adopting our son, D.J., was published a dozen years ago. For starters, D.J. isn't an infant anymore. And no one sits at home by the phone waiting for a call from a hot guy he met at a dance club or a prospective employer or an adoption agency. Now our phones go wherever we do, in our pockets or (more likely) in our hands, practically a part of our bodies. But it wasn't that long ago that someone waiting for an important, potentially life-changing phone call would be afraid to leave the house.

What else has changed?

Our country, of course, and by extension the world—whether the world liked it or not—on 9/11.

Two wars came, but just one—as of this writing—has gone.

Americans put an African-American in the White House. Twice.

Republicans put an idiot Alaskan on the national stage.

We saw advances on gay rights all over the world. Marriage rights were extended to same-sex couples in nine US states and the District of Columbia, as well as Spain, Argentina, the Netherlands, Canada, South Africa, and five other nations and counting. And now at least fifteen countries—including most recently France, under Socialist prime minister Jean-Marc Ayrault—have extended adoption rights to same-sex couples. When I wrote *The Kid,* Americans opposed full civil equality for gays and lesbians by wide margins. Today poll after poll shows that an ever-growing majority of Americans now support marriage rights for same-sex couples.

What else?

My boyfriend became my husband—in Canada, first, where Terry and I got married on our tenth anniversary, and then in our home state of Washington, where voters passed marriage equality in 2012.

Myspace, Facebook, Twitter, and Instagram were born.

Kim Kardashian, Sinead O'Connor, and Britney Spears got married.

Everyone I know got iPods, iPhones, and iPads.

Kim Kardashian, Sinead O'Connor, and Britney Spears filed for divorce after seventy-two, sixteen, and two days of marriage, respectively.

My mother passed away.

Myspace passed away.

Steve Jobs passed away.

D.J.'s mom, Melissa, is no longer living on the streets.

I wrote a couple of books, became the go-to guy for straight people in need of sex advice, and Terry and I founded the It Gets Better Project.

Nabisco introduced candy-corn-flavored Oreos.

Another big change: The number of gay couples adopting children in the United States exploded. In 2000, the same year *The Kid* was published, there were sixty-five hundred adoptions by gay American couples, according to a study by the Williams Institute at the University of California, Los Angeles. In 2009, nearly twenty-two thousand gay couples in the United States adopted children. This increase in the number of gay adoptive parents has been described as "stratospheric."

The Kid played a role in the gay-parenting boom. I get letters daily from gay men who were inspired to adopt after reading about how Terry and I became dads. Many of these men tell me that they had always wanted to be parents but that they had concluded fatherhood wasn't possible for them after they came out. Reading about our "journey to parenthood," as social workers everywhere describe adoption, demystified the adoption process and helped them realize that they, too, could be parents. Because, hey, if they gave a kid to *those* guys—that sex-advice columnist and his disc jockey boyfriend?—who won't they give a kid to?

Anti-gay "Christian" activists oppose gay marriage, gay workplace protections, gay military service, and, as they've made clear through their support of the fraudulent "ex-gay" movement, gay *existence*. So it comes as no surprise that they also oppose gay adoptions.

Opponents of gay marriage/employees/soldiers/adoptions/existence push one "big lie" to justify each item on their anti-gay agenda—gay marriage will harm society, openly gay soldiers will destroy military readiness, gay people can choose to be straight, and so forth. (In fact, gay people have been marrying in Canada for more than a decade, and Canada is doing just fine; a study by the Palm Center, formerly at the University of California and now independent, found that the repeal of the ban on openly gay soldiers has had "no overall negative impact on military readiness, including cohesion, recruitment, retention, assaults, harassment, or morale"; in 2012 the head of the largest "ex-gay" group in the country, Alan Chambers of Exodus International, admitted that his organization cannot "cure" homosexuality.)

The "big lie" advanced by opponents of gay adoption is this: When a selfish gay couple adopts, a loving heterosexual couple is deprived of a child. Children who could have been adopted by straight couples are being given to gay couples, they argue, and they claim that it's not just childless heterosexual couples who are being harmed. Children are being harmed.

In August of 2012, Bryan Fischer, a prominent anti-gay voice on the

Christian right and the host of a widely listened-to talk radio program, called for the creation of a new "Underground Railroad" that would "deliver innocent children from same-sex households." Fischer is the director of issue analysis for government and public policy at the American Family Association, and he exerts a powerful influence on Republican politics. And Fischer believes that children with gay parents should be *kidnapped* because getting your kids to school in the morning, making sure their homework is done, their teeth are brushed, that they have enough decent food to eat—basic parental responsibilities—become "a form of sexual abuse" when same-sex couples perform them.

Children, according to Fischer and others on the right, need a mother and a father, and denying children two opposite-sex parents isn't just tantamount to child abuse, it *is* child abuse. For many years opponents of gay adoption have dishonestly cited studies that demonstrated the advantages of having two parents, not two parents of the opposite sex, to justify their opposition to adoptions by same-sex couples.

In 2012, a new study that seemed to support the anti-gay-parenting position was released. The study, authored by University of Texas sociologist Mark Regnerus, was funded by two anti-gay think tanks. Regnerus claimed that he was comparing outcomes for children raised by gay parents with children raised by straight couples. He wasn't. He was comparing children with married straight parents—children from stable, intact homes—to children from broken homes. The study has been widely debunked. ("Among the problems is the paper's definition of 'lesbian mothers' and 'gay fathers,'" reads a report in *The Chronicle of Higher Education*. "A woman could be identified as a 'lesbian mother' in the study if she had had a relationship with another woman at any point after having a child, regardless of the brevity of that relationship and whether or not the two women raised the child as a couple. . . . That fact alone in the paper should have 'disqualified it immediately' from being considered for publication.") Only two young adults out of the 248 interviewed in the Regnerus study were raised from birth by same-sex couples.

Dozens of legitimate, sound studies of children with same-sex parents have demonstrated again and again that our kids on average are just as likely to be happy, healthy, and well-adjusted as children with opposite-sex parents. Case in point: UCLA released a study, published in October of 2012 in the *American Journal of Orthopsychiatry*, comparing (and tracking over time) children who were adopted out of foster care by gay men, lesbian women, and heterosexual couples. The study followed eighty-two Los Angeles County children, a quarter of whom were adopted by homosexual parents, and then followed up with them for two years after being placed. Researchers found that "children in all three types of households benefited from adoption: on average, they made significant gains in cognitive development—their IQ scores increased by an average of 10 points—and they maintained stable levels of behavior problems. What's more, the kids adopted by gay and lesbian parents actually started out with more risk factors, and were more likely to be of a different ethnicity than their adoptive parents, but after two years were on equal footing with their heterosexually-adopted peers." Coauthor Letitia Anne Peplau concluded, "There is no scientific basis to discriminate against gay and lesbian parents."

This study and the many others like it are supported by the reality that social workers, pediatricians, and family counselors nationwide see every day. Which is why mainstream child health and social services organizations unanimously support adoption by qualified gay parents. The American Academy of Pediatrics offers this endorsement of same-sex adoption: "The Academy supports the legal adoption of children by [same-sex] coparents or second parents. Denying legal parent status through adoption to coparents or second parents prevents these children from enjoying the psychologic and legal security that comes from having two willing, capable, and loving parents."

Fischer's bigoted rants stoke the vilest form of anti-gay bigotry: the belief that gay people, and gay men in particular, prey on children. The religious right continues to promote the myth of the gay sexual predator—gay people "recruit" by sexually abusing children—but that lie is fast losing its toxic cultural currency. It simply isn't borne out by crime statistics (pedophiles are almost always straight-identified men, as Jerry Sandusky was, and they are attracted to children of both sexes, but they have easier access—as coaches, for instance—to same-sex victims) or by personal experience (most straight Americans know openly gay people now, and the openly gay people they know aren't sexually abusing children). Anti-gay voices on the right are attempting to stuff the same old fears (gay people *prey on children*) into a brand-new bag (gay couples *steal children* from straight couples).

Gay couples aren't stealing children from straight couples. Even with more same-sex couples adopting children than ever before, there are *still* more children who need to be adopted than there are couples (or singles) who are willing to adopt them. The choice for children waiting to be adopted isn't between gay parents and straight parents. It's between parents and no parents. And as nearly half a million children languish in foster care across the United States, political organizations with the word *family* in their names spend millions of dollars every year lobbying for restrictions that would block many of those children from ever having families of their own.

Whenever someone asks me why the United States is such a mess about sex and everything that touches on sex—why the United States, out of all Western industrialized nations, will never stop fighting about abortion, sex education, birth control, the sex lives of politicians, the existence of gay people—I shrug and say, "Canada got the French, Australia got the convicts, the United States got the Puritans." But, in one area, the United States isn't doing too badly when compared to lands that are braver, freer, and that have, every now and then, elected *actual* socialist heads of state. And that's in adoptions by same-sex couples. On this issue, and pretty much this issue alone, the United States leads. It is legal for same-sex couples to adopt jointly in eleven states; adoptions by single gay people are legal in forty-five states; and second-parent adoptions are legal in thirteen states. Same-sex couples who live in states where they can't adopt are free to do out-of-state adoptions in states where they can. Our relatively liberal adoption laws weren't the result of an orgy of progressive, pro-gay legislation. In most states "liberal" adoption laws are something of a legislative oversight. Adoptions by same-sex couples and single gay people were never specifically *banned,* which allowed judges and social workers, their sights set on the best interests of children, to quietly approve adoptions by single gay people and same-sex couples.

Belgium, by way of comparison, created a "statutory cohabitation" law in 1998 that granted limited rights to same-sex couples. The country legalized same-sex marriage in 2003, but it wouldn't allow adoptions by same-sex couples until 2006. Portugal granted same-sex couples limited rights in 2001 and legalized same-sex marriage in 2010. But same-sex couples in Portugal are still barred from adopting children. The same pattern has repeated itself in other European nations where gay people have secured their civil equality: First comes marriage—or some form of marriage-lite (civil unions, domestic partnerships)—then come gays pushing baby carriages.

Here in the United States we're doing it in reverse. Same-sex couples have been adopting—and having children through surrogacy and artificial insemination, and raising children born to us in previous heterosexual relationships—long before the marriage equality movement in the United States got off the ground. Same-sex couples that wanted to start families didn't wait for permission or marriage licenses. We created our families and trusted that the culture would catch up. And that's just what seems to be happening.

When President Obama announced his support for marriage equality in an interview on ABC News in May of 2012, he emphasized the gay parents he personally knew. ("When I think about members of my own staff who are in incredibly committed . . . same-sex relationships, who are raising kids together . . . I've just concluded that for me personally it is important for me to go ahead and affirm that I think same-sex couples should be able to get married.") If the gay men and lesbians who work for Barack Obama had waited for the president to endorse marriage equality before starting their families, they never would've started their families. Instead they met, fell in love, started families, and trusted that the culture—to say nothing of the president they served—would eventually recognize their humanity and affirm their basic human rights. The effort to bring gay families into the established social order—the movement to extend marriage rights to same-sex couples—isn't about upending the traditional understanding of marriage. It's about recognizing new realities, and new kinds of families, and bringing these families inside our shared marriage tradition.

"I suppose marriage equality is socially liberal inasmuch as it tries to defend and integrate a previously despised minority," Andrew Sullivan writes. "But it is socially conservative in its attempt to envelop that minority in the traditions and responsibilities of family life."

Exactly.

Louise Pratt, a member of the Australian Senate, may have said it best, though. During a debate over a marriage amendment bill in September of 2012—a bill that, had it not failed 26–41, would have legalized same-sex marriage in that country—Pratt, whose partner is transgender, said this: "We exist. We already exist. Our relationships exist, our children exist, our families exist, our marriages exist, and our love exists. All we ask is that you stop pretending that we don't."

The president of the United States has stopped pretending that our families don't already exist. Nine states and counting have stopped pretending that our families don't already exist. It's only a matter of time before the other forty-one states—and the federal government— stop pretending.

Our son—who is being raised by same-sex parents in a state that has passed marriage equality—well, he most certainly exists. He's fifteen years old now, and he gets taller and more opinionated with each passing day. D.J. is a snowboarder, a skateboarder, a challenge, and a fan of rap music. (Rap music? Where did we go wrong?) He also came out to his parents a few years ago—as straight.

Terry and I knew our only son was straight long before he officially came out.

We knew before we became parents that the odds of having a gay son—or a lesbian daughter—were pretty slim. (According to a Gallup poll conducted in 2011, the average American believes that 25 percent of the population is gay. The best current estimates put the total of the US population that is gay, lesbian, and bisexual at roughly 3.5 percent.) And unlike the straight parents Terry and I have known, loved, and been raised by, we weren't emotionally invested in our child sharing our sexual orientation. We were open to a gay kid, of course, and being adopted by gay dads would've been a lucky break for any gay babies that happened to be gestating when we were in the process of adopting. But we knew going into it that our child's sexual orientation wasn't something we could control.

And it didn't take long for us to realize that the kid we wound up adopting wasn't gay. We had him figured for straight back when he was a trucks-and-guns-obsessed toddler, just as my parents suspected I might be gay back when I was a musical-theater-obsessed fifth grader. (Some guns-and-trucks-obsessed toddlers grow up to be gay, it should be noted, just as one or two musical-theater-obsessed fifth graders are rumored to have grown up to be straight. There are numerous con-firmed cases of the former but none of the latter as of this writing.) And the older D.J. got, the straighter he got. However complex or nuanced the question, D.J. has always been able to construct a monosyllabic response. He has never expressed the remotest interest in art or the-ater or books. He feels that farts are the height of wit and that all other foodstuffs should have been retired after pizza came along. By the time D.J. was in the fifth grade, Terry and I realized that we were es-sentially raising the kid who beat us up in middle school.

We weren't the first people that D.J. came out to as straight. Just as I first came out as gay to a couple of not-so-close friends to test the waters before breaking the big news to members of my immediate family (first my older brother Billy, then my mother, then my other siblings, then—years later—my father). The first person D.J. came out to as straight was John, a stay-at-home dad who lives across the street with his wife, Mishy, and their four kids. Heartbreakingly, D.J. swore John to secrecy, just as I had sworn my not-so-close friends to secrecy. D.J. wasn't ready to tell us, he told John, because he wasn't sure how we would react. Hearing that kind of broke our hearts.

We thought we had communicated to him that we loved him no matter what. And we hadn't just told D.J. that we would love him whether he was straight or gay; we went out of our way to make sure that he understood—and to make sure he knew we understood—that this wasn't a coin toss. We told him it wasn't a fifty-fifty chance he would be gay or straight. No, the odds were most definitely in straight's favor. (One night, years before he came out to us, D.J. and I sat and made a list of all of the couples we knew. Same-sex couples in one column, straight couples in another. Most of the couples on our list were straight, I explained, because most people are straight. I told him that one day his heart—and another organ that I neglected to mention at the time [keeping the convo age-appropriate]—would let him know if he was straight or gay or if he fell somewhere in between.)

D.J. finally told us he was straight about a week after he told John. We were standing in the front yard when D.J. tossed it out. "So you guys know I'm straight and stuff, right?" We said that we knew. Not because John had told us, although John had, but because we sensed it all along. We told him we loved him and that we never wanted him to be anyone other than the person he is. We told him that his being straight didn't change anything. Then we told him to go do his homework to drive that final point home.

D.J. was not supposed to turn out straight—at least not according to opponents of adoptions by same-sex couples. Another chief argument against gay couples adopting is that our kids will "adopt" the "gay lifestyle" when they "grow up." Gay parents sometimes offer clumsy responses to this argument. Don't get me wrong: It's among the easiest anti-gay arguments to refute. Terry and I have four straight parents between us, seven if you include stepparents. (My parents divorced and remarried; Terry's mother remarried after Terry's father died.) If a person's sexuality is determined by his parents' sexuality, then why aren't Terry and I straight?

And where did gay people come from before same-sex couples began parenting?

Tony Perkins, president of the anti-gay hate group Family Research Council, believes he has the answer to that last question: Gay people come from lousy straight parents. In a 2012 appearance on *Hardball* on MSNBC, Perkins told host Chris Matthews that good straight parents prevent gayness by "teaching their children the right way to interact as human beings" (i.e., the penis-in-vagina way to interact). And by "controlling" for certain "environmental factors," factors Perkins neglected to name, good straight parents can prevent their children from growing up to be bad gays.

Where do gay people with straight siblings fit into Perkins's theory on the cause of homosexuality? I have three siblings, all straight, and Terry has one brother, also straight. Mary Cheney, the lesbian daughter of former vice president Dick Cheney, has one sister, Elizabeth, and she's straight. Did my parents and Terry's parents and Mary's parents teach our siblings the right way to interact while failing to teach us those same lessons? Did they provide heterosexuality-inducing environments for our brothers and sisters while creating homosexuality-inducing microclimates just for us? Or—and this seems much more likely—is Tony Perkins full of shit?

Let's go with Perkins being full of shit.

The mistake many gay people make, though, when we attempt to refute the it-will-turn-kids-gay argument, is primarily one of tone. In our hurry to reassure straight people that having gay parents doesn't make kids gay, we sometimes sound like we agree that it would be some sort of tragedy if our kids grow up to be gay. But reassuring straight people that our kids are no more likely to be gay than their kids are, *without* sounding like gayness is a tragedy, is trickier than it sounds. (And it's important that same-sex couples get this stuff right: Many gay adults who were raised by same-sex parents report feeling shame when they realized that they weren't straight. Many of these kids had a difficult time coming out to their gay and lesbian parents as gay because they felt they were somehow giving ammunition to their families' enemies.)

I lost track of the number of times we were asked, when D.J. was very young, if we were going to try to "raise him gay." Terry would stand beside me rolling his eyes while I patiently explained that sexual orientation doesn't work that way. We couldn't control D.J.'s sexuality any more than our parents could control ours.

But if gay parents could turn their kids gay—if it works the way the Tony Perkinses and Bryan Fischers of the world would have us believe—how on earth did D.J. escape gayness? That kid didn't just have gay parents. He had *me,* America's Gayest Parent. I sang D.J. show tunes at bedtime for Christ's sake. ("Maybe This Time" from *Cabaret* was a particular favorite before D.J. outgrew lullabies and turned to rap.)

We can't say for certain yet that gayness is entirely genetic, although all current evidence points that way. But seeing as *my son* turned out straight, I think we can state with some certainty that gayness isn't contagious.

And now, a dozen years after I wrote *The Kid,* and with roughly a million books out there by fathers about fatherhood, what can I possibly say about parenthood that hasn't already been said? How about this: Having a child is like having a heroin problem. When you're high, *man,* you've never been so high. When you're high, *maaaaaan,* all you want is more children. But when you're low, *fuck,* you have never been so low. When you're low, *fuuuuuuuck,* you regret ever picking that first needle up.

Looking back, our low moments seem pretty mundane, and they will be familiar to most parents: sleep deprivation and projectile vomiting when D.J. was young; sleep deprivation and epic conflicts about who's in charge as D.J. moved into his teens. But the highs have been so sweet—and so unique—that they've gotten us through the lows. And the highs arrive when you least expect them, and they often come disguised as lows.

When D.J. was four years old we went on a trip to Paris. D.J. slept on the plane all the way over; Terry and I did not sleep. We arrived at our hotel in the wee hours of the morning completely exhausted. Terry and I wanted to go to bed. D.J. did not. D.J. would not. It soon became clear that neither of us would get any sleep so long as D.J. was in the room. *Someone* was going to have to take D.J. for a walk, Terry observed, and his tone of voice made it very clear just who he thought that "someone" should be.

I was pissed when I left the room with D.J. that morning—pissed at Terry, who had successfully played the more-exhausted-than-you card (every parent is issued a deck), not at D.J., who was only guilty of being wide awake.

But my anger faded and my exhaustion lifted as I strolled through the streets of Paris with D.J. on my shoulders as the sun was coming up. At one point I noticed some Parisians—not tourists like us, but honest-to-God locals—slipping down an alley and returning a moment later with bags of pastries. D.J. ran ahead to investigate. The baker at a patisserie was selling warm pastries out the back door of his not-yet-open shop. We picked up a large bag of warm sugar brioche, found a bench in a small park along the Seine, and sat together, talking and eating, as Paris came to life around us.

Ninety minutes earlier I would've given anything to be in bed in our hotel room, sound asleep. But at that moment, I wouldn't have wanted to be anywhere else, or with anyone else, on earth.

Another high: A few years later, we moved into a new neighborhood and one day D.J. and a friend were rude to a pack of girls who lived down the block. The girls' mother came over, introduced herself, told us what had happened, and helpfully suggested that maybe D.J. had "issues with women." We suggested that D.J. was an eight-year-old boy, and like a lot of eight-year-old boys, he didn't have much use for girls. That's no excuse for rudeness, of course, and we were sincerely grateful to our new neighbor for giving us a heads-up. We assured her that we would sit D.J. down and read him the riot act. And we did just that: Sitting at the kitchen table we explained to D.J. that he had to be nice to all the kids in the neighborhood, boys *and* girls. He didn't have to play with the girls on the block. But there would be swift and painful consequences if he wasn't civil to the girls.

"Anyway, D.J.," I added, as the conversation was wrapping up, "one day you're going to want to talk to girls, so it might not be a bad idea to talk to one or two now, at age eight, while the stakes are still low."

D.J. pulled himself up and said, nope, he would never have to talk to girls because he was gay. He hated girls, girls were gross, and he had no use for them. So he was *definitely* going to be gay. Terry and I both burst out laughing. We explained that disliking girls at age eight typically isn't a sign that a boy is going to be gay when he grows up. Quite the opposite, in fact. D.J. dug in: hates girls, girls are gross, gonna be gay. Terry pulled out a photo album and showed D.J. a picture from his ninth birthday party: The only other boy at Terry's party was his brother. All the other guests—all twenty of them—were girls. All of his friends, when he was D.J.'s age, were girls. Gross girls.

D.J.'s eyes went from the photo album, to Terry, to me, and back to the photo album. Then he broke into a fit of laughter. At first D.J. was laughing at Terry—all your friends were *girls*?!?—but the quality of D.J.'s laughter quickly changed. It was the laughter of recognition—self-recognition.

Five short years and one casual coming-out scene later, I would sit at the same kitchen table and talk with D.J. about birth control. We'd had the birds-and-the-bees talk years earlier (botched at first, later amended), but now he had a girlfriend and I thought a review was in order.

"Dad! We're not *doing* anything," D.J. protested. "We're only *thirteen!*"

I told him I didn't think he was *doing* anything, I didn't want him *doing* anything, and that he was way too young to be *doing* anything. But plenty of thirteen-year-old boys have gotten their thirteen-year-old girlfriends pregnant. At this point I showed him teen pregnancy statistics from the CDC. (Being confronted with such statistics is one of the chief terrors of having a sex writer for a parent.) Without a doubt, the parents of all these pregnant thirteen-year-olds assumed their kids weren't *doing* anything either, I said. And they were *wrong*.

"Sorry, D.J.," I said, "but if you're old enough to have a girlfriend, you're old enough to listen to your dad talk about condoms."

Same kitchen table, same laughter, same high.

There's one more high I'd like to share—a more recent one—but there's something I need to come clean about first.

At the start of this chapter I claimed a small measure of credit for the boom in families headed by same-sex couples. And while it's true that there are a lot more same-sex couples adopting today than there were a decade and a half ago, and while it's also true that a lot of gay male couples have been inspired to adopt by *The Kid* (an e-mail arrived from a gay man thanking me and Terry for inspiring him and his partner to adopt while I was working on this chapter), those facts need to be placed in context.

The truth is that my contribution to the gay-parenting movement pales in comparison to the contributions made by others. These men—and they're almost always men—are the true heroes of the gay-parenting movement. I speak of Tony Perkins, Bryan Fischer, Rick Warren, Joel Osteen, Marcus Bachmann, Mike Huckabee, Gary Bauer, Peter LaBarbera, Pope Benedict XVI, and Rick Santorum, as well as homophobic preachers and parents everywhere.

In January of 2011, *The New York Times* reported data that the Census Bureau had gathered on gay families. As it turns out, the states with the highest percentages of families headed by same-sex couples aren't the ones you would expect. Same-sex couples in the Bible Belt (i.e., Arkansas, Louisiana, Mississippi) are actually much more likely to be raising children than same-sex couples in the Sanity Belt (i.e., the West Coast, New England, the Great Lake states).

"A large number of gay couples . . . entered into their current relationship after first having children with partners in heterosexual relationships," Sabrina Tavernise reports. And why are gay people entering into heterosexual relationships? Tavernise quotes a representative gay parent: "People grew up in church, so a lot of us lived in shame," said Darlene Maffett, a lesbian woman who was married for eight years and had two children before finally coming out in 2002.

There would be far fewer families headed by same-sex couples if not for the efforts of Christian conservatives. The homophobia that Perkins and the rest of his hateful crew work so hard to promote convinces many young gays and lesbians—who fear being rejected by their families—to attempt to live a straight life. And what better way to nail the closet door shut than to marry an opposite-sex partner and quickly have some children? (The study also found that same-sex parents in the Bible Belt tended to have their children at considerably younger ages than same-sex parents in the Sanity Belt.)

Anti-gay Christian conservatives like Tony Perkins and Bryan Fischer have put more gay men and lesbians on their "journey to parenthood" than I ever have. The homophobia they promote, and the fear and self-loathing it instills in gay teenagers, creates more families headed by same-sex couples in the end than all the gay adoption memoirs and gay adoption agencies and gay surrogacy programs in the country *combined*.

Now, if you'll indulge me, here's that one last high I'd like to recount.

We had taken D.J. and two of his friends on a snowboarding trip. The adults were in the kitchen, cleaning up after dinner, while the three teenage boys sat around the dining room table taking the piss out of each other. It was good-natured stuff—crude but not cruel—until one of the boys turned to D.J. and said, "So you have gay parents. Guess that means you're going to be gay too."

There was a long silence. D.J. was fourteen then, straight and out and proud, with one girlfriend down (that relationship was short-lived) and God only knows how many to go. Terry and I looked at each other, not sure what to do. D.J.'s friend was baiting him—and baiting him with an unsubtle homophobic jab within earshot of D.J.'s gay parents!—but we hesitated to come to D.J.'s defense. He had long ago made it clear that he didn't need or want us to fight his battles for him.

"My parents are gay," D.J. finally said, breaking the silence. "But *their* parents were straight. Like your parents. So if anyone else is going to be gay around here, it's *you*."

Terry and I looked at each other, our jaws hanging open, not sure how to respond. What D.J.'s friend said to him was homophobic. And D.J.'s response to his friend was homophobic. But it was also genius.

Should we say something? Do something? Terry shook his head and stifled a laugh.

Another high disguised as a low. We let it go.

7. Crazy, Mad, Salacious

My dad liked cop shows.

He was a cop, a homicide detective assigned to Chicago's seedy gay neighborhood in the seventies. And like a lot of cops, what Dad most enjoyed about watching cop shows was pointing out where they got it wrong. There was just one show on TV that got police work even slightly right, according to my dad. *Barney Miller* ran on ABC from 1975, when I was eleven, to 1982, when I was seventeen. The officers on *Barney Miller* weren't beat cops. They were detectives, like my dad. Their jobs were tedious, like my dad's—all paperwork and bad coffee, no car chases, no shoot-outs. And the detectives were middle-aged and out of shape, like my dad. And like my dad, the detectives on *Barney Miller* policed a seedy gay neighborhood, New York City's Greenwich Village.

There was a recurring gay character on *Barney Miller,* one of the first on television. Very swishy, carried a purse, owned a poodle. Sometimes we would be watching television together when the gay character appeared in an episode, and my dad would always sit there in silence until he was gone. My dad liked cop movies too. And I remember watching one in particular with my dad—*The Choirboys,* a 1977 movie—in our living room sometime after it came out on video. And how's this for a coincidence? The cops in *The Choirboys* policed Los Angeles's seedy gay neighborhood. And in one scene, one of the guys—one of the cops—is handcuffed to a tree in a cruisy park and left there with his pants around his ankles.

And who should come upon this helpless, bare-assed cop? A swishy gay guy carrying a purse, walking a poodle. He takes one look at the cop and says, "I can't believe it. A naked man chained to a tree. That's a crazy, mad, salacious dream."

"I'll kill you if you touch me, you fag son of a bitch," the cop says. "I'll rip your damn kidneys out. I'll punch your spleen."

"You'd do that for me?" the swish replies. Then he saunters off with his poodle—which is, of course, dyed pink.

Watching that with my dad when I was a teenager made me want to die because I knew I was going to be some kind of fag when I grew up and so did he. But I wasn't ready to talk about the subject with him and he certainly wasn't going to go anywhere near it. So when gays popped up on TV—something that began to happen with much greater frequency just as I hit puberty—things got awkward.

We watched the park scene in *The Choirboys* in complete silence, just as we watched *Barney Miller* in silence whenever the recurring gay character was in an episode. Here was this subject we were both trying to avoid at all costs, and all of a sudden, we were ambushed by the television set. I was already painfully self-conscious about certain tell-tale mannerisms and interests of my own. My passion for musical the-ater, my complete want of male friends, and my inability to focus on anything else whenever Andy Gibb was on *Solid Gold* alarmed both my parents. I would sometimes force myself to listen to Top 40 hits, hang out with boys from the neighborhood, or watch a Cubs game. It wasn't until years later that I found out my mom and dad were fine—or would be eventually—with me being gay. The reason my dad got so quiet when gay characters appeared on TV? (A silence I interpreted at the time for simmering disgust.) It turns out he didn't want to make me feel bad by laughing.

But sitting in front of the TV with my silent father all those years ago, I made a resolution. I was going to be some kind of fag when I grew up, I knew that, but I wasn't going to be *that* kind of fag. I wasn't going to carry a purse. And I would never come upon a half-naked cop, chained to a tree in a cruisy park, late at night, because I wasn't going to be walking any poodles around cruisy parks late at night. Because I wasn't going to be the kind of fag that owned a poodle.

I was going to be a different kind of fag. I wasn't going to be like the ones on TV in 1982. And straight people—my dad, Ronald Reagan, Anita Bryant—were going to like me.

The gay men portrayed on television when I was growing up distressed me—they put me in an awkward position—but they didn't upset me. They didn't upset me then, and they don't upset me now. I've spoken to other gay men close to my age who seethe when they remember gay characters on television with their poodles and purses, their lisps and limp wrists. It never occurred to me to be angry.

But, still, I made up my mind not to be like them. I could see that straight people held effeminate gay men in contempt; they saw them as weak and ridiculous. Gay men with pink poodles were hated; real men wanted to punch their spleens.

Once I came out, of course, it didn't take me long to realize that, first, not all straight people are homophobes, and second, straight people who *are* homophobic don't make distinctions between masculine and feminine gay men. They hate us all, purses or no purses, poodles or no poodles. And the feminine guys I got to know after coming out? The guys I didn't want to be like? They weren't weak and ridiculous. They were strong, and they were brave. (And some of them were hot, and some of the hot ones were really good in bed.)

Now whenever a friend complains about gays on television, I immediately concede that, yes, most gay characters are stereotypes. Back then, and even now. But is the portrayal of heterosexuals on television any better? The gays on *Will & Grace* in the 1990s were caricatures, yes, but so were the straights on *Friends*. Do real-life straight people act anything like the crazy-ass breeders on *Desperate Housewives*? And do real straight people act like the fake straight people did on *Lost*? (Has anyone ever acted like the straight people did on *Lost*?) Do real straight people act like Tom Cruise on *Oprah*? On *Modern Family* the relationship between Cam and Mitch, a gay couple with a small child, is nearly sexless, which, knowing what we do about gay men, seems fairly unrealistic. But Claire and Phil, the harried straight parents of three teenagers, have an active sex life, which, knowing what we do about long-married straight couples, may be even less realistic.

Only an idiot looks to television to form a picture of what straight people are really like. Only an idiot . . . or a child. Perhaps a child who, like Lily on *Modern Family*, has gay parents.

When D.J. was old enough to use the remote, I felt as if I were regressing to my teen years, suddenly worried about how people of a certain specific sexuality were portrayed on television. Only this time it wasn't the homosexual characters I was worried about. It was the heterosexual characters. Because I knew my straight son was watching.

I knew D.J. was straight the same way my parents knew I was gay: I just knew it. I always knew it. I knew it in my gut. But, unlike my parents, I wasn't in denial. I didn't push it out of my mind or try not to think about it or hope that I might be wrong.

And I was conscious, as D.J. grew, that he was learning about his sexuality watching television, just as I once learned about mine watching television. And in those formative years, when D.J. was seven, eight years old, the treatment of heterosexuality on one show in particular offended me so much that I banned him from watching it. And I'm not talking about the *Real Housewives* franchise here. We wouldn't have let him watch *Real Housewives* if he had wanted to. And he didn't want to. Reality shows were, for D.J., just so many grown-ups shouting at each other. And D.J. didn't have to watch TV for a taste of that.

No, this was a show for kids on the Disney Channel, one of the most popular kids' shows on TV then. And it was a show D.J. adored. *The Suite Life of Zack & Cody* is about twin brothers who live in a hotel in

Boston, the Tipton, where their divorced mom works as a cabaret singer.

Zack and Cody were always getting into crazy scrapes and hatching harebrained schemes. They were preteens themselves—ten or eleven years old—just a year or two older than D.J. In some ways this show defied stereotypes. There's a character named London, a spoiled rich girl played by an Asian actress but—get this—she's *Asian*, yeah, but she's *dumb*. And then there's Maddie, a teenage girl who works at the hotel candy shop, played by a blond actress, but—are you sitting down?—Maddie is blond, sure, but she's *smart*. And then there's Mr. Moseby, the hotel manager, played by a black actor. But he's *fussy*. Don't know if he owns a poodle, as I haven't seen every episode, but he's definitely the poodle-owning type.

But what offended me—what worried me—was the behavior of one of the twins. Zack was sexually precocious in a deeply creepy way. (Can a prepubescent boy be sexually precocious in a way that isn't deeply creepy?) Zack was also the more charismatic twin: Zack was Lucy to Cody's Ethel. Zack was the athletic one, the risk taker. And in every episode Zack wanted, ached for, pined for, and *sexually harassed* Maddie, the smart blond. Maddie was sixteen or seventeen. Zack was in elementary school; Maddie was in high school. Zack was prepubescent; Maddie was postpubescent.

I didn't like D.J. to watch TV alone when he was young. So I'd plop down on the couch with a book and sit with him, which is how I caught the episode of *Suite Life* where Zack worries about Maddie hooking up with other guys. An episode where Zack instructs other little boys on the art of talking to babes. His advice? One lies to babes. In one particular episode, "A Prom Story," Zack walks up to Maddie and—well, let's just read the dialogue.

> ZACK, *looking Maddie up and down*: Hey, sweet thing. What's the special today? I hope it's tall, blond, and curvy.

I'm not sure how a teenager would react to being hit on by a ten-year-old boy in real life because it never happens. But somehow fictional Zack escapes the humiliation or the punch in the chest that any real-life Zack would immediately be subjected to. Instead, Zack emerges from this encounter with the impression that Maddie has just asked him to go with her to her prom. Zack runs up to Cody.

ZACK, *excited*: Did you hear that? Maddie wants to dance with
me at her prom. I'd better practice my kissing.
CODY, *nauseated*: Don't look at me.

That is a threefer right there. You've got a prepubescent horny boy joke, an incest joke, and a cliché homophobic reaction to the idea of two boys kissing, brothers or not.

Thanks, Disney.

D.J. watched *The Suite Life of Zack & Cody* with a look of concentration on his face, a look he didn't get watching any other shows, a look he certainly doesn't get when his parents are talking to him. He looked like he was filing things away for future reference. For a boy without older brothers, a boy without straight male uncles or cousins living nearby, we worried that the way Zack treats women could be a problem every bit as damaging to a young straight boy as those images of gay men with poodles were to me.

And that is why we banned D.J. from watching *Suite Life*—that and an episode where Zack drilled a hole in the wall so he could spy on girls using the bathroom. There are people who will be on sex-offender registries for the rest of their lives for doing exactly what Disney showed Zack doing.

Parental bans are not only ineffective—they're counterproductive. I knew this from my own childhood. My father banned us kids from watching *Three's Company* (too sexual) and listening to the music of Kiss (too satanic). So his children watched *Three's Company* at houses of our friends and hid Kiss records in the jackets of Beach Boys albums. And D.J. continued to watch *Suite Life*—at the houses of his friends, and when his parents weren't in the room monitoring his television viewing.

I cling to one hope. Despite my exposure to all those swishy gay men walking poodles on TV during my formative years, I grew up to be a different kind of gay. And despite the girl-crazy little boys D.J. saw on the Disney Channel, he seems to be growing up to be a different kind of straight. Maybe we'll both wind up defying the stereotypes.

The only problem with that is fate. You can defy a stereotype. You can work against it. But stereotypes are patient. Sometimes they wait you out; they wear you down; they lull you into a false sense of security. And then—bam—one day you wake up and you're the owner of a poodle.

When D.J. was five years old, he asked Santa for a poodle. And he didn't want any poodle; he wanted a *toy* poodle. A poodle he planned to name Pierre.

I tried to stop it—selfishly, for my own sake—but I framed every argument as concern for D.J. We can't do this to him, I told Terry. He's already got gay parents, and I'm one of them. The cross he has to bear is big and pink enough already. Were we really going to nail a poodle to it too?

But D.J. was adamant. He had a friend, a boy with opposite-sex parents—straight parents—and his friend with the opposite-sex parents had a toy poodle. These people recruited my son. That's what poodle people do. They lure you into the poodle lifestyle by targeting your children.

We did manage to talk D.J. into a less gay name for his poodle. Stinker has just one eye, is completely deaf, doesn't come when you call him, and runs into walls and chairs and trees. And D.J. loves him.

I know all about Stinker's habit of running into trees because I'm the one who somehow gets stuck walking the dog at night. We live on

Capitol Hill, which is Seattle's gay neighborhood. We live near a big park. Seattle's cruisiest park. It's called Volunteer Park, fittingly enough, as you can find a volunteer under every other bush. And you can find me there too, late at night, walking a poodle.

"It's not my poodle," I once wanted to scream at anyone who gave me a look. "It's my son's poodle. My straight son's poodle. Not mine."

But I'm used to Stinker now. I've adjusted. I've accepted myself as a gay man who owns a poodle; and like the fags in *Barney Miller* and *The Choirboys,* I proudly walk my poodle through a cruisy park late at night.

Family is ultimately a more powerful influence than television. Hopefully we can help D.J. adjust to girl-crazy, when his time comes, just as he helped me adjust to poodle ownership.

And just as D.J.'s father can walk a poodle around a cruisy park without being a total fag, I'm confident that one day D.J. will go girl-crazy without turning into a total Zack.

Or that's what I tell myself anyway, when I'm walking D.J.'s poodle in the cruisy park late at night. I'm sure it's only a matter of time now before Stinker runs headfirst into a tree that has a bare-assed cop handcuffed to it.

8. Folsom Prism Blues

Sally Kern is one of America's lesser bigots.

There are a lot of bigoted Republican state legislators out there—and a few Democratic ones, too, but they seem to have the good sense to keep their mouths shut—so it takes real effort for a bigoted state legislator to rise to national attention. In the fall of 2012, for instance, America became acquainted with two bigoted Republican state legislators. Loy Mauch, a Republican member of the Arkansas State House of Representatives, asked in a letter to the editor in the *Arkansas Democrat Gazette,* "If slavery were so God-awful, why didn't Jesus or Paul condemn it [in the Bible]?" (I got into no end of trouble with conservative Christians and Republicans when I pointed out the same thing—the Bible doesn't condemn slavery. Quite the opposite: The Bible *endorses* slavery.) Terry England, a member of the Georgia State House of Representatives, compared women to farm animals during a floor debate about a bill that would have required women to carry all fetuses to term—even dead ones. "Life gives us many experiences," England said during the debate. "I've had the experience of delivering calves, dead and alive—delivering pigs, dead and alive."

Sally Kern, a former schoolteacher, has been a member of the Oklahoma House of Representatives since 2005. Kern first rose to national attention in March of 2008 when she said that homosexuality posed a direct and immediate threat to the United States. ("I honestly think [homosexuality] is the biggest threat our nation has, even more so than terrorism or Islam—which I think is a big threat. . . . It will destroy this nation!") Kern made national news again in February of 2009 when she told a gathering of the John Birch Society—who knew those tinfoil asshats were still meeting?—that America needed a new "Great Awakening" to combat the homosexual menace. The gays have a secret plan to convince the world that homosexuality is a "superior lifestyle," Kern warned the Birchers, and America needs to be on its guard against our nefarious themes:

> You know, I've done a lot of reading on this. I wish I could describe to you their behavior. I will not because I would be redder than this suit. . . . This theme of equality and freedom is the approach that the homosexuals are using today—totally perverting the true intention of what our Constitution meant. The homosexuals get it—it's a struggle between our religious freedoms and their right to do what they want to do.

Straight Americans would be "shocked and repelled" if they were exposed to the depraved things that gay Americans do—and Kern means gay *male* Americans (Kern doesn't obsess about lesbians)—and if straight Americans don't wake up and start fighting the gay agenda, Kern warned the Birchers, the gays will eventually convince the straights that the homosexual lifestyle is superior and pretty soon all Americans will be engaging in "depraved" gay behaviors.

My first impulse after reading Kern's comments was to run home and take a picture of a plate of cookies that was sitting on my kitchen counter. That's actually what I did: I got up from my desk, walked out of my office, jumped on my bike, rode home, and took a picture of a plate of peanut-butter cookies sitting on my kitchen counter. I baked the cookies myself the night before—from *scratch,* thank you very much—because baking is something I enjoy doing for my family. You could call it a "depraved behavior," I suppose, if you consider carbs depraved, which many gay men do. The plan was to post the picture of the cookies on my blog and put this question to Kern: "Is this the kind of depraved behavior that you meant, Sally? Baking cookies for your family?"

Whenever a right-wing bigot like Kern starts dropping dark hints about all the top-secret, super-crazy sex stuff we gay people get up to when straight people aren't watching, lots of gay people reflexively point to all the *wholesome* things we do. It's a knee-jerk, defensive response. Kern says we're all depraved perverts; gays and lesbians write blog posts and send tweets about PTA meetings and baking cookies and running errands for sick relatives: "We take care of our families; we pay our taxes; we bake cookies. What's so depraved about *that*? We're really not so different!"

But we are different.

Kern has a point. Gay men *do* tend to have more interesting sex lives than straight people do. There are lots of sexually adventurous straight people out there, of course, just as there are lots of sexually conservative gay people. (For the record: Not all sexually conservative people are repressed, just as not all sexually adventurous people are liberated.) But gay people are more likely to be sexually adventurous than straight people. Yes, gay people bake cookies. Yes, gay people go to work and pay taxes and take care of our families. But let's be honest: If we use Kern's implied definition of "depraved"—she means "kinky"—then, yeah, gay men are generally more "depraved" than straight people. It's not that gay men are any likelier to be kinky than straight men. We're just likelier to be open about it. Telling your mom and dad you're a cocksucker is *hard*. Telling your boyfriend you want to be spanked before you suck his cock? That's *easy*.

And so long as a gay guy is safe and sane about his kinks, so long as he indulges in moderation and only with men who share his kinks, there's no harm, no foul, and no depravity.

I didn't post the picture of those cookies to my blog that day. Because even as I stood in my kitchen, hovering over the plate of cookies on the counter with my phone in hand, I knew that to post that picture was a mildly dishonest deflection and not an answer. Yes, I baked those cookies. Yes, baking peanut-butter cookies for your family is pretty damn wholesome. But the fact of the matter is my sex life *would* turn Kern's face redder than the Republican-red dresses she favors.[1] Even in our eighteenth year together—our fifteenth as parents—Terry and I still have a great sex life. We enjoy the kinds of "behaviors" that fascinate the Sally Kerns of this world. And while I could hide behind a plate of peanut-butter cookies, why should I have to? Our sex life is good and varied and keeps getting better. We meet each other's needs, we indulge each other's kinks, and we're having a blast. All married couples should be so lucky.

I would share a few specific examples, but Terry doesn't allow me to write about our sex life.

Back when we first met, Terry gave me a choice: I could write about my sex life or I could have sex with him. But I couldn't write about my sex life *and* have sex with him. I choose sex with him. Terry does allow me to share a rough outline: We're monogam*ish*, meaning we're mostly monogamous; we enjoy some run-of-the-mill kinks, nothing crazy, nothing dangerous (we never do anything that would endanger our bowel functions). One other detail Terry allows me to share: My husband looks good in leather.

My husband looks *really* good in leather.

I was actually looking at my husband decked out in leather when I

---

1 Listening to the tape of Mrs. Kern fuming about depraved sex acts, I couldn't help feeling a little sorry for Mr. Kern. I don't think Mr. Kern wants to get his kink on with gay dudes—although you never know with the homophobes—but odds are good that Mr. Kern, like so many straight men, has a few non-standard-issue sexual interests. If Mr. Kern has a kink or two (highly probable given the law of averages), he can't share them with his wife. Because according to Mrs. Kern, kinks that turn your face (and other things) red are for homosexuals. Kinks define homosexuality, according to Mrs. Kern. Which is kind of sad for Mr. Kern if he's kinky, which he very well could be.

suddenly remembered Kern's comments to the John Birch Society months after she made them. We were standing in a hotel lobby in downtown Chicago, each with a vodka and Red Bull in hand, surrounded by thousands of other gay men wearing leather. I pulled my phone out of my pocket and scrolled through the pictures until I found the one of the cookies.

Terry and I were attending International Mr. Leather (IML), an annual contest/beauty pageant/party for the gay leather/S&M/fetish crowd. The International Mr. Leather Contest, which has been held in Chicago every Memorial Day weekend since 1979, transforms its host hotel into the World's Biggest Leather Bar. Terry looks good in leather—have I mentioned that my husband looks good in leather?—and I've always had an affinity for leather bars. After years of talking about going to IML, we finally decided to take the plunge a few years ago. We've been back three times.

The Kerns of the world point to IML as proof that gay people are too depraved for even basic civil rights protections, much less marriage and family life. But everywhere Terry and I went at IML that first year, we met guys who had been together for five, ten, twenty, and thirty years. Some of the gay couples we met at IML were there to look, some were there to play, and some, like us, left kids back home with grandparents for the weekend. Despite what Sally Kern would have you believe, there doesn't seem to be anything mutually exclusive about conspicuous displays of wholesomeness (baking cookies) and conspicuous displays of depravity (attending an event like IML).

So perhaps instead of reflexively pointing to our homemade peanut-butter cookies when someone like Sally Kern levels a charge of sexual "depravity" against gay men, we should respond by pointing to our cookies *and* our occasional wild weekends. Gay people seem to have a much easier time reconciling love and lust, commitment and desire. We can have loving, stable relationships and our sexual adventures too. We can have homemade peanut-butter cookies *and* IML.

And maybe in that way—and only in that way—gay people *are* superior.

The International Mr. Leather Contest doesn't just attract thousands of gay men from all over the world to Chicago every Memorial Day weekend. It also attracts a certain hater from the Chicago suburbs.

Peter LaBarbera is the founder of Americans for Truth About Homosexuality (AFTAH), an anti-gay hate group based in Naperville, Illinois. AFTAH is "devoted exclusively to exposing and countering the homosexual activist agenda," according to its website.

LaBarbera was a reporter at the Moonie-owned *Washington Times* in the early 1990s before leaving to work for Concerned Women for America and a handful of other anti-gay groups.

"Formed as a part-time venture in 1996 by long-time gay-basher Peter LaBarbera, who reorganized [AFTAH] in 2006 as a much more serious and influential, if often vicious, operation," the Southern Poverty Law Center (SPLC) wrote in 2010, when it placed AFTAH on its list of anti-gay hate groups. AFTAH, according to SPLC, repeats bogus claims like the notion that there is "a disproportionate incidence of pedophilia" among gay men, or that a proposed bill in California would "promote cross-dressing, sex-change operations, bisexuality and homosexuality to kindergartners."

LaBarbera is best known in the gay community for "infiltrating" IML, an event that's easily infiltrated, as it's open to the public. (Even so, you have to pass through multiple screening checkpoints, produce ID to prove you're over twenty-one, and sign a waiver before entering the Leather Market, where merchants sell gear, porn stars stroll around in jockstraps, and bondage and flogging demonstrations take place.) Once LaBarbera manages to get inside IML—which he does by walking through the doors—he takes pictures of gay men in fetish gear or nothing at all. LaBarbera posts his pictures to AFTAH's website under warnings like, "Not for children! Graphic photos below with offensive depictions of real-life homosexual depravities!"

LaBarbera's campaign to expose the "depravities" at IML—an effort that earned him the nickname "Porno Pete" from gay bloggers—can be charitably described as pointlessly redundant. Every year IML attendees post tens of thousands of pictures to their own blogs, Facebook pages, Twitter feeds, and Instagram accounts. There's also a massive photo archive on IML's official website (www.imrl.com), where anyone with (1) an Internet connection; and (2) a passionate interest in "homosexual depravity" can view and download thousands of images of gay men in leather harnesses, dog collars, and rubber bodysuits.

If the gay men who attend IML are trying to keep their "homosexual depravity" secret, well, they're doing a piss-poor job of it. (They're doing about as lousy a job hiding their depravity as all those straight women reading *Fifty Shades of Grey* in public are doing hiding theirs.) And since no one has to attend IML to get his hands on pictures of all that homosexual depravity, there must be some other reason that LaBarbera feels compelled to sneak into IML and take pictures. I wonder what that reason could be.

Thinking . . . thinking . . .

I'm drawing a blank. Maybe a good reason will come to me before I finish this chapter.

AFTAH isn't just content to photo-document the atrocities at IML year in, year out. LaBarbera has tried to shut IML down by issuing boycott threats against the small number of Chicago hotels large enough to host the event.

"Would you want to sleep in the same bed where a homosexual orgy—or drunken, orgiastic encounter between two 'leathermen'— took place with body fluids and feces flying here and there? Neither would we," LaBarbera wrote on AFTAH's website in 2011. "Tell the Hyatt Regency Chicago that it is wrong and un-hygienic to profit off perversion-fests like IML." (I don't want to get too graphic here or anything, as this book is headed for the Library of Congress, but if feces is "flying here and there" when you have anal sex, *you're doing it wrong*. One doesn't have anal sex with an ass full of shit for the same reason one doesn't have oral sex with a mouth full of food—it's uncomfortable and it makes a mess.)

LaBarbera's anti-depravity crusade isn't limited to IML. In January of 2009, AFTAH rallied its right-wing Christian followers behind an effort to shut down a kink-and-swinging gathering in Columbus, Ohio. LaBarbera conducted a phone harassment campaign targeting the host hotel for "Winter Wickedness." AFTAH demanded that the hotel break its contract with the organizers and cancel the event.

"LaBarbera's tongue hangs out as he details all of the various demos and activities slated for this weekend's Winter Wickedness," gay blogger Joe Jervis wrote about the controversy, "but he fails to mention the *slight* detail that this is an event primarily for *heterosexuals*."

Why would LaBarbera and Americans for Truth About Homosexuality leave *that* little detail out of the "action alert" they sent to their anti-gay followers? Because Peter LaBarbera, like Sally Kern, wants people to believe that all gays are depraved perverts and all depraved perverts are gay.

Acknowledging the existence of kinky heterosexuals would complicate LaBarbera's efforts to convince his already-convinced followers that gay people, and only gay people, are capable of sending bodily fluids and feces flying all over a hotel room. (Straight people have anal sex too; in real numbers, more straight people engage in anal intercourse than gay people.)

LaBarbera did not succeed in shutting down Winter Wickedness, although attendees did have to run a gauntlet of local TV news cameras to enter the hotel. And he didn't succeed in fooling me with his "action alert" either. I knew right away that Winter Wickedness was a straight event. The hotel where it was taking place? The hotel LaBarbera was asking his followers to call?

A Holiday Inn.

There's not a lot gay men won't do—go look at the photos on IML's website if you don't believe me—but we draw the line at spending a weekend at a Holiday Inn in the suburbs of Columbus, Ohio.

Here are six words that I never thought I would type in this precise order: *In all fairness to Peter LaBarbera . . .*

Porno Pete appears to have lost interest in shutting down International Mr. Leather. He didn't attend the most recent IML; some other mole was dispatched from AFTAH World Headquarters. LaBarbera's compatriot was so distressed by what she saw in the Leather Market—gay men *shopping*—that she had to retreat to her car "to settle [her] nerves" before diving back in again and again. The steam also seems to have gone out of LaBarbera's efforts to harass IML's host hotel into dropping the event. Maybe it was the glowing feature about IML in the *Chicago Tribune* a few years ago. If the editors of a reliably Republican paper like the *Tribune* see IML as essentially harmless—as evidenced by their willingness to publish a long puff piece about it—what hope does LaBarbera have of convincing the average Chicagoan, much less the Hyatt Hotel Corporation, that IML is a feces-flinging "perversion-fest" that must be stopped?

But Porno Pete hasn't entirely lost his passion for large gatherings of gay men in leather, rubber, and bondage gear. His focus has simply shifted from gay men behaving badly in the city by the lake to gay men behaving badly in the city on the bay.

The Folsom Street Fair is an annual one-day leather/fetish street party that has been taking place on a Sunday in late September in San

Francisco every year since 1984. Unlike IML, which requires attend-ees to sign waivers before they can enter spaces where adults are wearing revealing outfits and purchasing sex toys, the Folsom Street Fair is, as attentive readers may have already deduced, a *street fair*. The guys, the goods, and the gear are out in the open. Attendees do have to pass through gates to enter the fair, there are signs at every entrance warning people they are about to enter an adult-themed fetish festival, and the whole thing takes place in the South of Market neighborhood, long home to San Francisco's leather bars, BDSM-gear shops, and sex clubs.

"Nothing screams 'Perversion!' like the annual Folsom Street Fair in San Francisco, America's first homosexual Mecca," LaBarbera wrote on AFTAH's website in August of 2012. "AFTAH has documented the unprecedented public perversions and nudity of this bizarre out-door 'fair' as police stand idly by." LaBarbera then invites his readers to peruse six different archives of pictures taken at Folsom by under-cover AFTAH operatives. (Needless to say, the attendees and organiz-ers of the Folsom Street Fair post thousands of pictures to Facebook, Twitter, and Instagram, and hundreds of photos are posted every year at the organization's official website: www.folsomstreetevents.org.)

Some ask why kinksters feel a need to have street fairs and conven-tions. Kinks are well and good, but why gather in groups to celebrate and practice them? Why do this stuff in public? Why create a commu-nity around kink?

Here's why:

> An Alabama minister who died in June of "accidental mechanical asphyxia" was found hogtied and wearing two complete wet suits, including a face mask, diving gloves and slippers, rubberized underwear, and a head mask, ac-cording to an autopsy report. Investigators determined that Rev. Gary Aldridge's death was not caused by foul play and

that the 51-year-old pastor of Montgomery's Thorington Road Baptist Church was alone in his home at the time he died (while apparently in the midst of some autoerotic undertaking). While the Montgomery Advertiser, which first obtained the autopsy records, reported on Aldridge's two wet suits, the family newspaper chose not to mention what police discovered inside the minister's rubber briefs.

That's from a report on the website *The Smoking Gun*.

Thorington Road Baptist Church issued a press release asking people to "refrain from speculation" about Aldridge's death. So I won't speculate about the death of the married Baptist minister—and former Liberty University dean—or the contents of his rubber briefs at the time he died. (A big, black dildo.) But I will say this: The pastor of Thorington Road Baptist would probably still be alive today if he had been indulging his passion for bondage, wet suits, diving gloves, hoods, rubber briefs, and black dildos on the streets of San Francisco during Folsom or at the Leather Market in Chicago during IML and not home alone in Montgomery, Alabama.

The late Reverend Aldridge's kinks aren't uncommon and neither is solo-bondage play. There are thousands of hours of digital video on Xtube and other amateur porn sites showing men—and it's always men—in elaborate "self-bondage" scenarios. Many of them are wearing wet suits, like Rev. Aldridge, and the hogtie seems to be a popular position with self-bondage enthusiasts. Bondage is inherently dangerous, particularly when combined with autoerotic asphyxiation, and no one should experiment with bondage alone, and a tied-up person should never be left alone. And Rev. Aldridge might be alive today if he had been shameless about his sexual depravity—that is, if he were part of a kinky community, just another masked-and-gagged face in the crowd at Folsom or IML.

I don't want to be Pollyannaish about this. Even simple BDSM is varsity-level sex play; some BDSM activities are Olympic-level. BDSM can be dangerous. A person can get hurt; a person can hurt others. But BDSM is infinitely more dangerous when people do it alone, or when they do it with someone who isn't a part of, and therefore answerable to, others in the kink community. An organized kink scene isn't foolproof: Experienced kinksters have died during BDSM scenes that went disastrously wrong; people have been sexually assaulted by predators that gravitated toward the kink scene. But most deaths in BDSM scenes gone wrong—all of them senseless and tragic deaths—are similar to Rev. Aldridge's death: People died playing alone while engaged in a self-bondage scenario that restricted their breathing. Considered in that light, events like Folsom and IML actually do a public good. They are probably even saving lives. People at Folsom and IML don't just engage in BDSM sex; they share skills and enforce community norms around safe BDSM play.

And, once again, in all fairness to Peter LaBarbera (I can't believe I had to type that twice), not every critic of Folsom or IML is an anti-gay nut running a hate group out of his basement. Some of Folsom's most annoying critics are gay.

Every year, after Folsom or IML or a pride parade with a BDSM contingent, letters appear in gay newspapers and posts appear on gay blogs expressing "concern." At a time when gay people are struggling for equality, the concern trolls fret in unison: *We can't afford to have leathermen and BDSMers and kinksters walking around in public. They're setting back the gay rights movement!*

Any attempt to shut down the Folsom Street Fair—or to ban leathermen or drag queens or go-go boys from pride parades—would be so poisonously divisive that it would do more harm to the gay rights movement than a thousand Folsom Street Fairs ever could.

And the Folsom Street Fair isn't and hasn't been exclusively gay for a long time. Thousands of straight kinksters attend Folsom, to the dismay of some gay attendees. The only difference between straight and gay Folsom attendees is that the straight ones aren't told that they're making all heterosexuals look like sex-crazed sadomasochists. (In my opinion, sex-crazed sadomasochists are the best kind of sadomasochists.) Straight people aren't fighting for their civil equality, of course; kinky straights can marry in all fifty states, kinky straights can serve openly in the armed forces, and no one is pledging to write anti-kinky-straight bigotry into the US Constitution. (Although kinky straight people have been discriminated against in divorce proceedings and child custody arrangements.) So maybe it's not the *same*—maybe it's not as politically risky—when straight people come out in bondage gear, leather chaps, and pony masks.

Despite the protests of anti-gay nuts and concern trolls alike, the Folsom Street Fair is almost thirty years old now; IML is well into its fourth decade; and pride parades, complete with go-go boys and drag queens and leathermen, have been taking place on Sundays in June in cities all over the country since the early 1970s. And everyone acknowledges, even our enemies, that the gay rights movement has made extraordinary strides in the forty-three years since the Stonewall Riots in New York City. We're not all the way there yet; we have yet to secure our full civil equality, but the pace of progress has been unprecedented in the history of social justice movements. The women's suffrage movement, for example, was launched in the United States in 1848. It took more than seventy years to pass the Nineteenth Amendment, which extended the vote to women. In 1969, at the time of the Stonewall Riots, gay sex was illegal in forty-nine states. Gay sex is now legal in every US state; gay marriage is legal in nine states and our nation's capital (and in all of Canada); and gays, lesbians, and bisexuals can serve openly in the military. (The armed forces still discriminate against trans people.) The president of the United States even mentioned the Stonewall Riots in his 2013 inaugural speech. And we've made this progress despite fierce opposition from the religious right, a deadly plague that wiped out a generation of gay men, and—

horrors—all those leather guys at Folsom and all those go-go boys and drag queens at Pride.

We couldn't have come so far, so fast if Folsom or pride parades were harming our movement. And I would argue that all those leather guys, dykes on bikes, go-go boys, and drag queens have actually helped our movement. They demonstrate to all people, gay and straight, that the gay rights movement isn't just about the freedom to be gay *or* straight. It's about the freedom to be whatever kind of straight, gay, lesbian, bi, or trans person *you* want to be.

Joining LaBarbera and his rinky-dink hate group in an obsession with the Folsom Street Fair is Bill Donohue, the head of the Catholic League for Religious and Civil Rights, an organization with a multimillion-dollar annual budget. Donohue has been having a highly public, er, stroke about the Folsom Street Fair since 2007.

Geologists have yet to discover a rock that Donohue can't find anti-Catholic bigotry lurking under, it should be said first. And no one on cable news has the balls to call Donohue on his own bigotry. Here's a Donohue classic: "Hollywood is controlled by secular Jews who hate Christianity in general and Catholicism in particular."

And Donohue had this to say to a man who was molested by a priest when he was a minor: "Most 15-year-old teenage boys *wouldn't allow themselves to be molested.* So why did you?" The blame for clerical sexual abuse scandals that have rocked the Catholic Church, in Donohue's mind, seems to rest squarely on the narrow shoulders of all those children who "allowed" themselves to be molested. (Doing Donohue one better, Father Benedict Groeschel, of the conservative Franciscan Friars of the Renewal, told the *National Catholic Register* that Catholic priests are the real victims. "Suppose you have a man having a nervous breakdown and a youngster comes after him. A lot of the cases, the youngster—14, 16, 18—is the seducer." Groeschel went on to say that boys with "holes in their lives" that needed filling were drawn to priests, and that priests who slept with minors shouldn't go to prison for their "first offense." So reassuring to know that Father Groeschel is a professor of pastoral psychology at St. Joseph's Seminary in New York, isn't it?)

So what happened in 2007 that brought Donohue's wrath down on the Folsom Street Fair?

The organizers of Folsom produced a promotional poster that featured male and female BDSM and leather fetishists arrayed around a table in a familiar tableau: It was Leonardo da Vinci's iconic *Last Supper,* with a shirtless, African-American leatherman sitting in for Christ and other leather- and-rubber-clad kinksters standing in for the apostles. Donohue's head exploded. He called the poster blasphemous, spat out press releases claiming that *The Last Supper* was "sacred" to Catholics, and finally he called for a boycott—*these people and their boycotts*—of Folsom's large corporate sponsors.

I was one of very few people who came to the defense of the Folsom Street Fair during the *Last Supper* controversy. Even my friend Andrew Sullivan, a man with an irreverent sense of humor and a booming laugh, slammed Folsom's *Last Supper* poster, calling it "a provocation . . . cheap blasphemy." In response, I posted scores of other *Last Supper* parodies that no one objected to when they were created, much less condemned as "blasphemous." Donohue didn't object when *The Simpsons* parodied Leonardo's suddenly sacred *Last Supper,* nor did Donohue object to *Last Supper* parodies featuring the casts of *The Sopranos* and *That '70s Show.* There were no objections I could find to *Last Supper* parodies that featured supermodels, Ronald McDonald, the Boston Red Sox, Count Chocula and other children's cereal mascots, flesh-eating zombies, *Star Wars* characters, Big Bird and the Muppets, dogs, cats, Popeye, Donkey Kong, and on and on.

Apparently there's nothing blasphemous about Tony Soprano or

Big Bird or a flesh-eating zombie sitting in for Christ—nothing blasphemous at all—but a leatherman crosses the line.

Fox News called and invited me to debate Bill Donohue about the Folsom poster. As qualified as I am to debate Bill Donohue (I was raised Catholic, my dad was a deacon, I've been known to shout), and as much fun as the interview sounded, I had to pass. First, it was Fox News, and I've made a policy of passing on Fox News. Second, the interview was scheduled for seven forty-five in the morning New York City time, which would've been four forty-five in the morning Seattle time. That's too early to get into a shouting match with a Catholic to whom I'm not related.

Donohue's obsession with Folsom hasn't let up in the five years since the poster controversy.

"Last Sunday, homosexuals paraded around naked in the streets of San Francisco at the annual Folsom Street Fair," Bill Donohue wrote in a news release on the organization's website after the 2012 Folsom Street Fair. "They did more than walk the streets nude—they beat each other with whips. The leather/fetish homosexuals led each other around like dogs with metal collars; they set up booths where visitors could get flogged; they sold hard-core pornography. . . . And after promoting lethal sex acts—the kind that causes AIDS—they raised money for AIDS."

"There were no arrests," Donohue glumly noted.

I have to break in here with a public service announcement: Not only has Folsom raised 5 million dollars for charity over its lifetime, more than 2 million dollars of that in the last few years, but leading someone around the streets of San Francisco on a leash doesn't spread AIDS. Whips and chains and flogging and pornography don't spread AIDS. In the early years of the AIDS epidemic, when HIV-prevention campaigns were entirely grassroots efforts (i.e., not reliant on government grants), HIV educators actually stressed the relative safety of BDSM play. Indeed, the onset of the AIDS epidemic forced sex educators to recognize that BDSM—both the gay *and* straight varieties—was safer than "normal" anal or vaginal intercourse. Someone who gets off having his ass spanked is actually *less* likely to contract the human immunodeficiency virus than someone who needs to have his ass fucked. Please make a note of it, Bill.

It's not just public nudity and flogging that annoy Donohue. "As always, the homosexuals mocked the Catholic clergy and religious," Donohue complained. "They dressed as cardinals, bishops, and nuns. There was even a group that disparaged the Jesuits, the 'Society of Janus'; their specialty is BDSM. The anti-Catholic aspects of this grand exhibition of moral destitution are not hard to understand: the participants are in a constant state of rebellion against truth."

Donohue seems to think that gay men are kinky just to annoy Catholics, and that the Catholic imagery you see at Folsom—kinky priests, kinky nuns, kinky Jesuits—is a gratuitous insult. In fact, many people, gay and straight, are kinky not to annoy Catholics, but because they *are* Catholics, and the Catholic imagery on display is included for a good reason.

The science writer Jesse Bering's most recent book, *Why Is the Penis Shaped Like That? And Other Reflections on Being Human,* included a chapter on the origins of kinks. It turns out that random but emotionally significant childhood experiences play a big role.

"This basic developmental system, one in which certain salient childhood events 'imprint' our psychosexuality, may not be terribly uncommon," Bering writes. "In fact, that early childhood experiences mold our adult sexual preferences—specifically, what turns us on and off, however subtle or even unconscious these particular biases may be—could even be run-of-the-mill."

Consider what Catholic schoolchildren are busily imprinting on as their sexualities develop. They are told to worship a man who was tortured to death. And what do we Catholics call His grisly execution? Oh, that's right: the Passion. Catholic children kneel in front of life-size representations—some highly realistic—of a ripped dude in a loincloth nailed to a cross with a look of ecstasy on his face. They're taught stories about gruesomely martyred saints. When I was in Catholic schools, I was told by nuns and priests that pain and suffering wouldn't just bring me closer to God—although they would do that— but that pain and suffering were gifts from God. I was told that pain and suffering were signs of God's favor. I was told that God tormented us—even us children—to test the depths of our love for Him.

And we were constantly warned to avoid sin, particularly sexual sins. Premarital sex. Homosexuality. Adultery. Masturbation. It seems that God created us horny but—*psych*—God doesn't approve of this sex business *at all*. It is easy, as a young Catholic, to embrace God's hatred of sex; sex seems so disgusting and squalid when you're a child. Then puberty comes along and suddenly your crotch is at war with your faith.

There's a good reason Donohue doesn't see Muslim or Hindu or Jewish imagery at Folsom or IML, another of his perennial complaints. Those religions aren't dominant in our culture: We are a majority Christian nation; Catholics are the largest single Christian denomination in the United States. And those other religions, each one messed up about sex in its own special way, don't have salvation narratives that lend themselves so readily to both the formation and expression of BDSM fantasies. (Sin, torture, torment, and a Big Sky Daddy who punishes you because he loves you.)

There's a direct link between the flogging scenes at Folsom and the flogging scenes depicted on stained glass windows in Catholic churches, in the Stations of the Cross, and in Mel Gibson's BDSM-tinged snuff flick, *The Passion,* a film that was shown in Catholic schools all across the country. ("[*The Passion*] relies for its effect almost entirely on sadomasochistic male narcissism," the late Christopher Hitchens wrote on *Slate,* ". . . massively repressed homoerotic fantasies, a camp interest in military uniforms, [and] an obsession with flogging.")

Not every child exposed to Catholicism during his formative years is going to be into BDSM when he grows up. Not all Catholics are kinksters and not all kinksters are Catholic. But a significant number of the men and the women flogging each other on the streets of San Francisco during Folsom—a disproportionate number, I would wager—were raised Catholic. Catholic religious imagery and dogma imprinted the shit out of their erotic imaginations when they were children, and the people selling whips at Folsom are reaping the rewards.

Because kinksters aren't born. They're made. And the Catholic Church creates them by the millions.

Finally, and in conclusion, I'd like to state that Terry looks *really* good in leather—wait, did I already say that? I did. But you don't have to take my word for it. I believe there's a picture of Terry at IML, decked out in his leathers, on Peter LaBarbera's website somewhere.

9. The Straight Pride Parade

There's something a little scary—scary in all the wrong ways—about a "Sexy Jane Doe" costume.

You can buy "Sexy Jane Doe" costumes, which are basically form-fitting body bags complete with toe tags, through Halloween catalogs or in those pop-up Halloween shops that occupy empty storefronts from late August through the end of October. "Sexy Jane Doe" is half of one of those adult his-and-hers Halloween costume sets that drive some people nuts. You know: Sexy Nurse & Doctor, Sexy Nun & Priest, Sexy Pirate & Pirate Captain. They upset people because the costumes for girls bare a lot of flesh, but the companion costumes for boys don't bare any flesh at all. And that is *so* sexist and *so* unfair and—wait a minute.

Someone is selling sexy *corpse* costumes?

Yes, someone is. "Sexy Jane Doe" is part of a *CSI*-inspired his-and-hers costume set and it's no exception to the clothed-male/nearly nude-female rule. The official name of the girl's costume in the set is "Jane Doe DOA Bodybag." It's a shiny, black, skintight, miniskirted body bag/dress that "hugs every curve," and comes with a zip-up-and-over-the-head hood and "toe-tag Jane Doe neckband." The boy gets a "Coroner" costume, which consists of a baggy black lab coat with the word *coroner* printed on it, presumably to be worn over street clothes, and a black surgical mask.

There's nothing sexy about "a man whose job is to deal with dead people looking at a sexy dead *stranger*," a blogger named Lilith wrote in a post at Feministing.com, "an online community for feminists and their allies." No argument from me there, Lilith, and I agree that a "deliberate power dynamic [is] being displayed" when a woman dresses up as a sexy corpse and lies down on an autopsy table to be ogled by a man in a not-so-sexy lab coat, which was how the "Sexy Jane Doe" and "Coroner" costume set was illustrated in the catalog. Nope. There's just nothing very sexy about that. (Well, I don't find it sexy. But sexy is subjective, and this his-and-hers costume set is probably sexy to *someone*.)

You know what else isn't sexy? The grousing I hear from friends and coworkers when ads for "sexy" Halloween costumes start appearing in early September. People I know to be reliably pro-pleasure lefties—people who are all for recreational sex and legal drugs and strap-on dildos—suddenly start sounding like right-wing religious conservatives when Halloween rolls around. A holiday for *children* has been transformed into an opportunity for stupid grown-up straight people to dress up in revealing outfits and make sex-crazed spectacles of themselves in public. And isn't that just *sad*?

No, it's not sad. It's awesome. And it's long overdue.

I'm often asked—I'm often confronted—about gay pride parades when I speak at colleges and universities. Usually it's a conservative student, typically someone who isn't happy about my being invited to campus in the first place, trying to score a point for the superiority of the heterosexual lifestyle. "Homosexuals like to pretend that being gay is about who you *love*," the conservative student will say, his voice dripping with sarcasm, "but look at your so-called gay pride parades, with men in their ass-less chaps and all those bare-chested lesbians." These exchanges typically end like this:

CONSERVATIVE STUDENT: You don't see straight people flaunt-
    ing our sexuality like that. We don't have straight "pride"
    parades.
ME: You should.

And it becomes clearer with every passing year—and with each new his-and-hers Halloween costume set sold—that straight people *do* have pride parades. They take place on October 31, the route meanders from one straight bar to another, and they keep getting bigger and sexier. (And, note to conservative student, straight people flaunt their sexualities in a million ways, large and small—kissing in ballparks, public marriage proposals, holding hands in grocery stores, bachelor and bachelorette parties, ruinously expensive weddings, baby showers, birth announcements, etc.)

Back in the bad old days—pre-Stonewall, pre–pride parades, pre–the-ability-to-live-openly—Halloween was *the* gay holiday. It was the one night of the year when a man could go out in leather or feathers and a woman could go out in a zoot suit with her hair greased back in a ducktail without having to fear arrest, exposure, and ruin.

In *Making Gay History: The Half-Century Fight for Lesbian and Gay Equal Rights*, an oral history, Shirley Willer describes pre-Stonewall life in Chicago, now one of the gay-friendliest cities in the country. "The annual Halloween costume balls [were] run by the Mafia," Willer said. "These balls were big events in Chicago, the only events where all bets were off and the police left us alone. . . . This was the one time of year when gay people could be gay. It was the only visible sign that there were literally thousands and thousands of gay people in the city."

Halloween resonated for pre-Stonewall queers because the closeted life was a never-ending, hugely stressful masquerade. If you were lucky in those days, you might be out to a few very close friends. But you were closeted at work and on the street and to your family. To survive, a queer person had to be very good at masks, at pretense, and at playing dress-up. But on Halloween gay men and lesbians could take off the disguises they wore the other 364 days a year and be the most outrageous, flamboyant versions of their true selves. Halloween allowed gays and lesbians to take a skill set honed under duress—the ability to pretend to be something we were not—and put it to use creating joy.

While Halloween is still celebrated by LGBT people, it's no longer the highest holiday on the queer calendar. Oh, we keep it, but we don't keep it holy. It's just another excuse for a party—and we're always on the lookout for an excuse to party—but Halloween has been downgraded, displaced by other and better excuses for parties, from pride parades to crowning a new Mr. Leather to the arrival of the weekend. There are still parties in gay bars on Halloween, of course, and you'll see people, many of them straight, parading up and down the streets of gay neighborhoods on October 31 in elaborate costumes. But Halloween belongs to heterosexuals now.

According to the National Retail Federation, Americans spent 7 billion dollars on Halloween in 2011, and nearly 70 percent of adults now celebrate the holiday. "Bars all over the country hold parties for the 21-and-up crowd and manufacturers crank out costumes that definitely aren't meant for family trick-or-treating," reports Martha C. White, on *Time*'s *Moneyland* blog.

Straight people in the United States needed something like the hyper-sexualized bash that Halloween has become. Straights in Brazil have Carnival; straights in Germany have Fasching—big public parties where straight people show their tits, shake their asses, and flaunt their sexualities. Booze companies in the 1990s spent millions in an attempt to make a national holiday out of Mardi Gras, a big public party where straight people show their tits, shake their asses, and flaunt their sexualities on the streets of New Orleans, but a national Mardi Gras didn't take. Instead straight people made a collective, subconscious decision to appropriate and redefine Halloween.

Straight people have also wisely chosen to collectively disregard the dire warnings of batshit fundamentalist nutbags like "Apostle" Kimberly Daniels, an evangelical preacher who sits on the Jacksonville City Council, and Mission America's Linda Harvey. Daniels warns that Halloween candies are infused with demonic spells (and you thought corn syrup was the problem) and that Halloween parties involve "sex with demons," "orgies," and "sacrificing babies." (Man, I'm not getting invited to the right parties!) Harvey, for her part, has warned straight people against celebrating Halloween. "We all can see [that Halloween] is a huge celebration in the LGBT world, especially for the gender-confused folks," Harvey said on her radio show shortly before Halloween in 2012. "The core of Halloween is glittering artificiality; you can pretend to be someone you aren't for a night, you can flirt with danger, you can divine a different destiny. . . . It's one of Satan's oldest tricks!"

Straight people have made the right choice to disregard Apostle Daniels, Linda Harvey, and all the other batshit fundamentalist nutbags out there and embrace Halloween. It was certainly a better choice than the one booze companies were attempting to make for them. Pride parades are now the big public celebration of queer sexualities in all their tawdry glamour, and Halloween is the big public celebration of straight sexualities, and it's every bit—every tit—as tawdry and glamorous.

And necessary.

Gay people don't resent straight people for taking Halloween from us. In all honesty, we were hardly using it anymore. And, besides, we know what it's like to keep your sexuality under wraps, to keep it concealed, to be on your guard and under control at all times. Even today, with more gay people living openly, there are still times in our lives when we have to put that straight mask back on and try to pass (in adolescence, on road trips through red states, in the locker rooms of gyms in small towns). And while heterosexuality isn't subject to the same sorts of institutionalized repression that homosexuality was and still is, straight people are subject to subtler forms of sexual repression.

Straight people move through life thinking about sex constantly, always horny and always slightly frustrated (which is a feature of human sexuality, not a bug—we're wired to be horny all the time), but social convention requires straight people (and gay people) to act as if sex were the last thing on their minds. That can be *exhausting*. And then there's the hash so many young straight people make of their lives. When gay people come out, we shrug off the pressure to conform about something so enormous—sexual orientation—that the shrugging off of other, lesser pressures to conform comes easy.

Straight people don't have to come out, as heterosexuality is assumed. And while that's good in many ways—less stress during adolescence is certainly good—it's not so good in other ways.

Young straight people are less likely to question choices that their families and societies are attempting to make for them. Even worse, the culture has a way of convincing young straight people that they're somehow freely making choices that have actually been foisted on them. From the expectation that you will settle down (What if you don't want to settle down?) to the expectation that you will have kids (What if you don't want to have kids?) to the expectation that you will choose an appropriate partner (i.e., someone your parents approve of over the kind of partner—or *partners,* plural—that actually excites you). A lot of straight people move through life following a script that others wrote for them. And many straight people only realize that they didn't want to settle down or have kids or marry the kind of person they married until it's too late (i.e., until after they've married and had kids with someone their parents like a lot more than they do).

People under those kinds of pressures, and people who've made those kinds of mistakes, desperately need pressure-release valves. And those are precisely the kinds of pressures—to conform to a certain romantic script, to live with sexual and reproductive choices that others made for you—that can make a person want to pull on a pair of ass-less chaps, smear glitter on her tits, and march down the middle of the street. Those are the kinds of pressures that cry out for some form of organized mass release. And they're the kinds of pressures that only something like a pride parade—straight or gay, Mardi Gras or Halloween, Carnival or Fasching—has the power to release.

Straight people needed one day in the year to let it all hang out, a day on which they could violate the social norms and expectations they hew to the rest of the year, a day to publicly cross-dress or undress, a day when they could be the piece of meat they know themselves to be and treat other people like the pieces of meat that they are.

And they got it: Halloween.

Right now things are a little unfair on the gender front. Okay, they're a *lot* unfair. Straight girls are expected to show flesh on Halloween; straight boys aren't. As an aside: An emerging, and perhaps encouraging, trend for ladies on the choice front is the pairing of sexy with ironic (e.g., sexy iPod nano, sexy Taco Bell Sauce Packet, sexy Chucky). In response to this sexy/ironic trend in the Halloween costume menagerie, *Slate* contributor Amanda Hess offers this: "When I see women dressed as sexualized fast-food sauces, I don't know whether to laugh or cry. In the new Sexy Halloween economy, the line between sexy and ironic appears to have evaporated. There's something hopeful about that—this new permutation of the trend rejects plastic corporate packaging and values a woman's cleverness instead. As long as she still looks hot."

And I don't think this new trend is a sign that the sexy Halloween costume industry has jumped the shark so much as they've discovered a treasure trove in self-mockery. How postmodern of them. They're incorporating the critique and mocking it at the same time, which allows wearers themselves to mock the "sexy" costume trend while going out in sexy costumes just the same.

After I talked about the phenomenon on a podcast recently, I got some tweets from female listeners who said I was missing the point. "We shouldn't be forced to wear sexy costumes if that's not what we want," one woman tweeted.

No one is forcing anyone to wear sexy costumes. Women who don't want to wear sexy costumes don't have to. And if the issue is choice—all the costumes for sale for women at the pop-up Halloween shops are "sexy" this and "sexy" that—well, women have the option of buying men's costumes (which can be taken in with a stapler), or making their own. Lots of gay men go to pride parades in fluorescent thongs—but not all gay men are required to. I've never gone to a pride parade in a thong (nor would I ever), but I've never felt pressured to go in a thong. Still I would defend to the death the right of other gay men to wear thongs at pride parades if that's what they want to do.

I see this attitude from the female tweeter as the pathologizing of other people's choices: Women who don't want to wear "sexy" costumes assuming that any woman who is wearing a sexy costume had to have been coerced, and must be unhappy, or is being abused, or she thought she was making a free choice but just doesn't realize that the culture put the zap on her head.

The sexy/ironic trend aside, I don't foresee things radically changing in this arena anytime soon, sadly. Because it comes down to something that defies logic, politics, and even free will: People who want to fuck men—straight and bi girls, gay and bi guys—show flesh because it works. Showing flesh attracts positive male attention. (Positive or negative, I guess, since it kind of depends on how you feel about male attention.) But engaging in that kind of sexual display—here are my tits!—is perceived by men and women, gay and straight, as feminizing. So while baring their tits is an effective way for girls to attract male attention, it's often a less successful mating strategy for men who are looking to attract female attention. Guys who show off their tits risk looking like they're trying to attract male attention too (i.e., they risk looking like fags). So straight guys who bare their tits on Halloween—or their abs or their asses (especially their asses)—aren't going to reap the same kind of rewards that tit-baring straight girls do.

And that's a shame because there are a lot of straight guys who shouldn't have to wear baggy lab coats on Halloween. (There's a "John Doe DOA" costume for sale, too, but it's a formless, shapeless head-to-toe body bag with a hole cut out for the face.) It would be wonderful to see straight boys out there celebrating their erotic power on October 31 the same way the gay boys do: by allowing themselves to be objectified at the same time that they're objectifying others. That would make the straight pride parades—all those Halloween-night bar crawls—feel as egalitarian as the gay pride parades on which they are unconsciously modeled.

"Every year around Halloween, I see some columnist or blogger or others talk about how 'Halloween is just an excuse for girls and women to whore it up all night,'" writes Nicolechat on another post at Feministing.com about sexy costumes. "But every time I read that, I think to myself, so what? What's wrong with having a night where we can say 'This is my body, and I'm not ashamed of it, or of using it to express my sexuality.'"

There's nothing wrong with it, Nicolechat, nothing at all.

Heterosexuals in North America have needed a holiday like this for a long, long time. And now they've got one. Halloween is yours now, straight people, please be good to it. And girls? Wrap those bandages loosely and by midnight your boyfriend's "mummy" costume will be just as revealing as that off-the-rack "sexy witch" outfit you bought at the costume shop.

Happy Heteroween.

10. Four Closet Cases

Shortly after I came out to my family, I started sneaking into gay bars on the—no, wait. Let me start over.

Shortly *before* I came out to my family, I was *already* sneaking into gay bars on the north side of Chicago. Looking back, I can see how dangerous this was. I wasn't quite eighteen yet, and I was more attractive than I realized at the time. It was the summer of 1982, and I was hanging around in gay bars, desperate for affection and affirmation, just as a deadly virus was taking root in the gay community. The Centers for Disease Control would give the virus a name that summer: "acquired immunodeficiency syndrome."

The insecurities and social awkwardness that rendered me incapable of realizing when someone was trying to pick me up may have saved my life in the summer of '82.

If my parents had known what I was doing at night, and where I was going, they surely would've intervened. But they didn't know what I was doing because I was working so hard to hide it—to hide myself—from them. Like a lot of gay teenagers, I was flying blind into adult social and sexual situations.

I don't remember much about the first gay bar I walked into, but I can vaguely remember what I had to drink: a Long Island Iced Tea, I'm embarrassed to say. I do remember what it felt like to walk into a gay bar for the first time, though. I had spent all day, every day, for the last six years of my life trying to hide my homosexuality from my family, from my friends, from my classmates, from my teachers, from strangers on the street and on the L. To step through that door and feel that pressure lift made me feel lightheaded. It was like stepping through an airlock; I'm surprised my ears didn't pop.

I quickly made some friends my own age, other teenagers who were slipping into gay bars at night, kids like me, who weren't out to their parents or friends from school. We became a posse.

We mostly went to the bars where the twentysomethings hung out, but there were always older guys in "our" bars, guys in their fifties, guys in their sixties. These men were in bars they were way too old for, and some of them pursued guys who were way too young for them. I felt sorry for the older gay men. My friends didn't. They made fun of the "old trolls," as they cruelly called them; although they would condescend to accept drinks from the old trolls just the same.

Unlike most of the other boys in my posse, I knew a little gay history. I could also add and subtract. When the older men in the bars were seventeen, it was 1942 or 1932—and it might as well have been 1642 for all the difference it made.

When the older men we were meeting in the bars were seventeen, I told my friends, it just wasn't possible to be an openly gay teenager. There weren't gay youth groups or gay bookstores or gay neighborhoods. "Give 'em a break," I used to tell my friends. "They missed out."

And when I got to know some of these older guys, I was shocked—shocked!—to discover that not all of them lusted after me and my friends. Some of them lusted after other middle-aged guys; others had long-term boyfriends at home. Most were closeted at work or to their extended families, and they needed to step through the airlock, just like I did, to escape the pressure of a half-closeted life.

But many, as I suspected, had indeed "missed out." Most of the older men I got to know that summer had married and had children long before the Stonewall Riots. They had known they were gay when they took their vows, but they didn't think they had any other options then—they had to pass; they had to find wives; they had to have children. There were no other options.

Consequently, their coming-out experiences had been messy, protracted, and painful. A few of them had come out willingly, but most told stories of getting caught or being discovered. The term hadn't been invented yet, but a few had been outed. Most of the coming-out stories ended with marriages dissolved, children estranged, and careers destroyed. Hearing their stories made me feel even sorrier for them.

Jim West, a prominent Republican politician in Washington State, had a messy, protracted, and painful coming-out experience—and that's putting it mildly. An elected official for more than twenty years, West was one of Washington's most prominent and powerful homophobes. During his two decades in the state legislature, West backed a bill that would have made it illegal for gay men and lesbians to work in schools and day care centers; he voted to define marriage as a union between a man and a woman; he personally killed a bill that would have protected gays and lesbians from discrimination; he proposed a law that would have made sex between consenting teenagers—gay or straight— a felony in Washington State.

West left the Washington State legislature in 2003 to run for mayor of Spokane, Washington. West won that race, just as he'd won every race he had ever entered, and immediately after being sworn in, West moved to veto a new law providing benefits to domestic partners of gay city employees.

When Spokane's daily newspaper, *The Spokesman-Review,* heard rumors that West was trawling the Internet for gay teenagers, the paper began trawling the Internet for West. It didn't take long to locate West in a Gay.com chat room, where he went by the handle "Cobra82." West offered a city internship to a reporter who he thought was an eighteen-year-old boy, with the understanding that the boy would have sex with him. (Now we know why West wanted to ban sex between teenagers: He wanted the teenage boys all for himself.) In May of 2005, *The Spokesman-Review* published a long story on West's secret double life, and on December 6 of the same year, voters turned West out of office in a recall election.

As chance would have it, I was in Spokane the day Jim West was forced from office. My husband had grown up there, and we were visiting his family. Spokane is a good place to be from, Terry likes to say—*far from*. Spokane is religious, conservative, sprawling, and overwhelmingly white, and it's not an easy place to be gay or African-American or Democratic or Jewish or an atheist or a pedestrian.

It certainly wasn't an easy place for my husband to grow up; he was physically assaulted repeatedly in high school. (When his mother complained to the principal, she was told that the abuse would continue so long as he insisted on "acting like that.") And Spokane can't have been an easy place for West to grow up either. But none of the sympathy I felt for the middle-aged gay men I met in the early 1980s extended to West—or to many closeted middle-aged men today.

Because I can still add and subtract.

West was born in 1951. He was eighteen in 1969, the year of the Stonewall Riots. He was twenty-six in 1977, the year that Harvey Milk was elected to the Board of Supervisors in San Francisco. West was thirty-one years old when I was eighteen and hanging out in bars in Chicago. West was thirty-four years old when Terry was being beaten in his Spokane high school, in a district that West represented in the Washington State legislature.

Jim West didn't have to live a lie. He could have lived as an openly gay or bisexual man—West, who had once been married, claimed to be bisexual in interviews about the scandal, though all of the pictures found on his work computers were of young men—but he chose not to. Unlike those older gay men I met in 1982, West and other closeted middle-aged men today didn't come of age at a time when no one could conceive of openly gay and lesbian people and communities. (Or politicians: Washington State has five openly gay members of its legislature; there was at least one openly gay member of Washington State's legislature every year that West himself was a member of the legislature.) Jim West had options. But he chose the closet and shame and lies and hypocrisy.

And like a lot of politically powerful closet cases, West covered for his homosexuality by pushing anti-gay legislation. No one would suspect him of being gay, West calculated, so long as he was the biggest bigot in the Washington State legislature.

Ted Haggard was born in 1956. He was thirteen at the time of the Stonewall Riots, and twenty-one the year that Harvey Milk was elected to the San Francisco Board of Supervisors. Haggard was the pastor of a mega-church he founded in Colorado Springs; and like West, he was a politically powerful, high-profile homophobe.

In 2006 Haggard was outed by Mike Jones, a Denver-based male escort that Haggard had been patronizing for years. The ensuing scandal didn't tell us much we don't already know about closeted gay men. The common themes that link West and Haggard are the enormous risks these men took to get their needs met, and the harm they were willing to do to other gay people in an effort to cover for themselves.

There was something new in the Haggard scandal—perhaps we should call it the Haggard flameout—and that was the refusal of Mike Jones to honor the callboy's code of silence, the omertà of gay hookerdom.

I have a friend who used to do sex work. He was based in Los Angeles at the time, and one of his clients was a movie star. A big movie star. A top movie star. A male sex symbol. This guy used to send a private jet to pick up my friend and fly him to isolated, far-flung resorts, to help him "unwind" after shooting a film.

I can't tell you who this movie star is. It's not that I'm afraid of being sued or that I necessarily disapprove of outing.[1] *I don't know the movie star's name.* No matter how many times I asked, no matter how much I pried, my sex worker friend simply wouldn't tell me the star's name. My friend wouldn't even tell me where he was meeting his famous client, lest the locations where his films were being shot offer a clue. My friend took the callboy's code of silence seriously.

On the website where Ted Haggard found Mike Jones, the callboys all describe themselves as discreet. That's a solemn promise not to blab to the wife if you're married; to the tabloids (or to prying friends) if you're a movie star; to your congregation if you're one of the most powerful evangelical ministers in the country. (Haggard was the head of the National Association of Evangelicals; Haggard spoke with then-president George W. Bush on a weekly basis.) Mike Jones never outed a client before Haggard. But Jones broke the callboy code of silence because Haggard's hypocrisy offended him. The fear that callboys can no longer be trusted will doubtless make the lives of men like Ted Haggard that much more lonely and difficult.

Back in the bad old days—back in the mythical 1950s, the era social conservatives pine for—most gay men were closeted, like the middle-aged guys I got to know that summer had been earlier in their lives, and in one way this made it easier for closeted men to arrange trysts. You could rely on the discretion of your sex partners back then because they were relying on yours. It was the era of mutually assured destruction, both in terms of nuclear warfare and gay sex. Your partner couldn't reveal your secret without revealing his own.

---

1 I don't disapprove of outing—but I wouldn't out this guy if I knew who he was. I don't believe in outing movie stars or harmless folks. I agree with what Frank Rich said in *New York* magazine (January 17, 2013): "My own feeling is that every person, regardless of sexuality, should make his or her own decisions about what to keep private and what to tell the world. That said, closeted gay hypocrites with political power—whether in elective office, corporate life, or the pulpit—who vilify or curb the rights of other gay people deserve everything that's coming to them."

Needless to say, a sex life infused with Cold War–style tensions didn't lead to many healthy or lasting relationships.

Today gay and bisexual men live openly, making the modern closet a much less crowded place. While all the best gay men used to be closeted, the only adults you find in the closet today are the fearful, the compromised, and the hypocritical. They're public figures whose lucrative careers in film or politics would collapse if they came out; gay men whose obscenely wealthy families would disown them if they lived openly; or gay men leading congregations that would dismiss them if they knew the truth about their pastor.

A less crowded closet doesn't just mean slimmer pickings for men like Ted Haggard, but highly unreliable ones as well. Decades ago you could be certain that the closeted gay man you were sleeping with would still be closeted ten or twenty years later. Now you never know. The closeted gay man you entrust with your secret today might be out next year. And if he has nothing left to hide, your secret is no longer safe. Better hope you parted on good terms.

Which is why so many powerful closet cases turn to callboys. It's not just the callboy's promise of discretion, but the sense that the old dynamics—mutually assured destruction—remain in force. A callboy can't expose your secret without exposing his own. There's still a stigma attached to selling sex.

So why did Mike Jones speak out?

Because today it is arguably more shameful to be a hypocritical closet case than it is to be an honest sex worker. (Although gay political organizations treated Jones pretty shabbily.) Even those delighted by Haggard's fall—and I count myself among their number—ached for his children, who suffered for the sins of their father. And let me be clear: Their father's sin was not his sexual orientation; it wasn't seeing rent boys or even using meth. Haggard's sin was hypocrisy. His sin was the closet.

As was—as is—Larry Craig's.

Craig isn't the only straight-identified man who has ever been arrested cruising for sex in a public toilet. Indeed, most of the men who are arrested for having "gay" sex in public restrooms have wives waiting at home. Craig wasn't even the first man arrested cruising for sex in that particular restroom at that particular airport on that particular day. Forty other men were arrested as part of the same sting operation at Minneapolis–St. Paul International Airport after complaints from annoyed travelers who wanted to use the bathroom for its intended purpose. The reason we heard about Craig's arrest, to the exclusion of all the others, was that Craig had the misfortune of being the only sitting US senator—the only rabidly anti-gay sitting US senator—cruising for sex in that particular bathroom on that particular day.

Craig, of course, claimed he was innocent and that his actions were misconstrued. Why was Craig tapping his toes while he sat on the toilet? Craig explained that he has a restless leg. Why did his foot slide under the divider, nudging the foot of an undercover officer in the next stall? Craig claimed he has a "wide stance."

Craig was born in 1945. He was twenty-four years old at the time of the Stonewall Riots. He was thirty-two when Harvey Milk—who was born in *1930*—was elected to the San Francisco Board of Supervisors. Like West and Haggard, Craig didn't have to live in the closet. And like West and Haggard, Craig was publicly straight but someone else entirely in the privacy of an airport stall, just as Jim West was someone else entirely in Gay.com chat rooms, and Ted Haggard was someone else entirely when he could get to Denver.

And George Rekers? He was someone else entirely in Europe.

Rekers is a psychologist and an ordained Baptist minister. He also cofounded the Family Research Council, an anti-gay hate group currently headed by Tony Perkins, and for many years Rekers served as an adviser to the National Association for Research & Therapy of Homosexuality, an organization that promotes "conversion therapy." In the early 1970s, when Rekers was a doctoral student at UCLA, he developed the infamous "Sissy Boy" Experiment that subjected dozens of boys, some as young as five, to harsh punishment if they displayed any non-masculine behaviors or interests. This research would be the bedrock for his thirty-year career as a conversion therapist. Rekers was one of eight contributors to the *Handbook of Therapy for Unwanted Homosexual Attractions,* published in 2009. In that book, Rekers specifically cited one of the boys in his study, Kirk Murphy, as a successful example of conversion therapy. One tragic fact shows Rekers's callous indifference to the real human toll of his pseudo-therapy: In 2003, *six years before this book appeared,* Murphy committed suicide.

In 2010 Rekers was caught returning from a two-week European vacation with a male escort. Rekers angrily denied reports that he was gay, and claimed that he took the male prostitute on the trip to "lift his luggage." Rekers claimed that he needed his luggage lifted for him because he has a bad back. Why take a gay male escort to Europe to lift your luggage? (Are there no bellmen in Europe?) Rekers stated that he hoped to talk the young man out of being gay during the trip. The young man told reporters that he gave Rekers nude "sexual massages" during the trip.

Rekers was born in 1948. He was twenty-one at the time of the Stonewall Riots and twenty-nine when Harvey Milk was elected to the San Francisco Board of Supervisors.

I have a great deal of sympathy for the older gay men I met in Chicago's gay bars in 1982. Their personal lives were messy. Like West, Haggard, Craig, and Rekers, they had victimized people; their wives, mostly, and their kids. But these men married and had children under duress in the 1940s and 1950s. They didn't have a real or meaningful choice; they were forced into their closets.

When I meet someone now who's in his fifties or sixties and is just coming out, I don't think ill of him. I'm glad for him. I hope he finds happiness, and I hope he makes up for lost time. But when I meet someone, or hear about someone, who is still closeted at that age . . . I don't feel much in the way of sympathy. I feel a certain anger-tinged impatience, to be honest. I have a difficult time regarding being closeted at fifty or sixty as anything other than a self-inflicted injury. Being gay isn't a choice. Remaining closeted all your adult life is. And it's not a tragedy; it's a moral failing. It's cowardice.

West, Haggard, Craig, and Rekers had a choice, and they chose to remain closeted and to use homophobia to deflect attention from their sexualities. Unlike the older guys I met in 1982, they didn't miss out. They opted out.

Fuck 'em.

11. Mistakes Were Made

There was a time in my life when I didn't believe in the existence of bisexual men.

Bi women? Yeah, sure, of course. They're *everywhere*. Truly bisexual women, girls gone momentarily wild, a small number of vocal LUGs.[1]

Bi men? Nope, no way, not feeling it.

I know better now, of course, but unfortunately I began writing a sex-advice column before I saw the light. So I infamously put "Bisexual men don't exist" into print. Once or twice.

My bad.

---

1 It turns out the LUG phenomenon, or Lesbian Until Graduation, was fueled more by male fantasy than reality—that and the ability of the small handful of actual LUGs out there to distort people's impressions. A study of 13,500 women and men, ages twenty-five to forty-four, conducted by the Centers for Disease Control and Prevention found that only 10 percent of those who held a bachelor's degree reported same-sex experience, compared to 15 percent who had only a high school diploma. University of Utah professor Lisa Diamond speculated that the results might be a reflection of the more common and accepted status of gay relationships in society in general, making it more acceptable for women to experiment with their sexuality outside of the college campus setting. Another interesting finding of the study related to sexual identity: While 13 percent of the female respondents claimed same-sex experiences, only 1 percent identified as lesbian to the 4 percent who identified as bisexual. And women were twice as likely to report same-sex behavior as men. Professor Diamond again: "A lot of data shows that women's sexuality is more hetero-flexible, more influenced by what they see around them." It also could mean that there is less of a social (and sexual) cost extracted for women experimenting with their sexuality than men. Men are still going to think a woman is hot (maybe even more so) if she's gotten it on with another woman once or twice. The same is not as true for men.

With the LUG issue settled, here's hoping the CDC turns its attentions to cholera or antibiotic-resistant gonorrhea or something more pressing.

But there were a lot of things I didn't know about sex when I started writing a sex-advice column. For instance, I didn't know where the clitoris was located. I mean, I had heard of clits; I knew they were down *there* somewhere; I just didn't know where exactly. And that's crazy, right? Who would give a sex-advice column to a gay guy who doesn't know where the clit is?

A nice straight boy from the tiny town of Pickett, Wisconsin, that's who.

Tim Keck is one of the cofounders of *The Onion,* which got its start in Madison, Wisconsin, in 1988. Fake news? Writing bullshit in AP style? Tim, along with *The Onion*'s other cofounder, Chris Johnson, invented that. I met Tim shortly after I moved to Madison with my boyfriend at the time. The boyfriend was getting his master's degree at the University of Wisconsin while I bided my time working in a video store. Tim and Chris had just sold *The Onion,* and Tim told me he was moving to Seattle to start a weekly paper. I told Tim to put an advice column in his weekly paper because everybody reads advice columns. Tim told me that was good advice and asked me to write it.

The column was supposed to be a joke. For six months, maybe a year, a weekly paper in Seattle was going to let a gay guy give sex advice to straight people. The plan was for me to treat straight people and straight sex with the same contempt that straight advice columnists had always treated gay people and gay sex. The salutation that would run at the start of every letter: "Hey, Faggot." It was going to be hilarious. And it *was* hilarious. But a strange thing happened after Savage Love started appearing in the back pages of *The Stranger,* Tim's new paper: Letters began pouring in from straight people who liked being treated with contempt—it was a new and different experience for them—and I was suddenly writing a real sex-advice column for straight people.

That wasn't the plan.

It took me a long time to realize that I couldn't just wing it. *I was going to have to look stuff up.* This was twenty years ago, remember, so I'm talking about looking stuff up pre-Google, pre-*Wiki*, pre-Internet. I couldn't just type "Where the fuck is the clit and what the fuck is it for?" into a search engine and paraphrase the results. I had to look stuff up in *books* that were kept on *shelves* in things called *libraries*.

As it turns out the clitoral glans—the bit commonly referred to as the clit—is in no way analogous to the bell at the top of the strong man game at a county fair (hit pad with mallet, puck zooms up, bell rings), as I may or may not have written in an early column. The clitoris isn't a joy buzzer at the top of the vaginal canal, as I may or may not have written in an early column. Although female genitalia in toto do, in fact, look like a canned ham dropped from a great height, as I wrote in an early column. (The "canned ham" comment prompted some readers to label me sexist and one to call me, and I quote, "a gynophobic little faggot." I strongly reject that characterization. First, I'm six feet one. Second, drop a canned ham from a great height—say, the top of a skyscraper—and what happens? One of the can's seams splits as it hits the sidewalk; the force from the fall compresses the can; pink meat is forced out through the split seam, creating a roughly symmetrical pink meat flower. And while pussy is something I could never bring myself to eat, I can eat an entire ham in a sitting. It seems to me that a truly gynophobic person would've compared female genitalia to something revolting and inedible. Like raw liver or lavender crème brûlée.)

So here's what I learned about the clitoris from books on shelves in libraries: The clitoral glans is the exposed part of a female sexual organ found in humans, a handful of other mammals, and *ostriches*. (Thank you, *Wikipedia*, for that last detail. But where were you in 1991 when I needed you?) In human females the clit is located above the urethral opening, which is itself located above the vaginal opening, which is itself located just around the bend from the anal opening. And there's more: Seventy-five percent of women can't come from vaginal intercourse alone because it doesn't provide the direct, focused, clitoral glans stimulation that most women require in order to climax.

To help straight boys understand the importance of the clit—a large part of my job—I tell them the exact same clump of fetal cells and nerve endings that become the head of the penis in males become the clitoral glans in females. Ignore the head of a guy's dick and he definitely won't be able to come. Ignore a woman's clit and she most likely won't be able to come.

I didn't know any of that before I started writing Savage Love. As a gay man in my early twenties, *I didn't need to know any of that.* I wasn't having sex with women and I had no immediate plans to mate with an ostrich.[2] But I know all about the clit now. Hell, I know more about female sexual organs than many women do. And while I've never gone down on a woman, I'm confident that I would know my way around a woman's genitals if I had to. I'm like an agoraphobic autistic savant who's never been to London, and has no plans to ever go to London, but who can quickly draw you a map of the entire London Underground on the back of a paper placemat *and* tell you which station is closest to Buckingham Palace. (Victoria Station is closest but the approach from Green Park is nicer.)

This book would run to several volumes if I were to clear up *everything* I've gotten wrong in the twenty years that I've been writing Savage Love. So I'm not going to do that. I don't really *need* to do that. Ever since readers forced me to turn my fake sex-and-relationship advice column into a real sex-and-relationship advice column—which required me to drop the "Hey, Faggot" salutation after a few years—I've viewed Savage Love as a conversation I'm having about sex with

---

2 And I still don't, despite the fact that gay marriage is legal now where I live. So much for the slippery slope theory of human/ostrich mating.

friends in a bar after we've all had a drink. A *few* drinks. While I like to think I'm usually right about sex-and-relationship stuff, and while I'm a pretty informed guy (particularly now, after looking stuff up for twenty years), I do sometimes get things wrong. And when I do my drunken friends set me straight. They send me angry e-mails; they argue with me in comments threads; they furiously tweet at me. Pretty soon everything is cleared up, or at least everyone has had a chance to be heard, and we're on to the next week's column.

Bi men tried to set me straight back when I first put "bisexual men don't exist" in print.

But "bisexual men don't exist" was the received gay wisdom at the time and I regurgitated that bit of wisdom more than once—usually in jest (I knew some bisexual men)—because: (1) It jibed with my own experience, that is, most of the bi guys I dated turned out to be closeted gay men (which turned out to be a problem with my sample and not a problem with bisexuality; more on that in a few hundred words), and (2) it didn't seem like *that* big a deal. I saw my disbelief as inconsequential. I wasn't the audience of preschoolers at a production of *Peter Pan*, and bisexual men weren't a crowd of Tinker Bells—their existence didn't depend on the power of my belief. ("Clap louder, Dan, or Bisexer Bell won't continue to be attracted to men *and* women!") And I saw the back-and-forth with ticked-off bi guys in the column as just more of the playful assholery that made Savage Love great. I see now that my gay-received-wisdom shtick was hurtful to some.

But there were bisexuals out there who saw the humor. I was even invited to sit in a dunk tank at one bisexual organization's annual Valentine's Day bash. I accepted the invite, donned full drag, and got dunked, over and over again, in an unheated ballroom in *Seattle* in *February,* raising hundreds of dollars for the group. (This was after I had gotten into it in print with a bisexual reader who said that she didn't fall in love with *genitals*. She fell in love with *people*. I took offense on behalf of all *monosexuals,* the term she used to describe non-bisexuals, because my husband isn't a dick with legs. Well, he's not all the time. Sometimes he's an ass with arms.)

As a result of the jokes, the dunk tanks, and my pushing back against the "monosexual" label (bisexuals didn't like being told they didn't exist; I didn't like being lumped into the same sexual category as Rush Limbaugh and Charlie Sheen), I was labeled bi-phobic ("An aversion toward bisexuality and bisexual people as a social group or as individuals"). The label has stuck. Google "bi-phobic" and I pop up on the first page of results.[3]

The chief reason it took me longer to come around on the existence of bisexual men than, say, the location of the clitoris was that science— *science!*—was getting it wrong too. It wasn't as if I went and looked up clitoris but refused to do the same for bisexuality. I looked up bisexuality. And much of what I read reinforced my preconceptions and my prejudices.

The single most damaging thing I read—and, regrettably, blogged about—had to be the results of a 2005 study conducted by psychologists at Northwestern University and the Centre for Addiction and Mental Health (CAMH) in Toronto. The researchers placed advertisements in gay and alternative newspapers, recruiting 101 young adult men for a study about identity and attraction. While a third of the guys recruited for the study identified as bisexual, and while these bisexu-

---

3 Sometimes right-wingers stumble onto something about me on a bisexual website, or a cruising website, or a trans website, and are shocked to learn that there are queers out there who hate me as much as they do. Or more. I've managed, in my time, to piss off lesbians, bis, asexuals, trans people, poly people, kinky people, and even other gay men. Especially other gay men—there are gay men out there who hate what I have to say about bathhouse sex, park sex, and anonymous sex. (Suggesting to gay men that anal sex isn't a first-date activity, as I have, is hugely controversial in some circles.) Sometimes I'm wrong, and that's why my fellow queers are upset, but that's not always the case. Sometimes they're upset because I'm right. And some hate me because I am, and I quote, "a gay, white, cis-gendered, able-bodied gay man focused on gay-marriage priorities." The person who said that? A queer activist who goes by Fister Limp Wrist. The anger of other queers makes life difficult for right-wingers who want to paint me as the leader of all bomb-throwing sex-radical queers. Sorry to disappoint, right-wingers, but the true sex radicals see me as hopelessly conservative and dangerously "heteronormative."

ally identified guys existed, the researchers at Northwestern and CAMH were unable to document bisexual "genital arousal patterns" in their bisexual male test subjects. Men who identified as bi *claimed* that they were aroused by pornography that featured either men or women, but their genitalia—the dicks of these men had been wired up to sensors—told a different story.

"A new study casts doubt on whether true bisexuality exists, at least in men," *The New York Times* reported in the summer of 2005. "The study, by a team of psychologists in Chicago and Toronto, lends support to those who have long been skeptical that bisexuality is a distinct and stable sexual orientation. People who claim bisexuality, according to these critics, are usually homosexual, but are ambivalent about their homosexuality or simply closeted. . . . In the new study, a team of psychologists directly measured genital arousal patterns in response to images of men and women. The psychologists found that men who identified themselves as bisexual were in fact exclusively aroused by either one sex or the other, usually by other men."

The New York Times noted in its report that the study—the largest at the time of the estimated 1.7 percent of men who identify as bisexual (yes, even with that tiny sample size of 101 subjects, this study was then the *largest* to date)—would need to be "repeated with larger numbers of bisexual men before clear conclusions could be drawn." But the study was widely held up, in *The New York Times* no less, as coming close to proving something many gay men had long suspected and loudly asserted: While women could be gay, straight, or bi— researchers had no trouble documenting bisexual arousal patterns in women—men were "Straight, Gay, or Lying," as the nation's paper of record put it in the freakin' *headline*.

Here's the great thing about science: What science gets wrong, more science sets right. (What religion gets wrong, by way of contrast, more religion rarely sets right.) But before we get to how science finally got bisexual men right—before we get to how researchers were able to document the existence of bisexual arousal patterns in males and prove, once and for all, and to the satisfaction of jerks like me, that bisexual men really and truly do exist, prompting me to write a blog post titled "Case Closed: Bisexual Men Exist!"—allow me to unpack the reason some people still see me as bi-phobic and always will.[4]

I can sum it up in a sentence: I'm unwilling to pretend that something that *is*, isn't.

And here's a thing that *is*: Many gay men briefly identify as bisexual during their coming-out processes.

I did.

Telling my friends that I was bi was easier than telling them I was gay. Being bi meant I hadn't gone over to the dark side entirely; I was different, sure, but I wasn't *that* different. I liked boys, and that was news, but I still liked girls. So, hey, no need to panic: I could wind up with a girl in the end and not a boy in my end. (Sorry about that.) The news that I

---

4 Because I've been tagged as bi-phobic for so long—and because it helps bisexuals win the oppression Olympics to claim that they're even persecuted by fags—pretty much anything I say about bisexuals is filtered through a bi-phobic lens. A lesbian called my podcast to complain that her bisexual girlfriend actually liked dick (gasp!) and wanted to have a threesome with a man. I'm in favor of people meeting their partner's needs (see "The GGG Spot"); I've made it a policy in my own life to always err on the side of having the threesome; and I have a pronounced pro-dick bias. So I urged the caller to be open to the idea of the odd threesome with her girlfriend and a man. When I added that the caller shouldn't date bisexual women if she didn't want to be with someone who liked dick, bisexual activists interpreted that as my saying that lesbians shouldn't date bisexual women.

That was, in all honestly, something I recommended much earlier in my advice-slinging career (see below). But I wasn't advising this particular lesbian to dump her girlfriend and date only lesbians. I was telling her to accommodate her partner's needs, which is my standard advice for all people, regardless of sexual orientation, and in her case her partner needed dick now and then.

As noted above: I did once suggest that maybe—*maybe*—bisexuals should date each other. If gays and lesbians are so awful to bisexual people, and if straight people are awful to bisexual people, why not date each other? I'm not suggesting—not anymore—that monosexuals shouldn't date bisexuals. We can and we should and, if I were single, I certainly would. (I'd like to dedicate that last sentence to Eric, my insanely sexy bisexual friend, and someone I could definitely see myself dating if I were single.) I get letters every day from bisexual men and women who complain about how unfairly they're treated by both bi-phobic gays and straights. When I say, "Why not date other bisexuals?" thereby avoiding both bi-phobic gays and straights, bisexual activists spin in circles, claiming that I want to see bisexuals herded into the dating equivalent of internment camps.

was bisexual wasn't a comfort to everyone. "So friction is friction?" my girlfriend at the time asked with barely concealed contempt when the news reached her. (I didn't have the courage or the decency to tell her myself.)

I knew I was gay when I came out to my friends as bi. I had never really been attracted to girls. When I messed around with my girlfriend, and when I'd messed around with the girls I'd been with before her, I would close my eyes and pretend that I was with a boy. Because guess what? Friction *isn't* friction. (Yes, I had sex with girls—several girls—without discovering where the clitoris was. I never laid eyes on it, much less finger or tongue. I was a lousy straight lay.) But I told my friends I was bi because I was afraid. I didn't think they could handle the truth, and I knew that friendlessness was something I couldn't handle. So I lied.

Most of the guys I dated in high school and during my freshman year of college had told the same lie. This is the problem with my sample that I mentioned earlier. Around the same time I was lying to people about being bi, *the gay boys I was dating were lying about being bi.* Eventually everyone I knew who identified as bisexual—everyone I knew *personally,* everyone I knew *biblically*—came out as gay. They were all close to my age, they were all "young adult men," and they were all lying about being bi for the same reason I did: They were afraid.

This was why it was so easy for me, as a young adult, to accept the gay received wisdom. In my personal and biblical experience, bi guys were gay guys who hadn't come all the way out yet. When I first started writing Savage Love, I didn't know a single bi-identified guy who hadn't subsequently come out as gay.

Identifying as bi during the coming-out process wasn't unique to the gay experience in the early 1980s. I met a high school student at a conference in 2011 who was in the midst of what he described as his "second coming out." Bryce Coder is a gay kid from a small town in

Ohio. He told his family and friends that he was bi when he was a freshman in high school, but, as a sophomore, he had to come out to everyone in his life all over again. Why did he lie about being bi? He was afraid.

"I came out as bi because I didn't feel like my family would love me if there was no possibility of me being with a woman," Bryce told me in an e-mail recently. "I worried my parents would reject me if I couldn't give them a grandchild or get married one day. It was purely out of fear of rejection."

The British pop star Mika cultivated an air of sexual ambiguity—something very few straight men do (David Bowie and Ira Glass are the only other examples I can think of)—before telling an interviewer in 2009 that he was bisexual and could "fall in love with anybody—literally—any type, any body." Three years later Mika told another interviewer that he had "found the strength to come to terms with [his] sexuality."

"Yeah," Mika told *Instinct Magazine* in 2012, "I'm gay."

Here's why some people insist that I'm bi-phobic: I admit that when I meet a teenage boy who identifies as bisexual, a little voice in my head says, "I was too at your age." Or when I meet a British pop star who has been out for less than a year and who identifies as bisexual, that same voice says, "Yeah, I was too at this stage of the coming-out process." I don't say anything out loud, of course, and the fact that I lied about being bisexual when I was a teenager doesn't mean the person I've just met is lying about being bisexual. But my experience—and mine is common among gay men—does leave me doubting the professed bisexuality of high school sophomores and British pop stars alike.

While almost all LGBT people seem to enjoy speculating about the "real" sexualities of various celebrities, some LGBT activists view doubting a person's professed sexual identity—even if those doubts remain unexpressed—as a sort of low-level hate crime. It angers bisexuals in particular, as their sexual identities are questioned more than most. "If we respect a person's identity, we empower them," reads an epic bisexual manifesto that a reader directed me to. "We need to respect whatever [someone says], whether or not it jibes with our assumptions about them." This requires us to accept that the Reverend Ted Haggard is, as the Reverend Ted Haggard has claimed to be, "completely heterosexual." Seems like a stretch.

I've never berated a bi-identified teenage boy or a British pop star. I don't tell the ones I meet that they aren't or might not be bisexual. But I know that a bi-identified thirty-six-year-old man who has been out as bi for a decade is much likelier to actually be bisexual than a bi-identified sixteen-year-old boy. Bisexuality is not a phase *for bisexuals,* but for many gay men identifying as bisexual it is. If I have to pretend not to know that in order to avoid being labeled "bi-phobic," well, I guess I'll just have to live with that label.

I can see now why this is all so enormously frustrating for bisexual men. Many gay men think all bisexual guys are lying because a lot of men who claim to be bisexual *are* lying. But it's not bisexual guys who lie about being bisexual. It's gay men like me and Bryce and Mika who lie about being bi. And what do we do after we stop lying about being bi? We insist that all bisexual guys are liars because we were liars.

There are some bona fide bisexuals out there who *do* lie about their sexual orientation, however. But they're not lying about being bisexual. They're lying, actively or passively, about being straight. Which brings us to another thing that *is*: Most bisexual men—adult bi men, not scared gay boys—wind up in opposite-sex relationships. (Most bisexual women do too.) Some chalk it up to societal pressure; others point out that, since there are more straight people in the world than lesbian, gay, or bi people, the odds of a bisexual person meeting and falling in love with an opposite-sex partner are astronomically higher. But it's a thing that *is*.

"I am bisexual. Most of my friends are bisexual," says Neal Boulton, the bisexual former editor of *Genre* and *Men's Health,* and the creator of *Bastard Life,* an online magazine for gay, straight, and bi readers. "And nearly every bisexual I know has settled nicely into an opposite-sex relationship—or marriage. It's just a fact. It's so often just what we do. Now monogamous? That's another story."

Which brings us to another awkward thing that *is:* Many bisexual men admit to being sexually attracted to both sexes, but only *romantically* attracted to one sex, and that sex is usually the opposite one. The Toronto Bisexual Network tiptoes up to acknowledging this fact in its official definition of bisexuality: "Bisexuality is the potential to feel attracted to and to engage in sexual *and/or* romantic relationships with people of any sex or gender. A bisexual person *may not be equally attracted to men and women.*" (So much for falling in love with people and not genitals, huh?) This may be—just may be—another contributing factor to the whole most-bisexuals-wind-up-with-opposite-sex-partners phenomenon. And while it annoys bisexual activists when this subject is raised, gays and lesbians who were looking for love and found themselves in bed—or in relationships—with bisexuals who were only looking for sex would argue that the reality is far more annoying than the subject.[5]

Bi guys with opposite-sex partners may not be straight, but their relationships make 'em look straight. And unless bi men in committed, romantically exclusive (if not sexually exclusive) opposite-sex relationships make an effort to come out to everyone they meet—unless

---

5 From a recent letter from a bi man seeking advice: "I'm bisexual, married, and in my mid-30s. I made it clear to my wife very soon after we met that I was attracted to both men and women, and she was fine with that. My interest in guys has always been limited to the physical." This guy gets credit for being out, and I gave him the best advice I could. But it has to be said: A bi guy like this has one wife but he may approach hundreds of gay men for sex—and only for sex—during the life of his one marriage. A gay man looking for a romantic partner who winds up in bed with one or two bisexual guys like this—a gay guy who has been misled, perhaps, or who fell in love despite the bisexual guy's stated limitations—may conclude that being with bisexual guys isn't worth the risk of another heartbreak. It's like test-driving a car you'll never own. It's another thing that *is.*

they're very vocal about being bi—reasonable people, gay and straight (and bi!), will assume that they're straight.

I don't think it's deceitful for bisexual guys in long-term opposite-sex relationships to allow others to round them down to straight (or up to straight, if you prefer). There are a lot of bisexual women in same-sex relationships who don't go out of their way to come out to people as bi (indeed, many lesbian-identified women are bisexual), and a close friend of mine is a bi man in a same-sex relationship. He's been with his male partner for so long that his newer friends assume he's gay and some of his older friends have forgotten he's bi. Sexual orientation is one thing; sexual identity—real, perceived, or asserted—is another.

Sexual orientation is relatively simple: It's who you wanna do. Sexual identity, however, is more complicated and more nuanced. Sexual identity is a combo platter: It's equal parts who you wanna do, who you're actually doing, and what you wanna tell people. Sexual identity, unlike sexual orientation, involves a degree of choice. You may not be able to control who you wanna do, but you do get to decide what you're going to tell people—yes, even if you're Ted Haggard. (I may owe an apology to Ted Haggard, I guess, as it's possible that his sexual identity is as complicated and nuanced as a canned ham dropped from a great height. But he sure does come across like a tormented closet case to me.)

Bisexual men with female partners should, though, at the very least be *out to their female partners.* But judging from the e-mails I get at Savage Love, and from the many men-seeking-men ads on Craigslist and elsewhere, an awful lot of bisexual guys aren't out to their female partners. A half a dozen letters like this one arrive in my in-box every day:

> I am a 30-year-old bi male recently engaged to a wonderful woman. I have never told my fiancée about my bi past, and didn't think it was a big deal because I am more attracted to women, and was only in one male/male relation-

ship . . . but now that we're engaged, I am feeling guilty for keeping this quiet. Is it too late? Should I stay quiet? I don't want to lose her.[6]

Closeted bi guys—those who sneak around with men (often with gay men) behind the backs of their wives and girlfriends—are another thing that *is*. And they're a thing you should avoid talking about if you don't want to be labeled bi-phobic. But I can't avoid talking about them because they write to me all the time asking for my advice. (My advice to this particular "30-year-old bi male": You should come out to your fiancée. Keep reading for all the reasons why.)

I don't hate bisexual men generally and I don't even hate closeted bi guys specifically. I recognize that the stigma attached to male bisexuality—a stigma that I helped to promote before I saw the error of my gay ways—keeps a lot of bi guys closeted. (It's difficult to come out to your wife or girlfriend about being bi if she's convinced that male bisexuality is a myth, that all bi guys are secretly gay, and that you'll eventually leave her for another man.) But hate bisexual guys? Me? No way. It would be more accurate to say that I like bisexual guys so much that I wish there were more of them. I hope, for instance, that this bi guy has the decency to come out to his fiancée before he marries her, because she deserves better *and so does he.* Being closeted is awful and I wouldn't wish it on anyone. Hiding the truth about your sexuality from someone you love is painful and exhausting—which is why I stopped doing it when I was a teenager.

And, I'm proud to say, I've heard from many, many bisexual men who were inspired to come out as bi after reading my column.

---

6 There are worse examples I could have chosen—letters from bi guys cheating on their wives are common. But so are letters from straight guys cheating on their wives, gay guys cheating on their husbands, and lesbians cheating on their wives. People who aren't screwing up, or being screwed over, don't write to sex-advice columnists for advice. Pretty much all of my samples are hopelessly skewed.

Thanks to your advice I admitted I am bi, got out of a relationship with a woman who couldn't accept it and into a relationship with one who loves it. I go to the gay bar, feeling proud and confident, she joins me, loves the show, and so far it has been fantastic. I have spent many years learning to love myself, sometimes to no avail. At first I thought that meant only loving the "good" part of myself. Slowly, I have learned that loving myself means loving and accepting all of myself—including a few strange desires and dreams. I am a proud kinky, bisexual man now and you have helped me in this process.

Not a bad day's work for a bi-phobic asshole like me, huh?

Not only would it be great if more bisexual guys were out to their female partners, it would be great if more bisexuals in opposite-sex relationships—male and female bisexuals both—were out to their friends, families, and coworkers. Bisexual activists and bloggers complain about "bisexual invisibility" and "bisexual erasure." The site Queers United defines the latter as "the conscious or unconscious effort by individuals and groups to ignore, remove, or alter aspects of bisexuality in an effort to diminish the idea that bisexuality is a valid sexual orientation."

Some complaints about bisexual erasure are valid. For instance, gay people who claim—as I once did—that there's no such thing as bisexual men are certainly guilty of bisexual erasure. Most of the other examples cited on bisexual blogs are from pop culture. Mike Manning, for instance, was a cast member on the 2009 season of MTV's *The Real World*. Although Manning was bisexual and hooked up with both men and women during filming, all of his presumably numerous hookups with women—we're talking about *The Real World*—were edited out. Evidence of Manning's bisexuality was literally erased by the show's producers. Young gay and straight MTV viewers who believed that all bi men are secretly gay had their misconceptions reinforced, while MTV's young bisexual viewers were deprived of, well, if not a role model—again, we're talking about *The Real World*—then at least a little representation.

But some accusations about bisexual erasure are deeply silly.

"Whenever, say, some prominent heterosexually married male public figure has a same-sex affair, literally everyone rolls their eyes at the 'closeted homosexual,'" a twenty-six-year-old bi man living in Brooklyn told *Salon*'s terrific sex writer Tracy Clark-Flory, in a 2011 article on bisexuality. "I'm not sure I remember ever hearing someone seriously entertain the possibility that the philanderer was bisexual."

This seems to me an instance where bisexual erasure and bisexual invisibility—complete erasure, complete invisibility—work to the benefit of the bisexual community. No one suggested that Larry Craig might be bi after the married anti-gay Republican "family values" senator from Idaho was arrested for soliciting gay sex in a public toilet at the Minneapolis–St. Paul International Airport in June of 2007. And, if at the time, I had suggested that everyone really ought to "entertain the possibility" that Larry Craig could be a closeted *bisexual* Republican hypocrite, and not a closeted homosexual hypocrite, I would have been accused of invoking one of the worst stereotypes about married bisexual men: They can't keep the monogamous commitments they make to their wives. Here's a darker example: John Wayne Gacy married a woman—and had two children with her—before he kidnapped, raped, tortured, and murdered at least thirty-three young men and boys. I could ask people to "entertain the possibility" that Gacy was a bisexual serial killer in an effort to combat "bisexual erasure," I suppose, but I can't imagine the bisexual community really feels cheated every time Gacy is identified as a "gay serial killer."

Another deeply silly example of "bisexual erasure": Imagine you've just met a man at a party. The man introduces you to a woman. "This is my wife," the man says. If you thought, "straight man, straight couple," some bisexual activists—the unhinged ones—would accuse you of engaging in bisexual erasure, because the man you met could be bisexual. I've gotten into arguments with readers who insist that the onus isn't on the bisexual man with the wife to come out to you as bi. The onus is on you, me, and everyone else at the party to refrain from making assumptions. While it's true that the overwhelming majority of men are straight, and while this man's female spouse is solid, if not conclusive, evidence that he *could be* straight, it's bi-phobic of you to assume the man *is* straight just because he has a wife. "I'm not going to assume this man is straight," you should've told yourself when you thought, "straight guy," after meeting his wife. "There's a chance he could be bisexual. Furthermore, I'm not going to assume that his failure to identify himself as bisexual is evidence that he is comfortable being perceived as straight. I'm going to draw no conclusions *whatsoever*. He's a man with a wife, and he could be *anything*."

Human beings make assumptions about other human beings all the time, and so long as our assumptions aren't warped bigotry—all gays are sluts, all Muslims are terrorists, all blonds are dumb, all bisexuals are closet cases—they're harmless. If you wouldn't think less of the married man you met at the party if you found out later that he was bisexual, there's nothing bi-phobic about the reasonable assumption you made. I'm a gay parent and I can't count the number of times when I've been out with my son by myself—particularly when he was an infant—that well-meaning, well-intentioned people asked where my wife was. Another perfectly reasonable assumption: Most men wearing wedding rings (on their fingers) and small children (on their backs) are married to women. This assumption—that I was straight and married and my wife had to be somewhere—was entirely reasonable, and so long as the people who made it didn't throw up on my shoes after I told them that my wife had a dick, I didn't feel invisible, erased, or offended.

But the truly shameful erasure from the conversation here is that no one contributes more to this problem than bisexuals do. No one erases bisexuals quite as effectively as bisexuals do. While I recognize that the reluctance of many bisexuals to be out is a reaction to the hostility they face from non-bisexuals—the fear and loathing of so many prejudiced monosexuals—cowering in the closet isn't the solution. More and more people have come to accept gays and lesbians because we came out. But with most bisexuals winding up in opposite-sex relationships, and with most allowing people to assume they're straight (including their own friends, family members, and even spouses), millions of people who know bisexuals don't know they know bisexuals because the bisexuals they know aren't out to them.

A. J. Walkley is a "monogamous, bisexual, cisgender female . . . in a relationship with a cisgender male" who, with Lauren Michelle Kinsey ("a monogamous, bisexual, cisgender female . . . in a relationship with a cisgender female") cowrites the *Bi the Bi* blog for the Gay Voices section of *The Huffington Post.* (Gay Voices? That's an example of bisexual erasure right there, isn't it?) Walkley, in a joint post written with Kinsey, debated some of the issues I've raised about bisexual responsibility for bisexual invisibility. After she trashes me in one long, butt-covering paragraph, Walkley grudgingly concedes that I may be right:

> However, I would be remiss to fail to acknowledge the fact that, on some level, Savage has a point. I do believe that bisexual people make up a significant part of the global population, and we are most likely the majority of the LGB population. You would never know it, though, *because most of us are still closeted* for, as you acknowledged, Lauren, a whole slew of reasons. It's almost a "chicken or the egg" question: Does society and the LGBT community at large need to become more accepting before bisexuals come out en masse, or do bisexuals need to come out before more acceptance is possible? [Emphasis added.]

Walkley has a point—but it's a self-serving, self-defeating one. Yes, society needs to become more accepting of bisexuals. But that's not going to happen until the millions of bisexuals who've disappeared into opposite-sex relationships come out to their family, friends, and coworkers. If gays and lesbians had waited for society to become more accepting before we started coming out en masse, no gay or lesbian person would ever have come out at all. It's ridiculous to suggest that bisexuals coming out in 2013 face greater levels of hostility than gays and lesbians did coming out in 1969.

And if bisexuals did come out en masse they could rule the—well, not the *world*. But bisexuals could definitely rule the parallel LGBT universe. In 2012, a researcher at the Williams Institute at the University of California released the results of a study that attempted to estimate the LGBT population of the United States. Some of the numbers that "Gary J. Gates, Williams Distinguished Scholar" came up with were disputed—just 3.5 percent of the population is LGBT? There are only eleven million LGBT people in the whole United States?—but the most interesting finding was that there are *more* bisexual adults (1.8 percent of the population) than gay and lesbian adults combined (1.7 percent of the population). Not only do bisexuals exist, they outnumber us homosexuals.

I'm sorry, bisexual activists, but you're doing it all wrong. Instead of berating me for my alleged bi-phobia—and if *I'm* the enemy, you're in real trouble—berate your closeted compatriots.

If bisexuals came out en masse, you could run the LGBT movement. And if you concluded that my inability to pretend that some things that are, aren't, proved that I was irredeemably, hopelessly bi-phobic, well, then you could kick my ass out.

Okay, let's get back to science—*science!*—and the study that finally proved that bisexual men do, in fact, exist.

"In an unusual scientific about-face," *The New York Times* reported in August of 2011, "researchers at Northwestern University have found evidence that at least some men who identify themselves as bisexual are, in fact, sexually aroused by both women and men."

So what did researchers at Northwestern do differently the second time around? How did they demonstrate that bisexual arousal patterns exist in males? They controlled for something researchers failed to control for in the past: Not all guys who claim they're bisexual are telling the truth. They controlled for *liars.*

"Past research not finding bisexual genital arousal patterns among bisexual men may have been affected by recruitment techniques," A. M. Rosenthal, the lead author for the new study, concluded. "For example, bisexual men in those studies needed only to identify as bisexual and to self-report bisexual attractions (e.g., Rieger et al., 2005). Thus, the bisexual samples of previous studies may have been populated by men who had *never or rarely behaved bisexually and perhaps identified as bisexual for reasons other than strong arousal to both sexes."* [Emphasis added.]

Let me translate that into English: Most of the bisexually identified guys in earlier studies—almost all of them college-age guys, most barely out of high school—were gay guys. They were bisexual like I was bisexual, bisexual like Bryce was bisexual, bisexual like Mika was bisexual. Which is to say, *they weren't bisexual at all.* Or, as the 2011 study's authors put it, "past studies may have unintentionally oversampled bisexual-identified men with homosexual arousal patterns." But instead of doubting their subjects' bisexual identities—which, remember, is a terribly bi-phobic thing to do—researchers wound up casting doubt on bisexuality.

This time researchers didn't recruit subjects from gay and alternative newspapers, but from sources "likely to be frequented by men with bisexual erotic interests." Researchers trawled online sex ads for men who were seeking "to have sex with both members of heterosexual couples." They only accepted men who "had at least two sexual partners of each sex and a romantic relationship of at least three months' duration with at least one person of each sex. These inclusion criteria were employed to increase the probability of finding men with a bisexual genital arousal pattern (rather than those who identify as bisexual for other reasons)." Despite the added effort to find actual bisexual guys this time out, in the end Northwestern researchers dropped men that had been recruited for the study because they didn't believe them to be bisexual.

And how many of the guys with "bisexual erotic interests" found in places "likely to be frequented by men with bisexual erotic interests" did researchers wind up cutting? *Nearly half.*

So how's this for irony? The authors of this study—a study that has been quite rightly embraced, celebrated, and promoted by bisexual individuals, organizations, activists, and bloggers—were only able to document bisexual arousal patterns in bisexually identified males by doing precisely what many of those same bisexual individuals, organizations, activists, and bloggers condemn as bi-phobic: *They refused to accept the professed sexual identities of nearly half of their subjects.*

They controlled for *liars.*

I have had the disorienting experience of being accused of being bi-phobic for hesitating to accept the bisexuality of high school sophomores and British pop stars by people who were literally—*literally*—waving the results of this study in my face.

And this is why I drink.

12. On Being Different

Terry found a vacation rental for us in Hawaii.

The house was just steps from the beach—a very important detail for my husband—and it had six bedrooms. That's not the kind of vacation home we can typically afford, but there had been a last-minute cancellation, some other family had forfeited a large deposit, and my husband, ever the bargain hunter, snagged us a deal.

Six bedrooms! We invited two other couples, both gay, to join us. They were thrilled. Our then thirteen-year-old son invited two of his friends, both straight, to join his boring gay dads and their boring gay friends at the beach for two weeks. Their parents were thrilled.

It was on that beach in the summer of 2011 that I read Merle Miller's essay "What It Means to Be a Homosexual" exactly forty years after it first appeared in *The New York Times Magazine*. Miller was a famous public intellectual; he was a war correspondent during the Second World War, a novelist and a historian after. He went on to be an editor at *Harper's* and *Time* magazine. Miller came out in "What It Means to Be a Homosexual," which was published later that year in book form as *On Being Different*.

As my son and his friends roughhoused in the surf with Terry and the spryer halves of the two couples who joined us, I was sitting on the beach reading this passage:

> The fear of it simply will not go away, though. A man who
> was once a friend, maybe my best friend, the survivor of five

marriages, the father of nine, not too long ago told me that his eldest son was coming to my house on Saturday: "Now, please try not to make a pass at him."

He laughed. I guess he meant it as a joke; I didn't ask.

And a man I've known, been acquainted with, let's say, for twenty-five years, called from the city on a Friday afternoon before getting on the train to come up to my place for the weekend. He said, "I've always leveled with you, Merle, and I'm going to now. I've changed my mind about bringing _____ [his sixteen-year-old son]. I'm sure you understand."

I said that, no, I didn't understand. Perhaps he could explain it to me.

He said, "_____ is only an impressionable kid, and while I've known you and know you wouldn't, but suppose you had some friends in, and . . ."

D.J. came out to his boring gay dads as straight when he was eleven; both of the teenage boys he invited to Hawaii with us were straight. And the parents of D.J.'s friends? They were straight.

And they understood.

Which is why they didn't hesitate to say yes. The parents of D.J.'s friends knew they could trust us and our friends—two gay men they knew, four other gay men they'd never met—alone with their sons. (They also knew that their sons would be eating decent meals, brushing their teeth twice a day, and getting to bed at a reasonable hour—Terry and I have a reputation among D.J.'s friends and their parents for being joy-killing, rule-enforcing hard-asses.)

What worried Miller's friends—the "it" that his friends and acquaintances feared—was seduction. Gay men, given access to young boys, would "seduce" them into the gay lifestyle. My parents used to believe that. Among the questions I got when I came out to my family was whether an older gay man had ever seduced me.

I have known quite a few homosexuals, and I have listened to a great many accounts of how they got that way or think they got that way. I have never heard anybody say that he (or she) got to be a homosexual because of seduction.

I have known quite a few heterosexual parents since Terry and I adopted D.J. nearly a decade and a half ago. Despite the fact that more same-sex couples are adopting today than ever before, Parentlandia remains overwhelmingly straight. And not once in all the time since we became parents has a straight parent expressed the slightest anxiety about his or her son or daughter spending time with D.J., or with us, or with our gay and lesbian friends, despite the best efforts of anti-gay "Christian" conservatives to prop up the old bigotries and fears.

Have I mentioned that one of D.J.'s dads is a notorious sex-advice columnist, a recovering drag queen, and a political bomb thrower?

It has gotten better. Not perfect.

Better.

Billy Lucas was a fifteen-year-old kid growing up in Greensburg, Indiana. Lucas wasn't openly gay—he may not have been gay at all—but he was perceived to be gay by his peers and relentlessly bullied. Classmates told him to kill himself; they told him he didn't deserve to live; they told him that God hated him. School administrators, according to a lawsuit filed by Lucas's family, witnessed the abuse and did nothing to stop it. Some may have participated in the bullying of Lucas.

On Thursday, September 9, 2010, Lucas hanged himself in his grandmother's barn. His mother found his body.

Lucas's death moved Terry and me to start the It Gets Better Project. The idea was simple: There were LGBT kids out there who couldn't picture futures with enough joy in them to compensate for the pain they were in now. We wanted to reach those bullied and isolated lesbian, gay, bisexual, and transgender youth. We wanted to talk to them about the future, about their futures, and offer them encouragement. We were particularly interested in reaching LGBT kids growing up in places like Greensburg, Indiana, and other parts of the country where there aren't support groups for queer kids or Gay-Straight Alliances in the schools. We particularly wanted to reach gay, lesbian, bi, and trans kids with parents that would never allow their kids to attend an LGBT youth support group.

"You got to give 'em hope," Harvey Milk said. By sharing our stories, and encouraging other LGBT adults to do the same, we wanted to give LGBT kids hope.

Four weeks after we posted the first video to YouTube, the president of the United States uploaded his own *It Gets Better* video. (It took Ronald Reagan seven years to even say the word AIDS—it has gotten better.) More than fifty thousand videos have been posted as of this writing, they have been viewed more than fifty million times, and we have heard from thousands of LGBT kids who have been helped by the project.

The It Gets Better Project has generated a lot of goodwill and raised awareness about the challenges faced by LGBT youth. But the project was motivated by anger. Kids were being brutalized and bullied— sometimes bullied to death—for being queer. And not just by their peers: The LGBT kids who most needed to hear from us were the ones whose own parents were least likely to approve. LGBT kids are four times likelier to attempt suicide; LGBT kids whose families are hostile—LGBT kids who are being bullied by their own parents—are at eight times greater risk for suicide.

When we uploaded that first video, it was with a sense of defiance. We were going to talk to these LGBT kids whether their parents wanted us to or not. We were going to talk to them whether their preachers wanted us to or not. We were going to talk to them whether their teachers wanted us to or not. These kids were being told that LGBT people were sick, sinful, and unhappy, and we were going to expose the lies and call out the liars—even if the liars were their own parents.

Anger motivated us to start the It Gets Better Project, just as anger motivated Miller to write his groundbreaking essay. Gay people were coming out and demanding their rights in the wake of the Stonewall Riots, which prompted an explosion of commentary, much of it as bigoted, misinformed, and vile as the insults that Billy Lucas had to face every day. Miller, in an explosive coming-out scene, announced to two colleagues that he was "sick and tired of hearing such goddamn demeaning, degrading bullshit about me and my friends."

That exchange—that anger—led Miller to write "What It Means to Be a Homosexual" and to come out in the most public possible way. The social change we've witnessed over the last forty years was never a given. Change began when people like Merle Miller decided that they had finally had enough. Change began when LGBT people began to stand up for themselves and their friends.

> I am sick and tired of hearing such goddamn demeaning, degrading bullshit about me and my friends.

In that single sentence Miller captured the anger that has motivated LGBT activists from the Mattachine Society to the Stonewall Riots to ACT UP to the It Gets Better Project. Every LGBT rights activist I've ever met is someone who grew sick and tired of hearing such goddamn demeaning, degrading bullshit about themselves and their friends and decided to speak up and fight back.

That's what the LGBT movement is at its core: people standing up for themselves and their friends and their lovers and people with HIV and bullied LGBT kids. The LGBT movement is still facing down the liars and pushing back against the degrading bullshit. Gay people of

Miller's generation knew that gay life, as described by the shrinks and the religious bigots, looked nothing like gay life as they lived it. Miller, in anger, came to the defense of himself and his friends and helped to change the world. Today, in anger, we come to the defense of LGBT kids, gay kids growing up in parts of the country where goddamn demeaning, degrading bullshit is being screamed in their faces.

And we are sick and tired of it.

I'm often asked if I wish there had been an It Gets Better Project when I was a gay kid growing up on the north side of Chicago.

There was.

It wasn't on YouTube, which didn't exist when I was a kid, or on television, which didn't acknowledge the existence of gay people when I was a kid, and the president of the United States certainly wasn't a part of it.

Here's what the It Gets Better Project looked like in 1976: I was with my mom and dad and brothers and sister at Water Tower Place, a shopping mall near downtown Chicago. We were going to the movies— *Logan's Run*—and in front of us in line were two young gay men. They were holding hands. I was eleven years old. I was old enough to be aware, painfully so, of being different than other boys. My mother glared at the gay men in line, shook her head, and said, "They're weird," to my father, and put a protective hand on my shoulder and pulled me closer to her. She didn't reach for my brothers or my sister. Just me.

While my parents could only see dangerous perverts—it was the only thing their upbringing allowed them to see—I saw a future. I'd always known that I was different and now I knew how. I was different like them; they were different like me; I was going to be like them when I grew up. And they didn't look unhappy. They looked happy and free. They looked like they were in love.

Just by being out, just by being themselves, by taking each other's hands in public, those guys in that line at Water Tower Place gave me hope.

"Somewheres in Des Moines or San Antonio there is a young gay person who all of a sudden realizes that she or he is gay," Harvey Milk said in 1978 in his famous "hope" speech. "And that child has several options: staying in the closet; suicide. And then one day that child might open a paper that says 'Homosexual elected in San Francisco' and there are two new options: the option is to go to California, or stay in San Antonio and fight."

I was one of those kids that Harvey Milk was talking about when he gave that speech. I was thirteen years old in 1977, when Milk was elected to the San Francisco Board of Supervisors after three previous runs for office, and I only knew a few things about being gay at that time: My parents thought gay people were sick, my peers thought gay people were disgusting, and that woman who sold orange juice on the television thought gay people were pedophiles. I briefly contemplated suicide as a teenager, not because I was particularly depressed or un-happy, but because I wanted to protect my parents. I was a good kid, a well-behaved mama's boy, and I had concluded that my mother and father would rather have a dead kid than a gay one.

But hearing about Milk's election reinforced the message those two men waiting in line at Water Tower Place had unwittingly sent me a year and a half earlier. There was a place for me in this world. I had options other than staying in the closet or committing suicide.

"I know that you cannot live on hope alone," Milk said, "but with-out it, life is not worth living. And you, and you, and you have got to give 'em hope."

Hope can save lives—hope has saved lives—but we can do better than hope. By pushing back against the goddamn demeaning, de-grading bullshit that is still being hurled at us, by defeating it once and for all, we can deliver change.

———

> [The] closets are far from emptied. There are more in
> hiding than out of hiding. That has been my experience
> anyway.

I don't think that's the case today; not in the West, at any rate. Our closets aren't empty, of course, but the closet is the exception now, no longer the rule. (And the closet cases—the Wests and Haggards and Craigs and Rekers—are ridiculous figures, not tragic ones.)

In 1971, when he was fifty and just coming out publicly, Miller was awed by the strength, self-possession, and impatience of gay men and lesbians who were coming out in their early twenties. Just over ten years later—in 1982—I would come out to my family when I was still in high school. I recently heard from the father of a thirteen-year-old boy. His son, a middle school student, had just come out and his father wanted advice on parenting a gay kid. He didn't want to fail his son.

We've gone from a world where Merle Miller couldn't come out until middle age—the world he describes in *On Being Different*—to a world where thirteen-year-old boys are coming out to their families and all their dads want to know is how they can best support their gay sons.

It has gotten better. Not perfect. Better.

But you can't know how far you've come if you don't know where you started. Adult gay men and lesbians don't raise the next generation of gays and lesbians; our history isn't passed from parent to child. That's why it's critically important for gay men and lesbians, for bisexual and transgender people, to learn their history.

Straight people with LGBT family members, friends, and coworkers should know the history of the LGBT rights movement too. *All* straight people should know the story of the gay liberation movement, because it is also the story of straight liberation. The LGBT rights movement liberated straight people from their prejudices and their fears; it helped straight people see through the goddamn, demeaning bullshit; the movement for LGBT equality helped straight people rebuild relationships with the lesbian, gay, bisexual, and transgender family members and friends that their prejudices had estranged them from.

People like Merle Miller and, yes, those guys in line for *Logan's Run,* came out because they were sick and tired of the goddamn demeaning, degrading bullshit that LGBT people were subjected to. And by coming out at a time when it was so much more dangerous, personally and professionally, Miller helped to remake the world. Miller and all the gay men and lesbians who came out in the 1950s, '60s, and '70s— men and women who came out in big ways (by writing cover stories for *The New York Times Magazine*) and small (by taking their lover's hand in line at a movie theater)—made the world a better, safer place for all the gay, lesbian, bisexual, and trans men and women who would come after them. They made it a better, safer place for me. They made it possible for thirteen-year-old gay boys to come out to their fathers.

They made it better.

I'm roughly the same age now that Miller was when he wrote his groundbreaking essay. I'm creeping up on fifty. Like Miller, I have a mild case of writer's block; I've worked as a writer and an editor, and like Miller, I'm "an infrequent visitor to gay bars and was never comfortable in them." (I feel about gay bars the way many American Jews feel about Israel: happy to have a homeland, don't want to live there.)

Writing in 1971—when homosexuality was still a crime in forty-eight states—Miller observed, "I think social attitudes will change, are changing, quickly too."

When I finally came out in 1982, telling my Catholic parents I was gay didn't just mean telling them I was like those guys at the movies my mother wanted to protect me from. It meant I would never marry and I would never have children. I would certainly never be trusted alone with someone else's child.

But there I was, just four short decades after Miller wrote *On Being*

Different, just three short decades after I sat down with my mother and forced the words "I'm gay" out of my mouth. There I was, sitting on a beach next to my husband, while our teenage son dove through waves with his friends, two boys who were entrusted to our care by their straight parents.

"In the battle between reality and fundamentalism of all varieties, reality always wins—if it is given the freedom to breathe and we show the courage necessary to accept it," author and political commentator Andrew Sullivan writes in response to reading Miller's essay. "Even then it takes time. But when a truth has been suppressed by a massive lie for centuries, its eventual emergence is almost a miracle."

That day on the beach, reading Miller's essay and recalling what coming out meant when Miller did it and what it meant when I did it, it did feel like a miracle.

Thank you, Mr. Miller, for telling your story; thank you for your anger; thank you for fighting back against the demeaning, degrading bullshit. We couldn't have made it to that beach without you.

13. Extended Stay

I would need the room for a week. That's what I told the reception-ist at the Extended Residence Stay America Comfort Suites Inn Whatever when I checked in that Sunday night in March.

At least a week, I said, maybe longer.

My mother had already been in the hospital across the street for a week when I got to Tucson. She had been no stranger to hospitals over the last five years. She'd wake up one morning to find that her breathing was more difficult, or that some new infection was exploiting her weak-ened immune system, or that some new debilitating side effect from the powerful drugs that were keeping her alive had emerged. Her husband would rush her to a hospital and she would come home a few days later having accepted some previously feared development—being hooked up to an oxygen tank, having to use a walker—as her new normal.

The plan: I would stay in Tucson for three or four days and help my stepfather and aunt look after my mother. Then my brother Billy would fly in from Chicago, take over the helping-out duties and the hotel room; I'd go home, and we'd figure out what to do next.

I had gone straight to the hospital from the airport when I arrived in Tucson that afternoon. My mother was weak but alert, sitting up in bed. She nodded hello. The oxygen mask she was wearing made it hard for her to speak. Every couple of seconds a whirring machine next to her bed forced pure oxygen into her battered lungs with a thump. Shouting to be heard over the oxygen machine, I played cards with my mother, something we had always enjoyed doing. I taught her a new game. Things seemed decidedly less grim than they were when my aunt called me in Seattle the previous day. My mother didn't seem to be getting any worse, my aunt told me, but she wasn't getting better either. My stepfather didn't want to alarm us—or my mother—by asking her children to rush to Tucson. But my aunt didn't want it on her conscience if my mother died without her children at her bedside. Get on an airplane, my aunt said. Get on an airplane now.

My mother had pulmonary fibrosis, a degenerative lung condition, and she knew—we all knew—that dramatic turns for the worse were a possibility. She knew that pulmonary fibrosis would eventually end her life, and she'd done some research into just what sort of an end she could expect. It wasn't going to be pretty. Her lungs were gradually filling with scar tissue. She would, when her time came, slowly and painfully suffocate to death. But eight weeks before she wound up in a sprawling, dung-colored hospital in sprawling, dung-colored Tucson, my mother's doctors had given her two to five years to live.

She'd recently marked the five-year anniversary of her diagnosis, an anniversary very few pulmonary fibrosis sufferers live to see. She was scared, as her fifth anniversary approached, that she wouldn't "beat five." But her spirits lifted when her fifth anniversary came and went, and again when her doctors gave her those two, and maybe more, years to live. That's when she decided to go on a trip with her husband, driving to California and New Mexico and Arizona, to visit her sisters. She was looking forward to attending her first grandson's high school graduation in Montana, her grade school class's fiftieth reunion in Chicago, the tour of a Broadway show that I got her tickets to for her birthday.

While my mother was on her way to Tucson in the spring of 2008, a debate was raging in Washington State. Medical rights activists in

Washington had gathered enough signatures to put a physician-assisted-suicide law on the ballot. The proposed law, modeled on a law approved by Oregon voters in 1994, would allow physicians to prescribe lethal doses of medication to terminally ill patients. Two physicians would have to verify the patient had less than six months to live, wasn't being coerced, and was mentally sound. And the doctors could only prescribe the drugs. The patient would have to take them—the patient would have to administer them herself.

The fiercest critic of the proposed law was Joel Connelly, a columnist for the *Seattle Post-Intelligencer*. Connelly, a liberal Catholic, wrote column after column blasting Washington's Death with Dignity Act, the ballot measure's official title. The purpose of a "democratic society," Connelly argued, was to "safeguard and enhance life, especially among the youngest, the weakest, and the suffering." He urged voters not to "transform a crime into a 'medical treatment.'"

Early one morning, a few weeks after I got back from Tucson, I was lying in bed listening to the radio. I had been up most of the night. I found it difficult to sleep after coming back home from Arizona, and so, at the urging of a friend, I began taking Ambien, a prescription sleeping pill. It wasn't until I tried to stop taking Ambien that I learned that insomnia is one of the drug's possible side effects. That's why I was awake, at five that morning, when a report came on about the impending vote on Washington's Death with Dignity Act. Two women who had both recently lost their husbands were interviewed about the proposed new law. One of the widows planned to vote for it and the other planned to vote against it.

The woman planning to vote for the initiative—the woman whose husband died of brain cancer—came away from the experience convinced that terminally ill people should have a choice at the end of their lives. The terminally ill should have the freedom to end their suffering, she said, and hasten their inevitable, rapidly approaching deaths. And the woman planning to vote against the initiative wanted—well, she wanted what we all want. She wanted a good death, "a natural death," a death like the one her late husband "enjoyed." Asked to imagine her own death, she said she hoped for a painless death and that at the end she would be "enveloped in the love of a good caregiver."

We should all be so lucky. It'd be ideal if each of us passed from existence to nonexistence enveloped in the love of good caregivers and under the care of competent "pain management" professionals. But not everyone is so lucky. Even with the most loving caregivers and competent pain managers standing by, some of us are fated to endure deaths that are as gruesome and protracted as they are painful. Some deaths cannot be "managed." Sometimes loving caregivers can't "envelop"; they can only stand helplessly by and bear witness.

The widow who planned to vote for the Death with Dignity Act was given the last word: "You don't know how you're going to feel at the end of your life," she said. "I want to have choices available to me."

Exactly.

Washington's Death with Dignity Act was about choices. If voters approved the law, the widow who opposed physician-assisted suicide would not be compelled to end her life with the assistance of a physician. She could still choose to die a "natural death," surrounded by good caregivers and pumped full of the strongest pain medications available. (I fail to see what's so "natural" about pain medication— God didn't exactly give us a gland that secretes morphine when we need it.) But if voters rejected Washington's Death with Dignity Act, the widow who supported the law—the widow who wanted a choice— would not have the same freedom. She would not be able to choose to end her life, and end her suffering, if her pain was too much for her to bear.

Legalizing physician-assisted suicide doesn't force lethal drug cocktails on those who reject physician-assisted suicide for religious reasons, just as legalizing abortion or gay marriage doesn't impose anything on those who disapprove of abortion and gay marriage. Even where these practices are legal, those who oppose abortion, gay marriage, and physician-assisted suicide are not required to have abortions, marry same-sex partners, or ask their doctors for a lethal dose of drugs.

And there's nothing about physician-assisted suicide—or, as it should be called, end-of-life pain management—that precludes the presence of loving caregivers. You can be surrounded by love, have access to the best medical care available and the morphine that God was so cruel as to hide in poppies (where it lay undiscovered until 1804), and still reasonably and rationally conclude that you would rather not spend the last few moments of your life in blinding pain or gasping for breath or pumped full of just enough morphine to deaden the pain without quite deadening you.

Moments after I got back to my mother's hospital room from the Extended Suites Whatever on Monday morning, a doctor pulled my stepfather and me into the hallway. It wasn't good news. It wasn't pneumonia, as they had hoped, and my mother wasn't suffering from a virus. It wasn't some rare desert fungus. Her lungs were failing. Nothing more could be done. One of her battered lungs had a large and widening hole; the other was starting to come apart. We stared at the doctor dumbly, uncomprehendingly, until one of us—I don't know if it was my stepfather or me—finally said, "This is it?"

The doctor nodded. This was it.

My stepfather stepped out of the intensive care unit to find my sister and my aunt, who were sitting with my nephew, Cody, who was too young to come into the ICU. He would break the bad news to them, he said, and confer about how we should break the bad news to my mother. I slipped back into my mother's hospital room to sit with her. I took her hand. This was it, but I couldn't show it. She smiled at me weakly. I didn't tell her what I knew; it wasn't my place. We would wait together for her husband of twenty years to return.

Suddenly, the doctor was at the door to my mother's room again. He waved me out into the hall. He needed a medical directive. Immediately. My mother's vital signs were tanking. If they were going to put a tube in her, and put her on machines that could breathe for her, it had to be done now. I asked if I could go get my stepfather and the doctor said no. He needed a decision from my mother. Now.

So it fell to me to tell her she was going to die and quickly lay out her rather limited options. She could be put under and put on machines and live for a day or two in a coma, long enough for her other two children to get down to Tucson and say their good-byes, good-byes that she wouldn't be able to hear. Or she could live for maybe another six hours if she continued to wear an oxygen mask that pushed air into her lungs with so much force it made her whole body convulse. Or she could take the mask off and suffocate to death. Now.

It was her choice.

"No pain," she said, "no pain."

A nurse was in the room with us and she promised to give my mother enough morphine to deaden any pain. And then my mother made her choice: She would take off the mask and go. Now. I told the doctor and then ran into the waiting room to get my stepfather, my sister, and my aunt. Things were worse than they were five minutes ago. Get in here, I sobbed, get in here.

Now.

When we were all back at her bedside, my mother looked up at us, oxygen mask still on. Then she arched an eyebrow, shook her head, and said, "*Shit.*"

My mother used profanity sparingly, and only in quotation marks and italics. When she said "shit," we understood what she meant. And what she meant was this: "The kind of person who casually uses profanity might be inclined to say 'shit' at a moment like this, but I am not the kind of person who uses profanity. I am a good and decent Catholic grandmother. And I certainly wouldn't use a word like that at a moment like this. But if I *were* the kind of person who used profanity, 'shit' would be the word I would use right about now. But I'm not that kind of person."

She was making a joke. She was trying to cheer us up.

A haggard looking priest arrived to perform last rites, and it helped my mother brace for what she fea— uld be an extremely painful final few minutes. Th— ayer. I could see it helped. I could se— er. It gave *me* comfort. To— th learned at St. Ignatius rrible silence, solemniz-

uld be with us always, gain.

" But the mask was good-byes reduced to wracking sobs; floor beside our other's ear so she good-byes over the whir and ne, while my clearly shattered stepfather ly to get my other brother on his cell phone. Our good-yes were all chaos and hurry and pain.

My mother held tight to our hands. She had a terror of physical pain, and she was worried that the nurse would give her just enough morphine to make communication impossible but not enough to actually alleviate her pain. The nurse tried to reassure her but my mother was panicking, her grip growing tighter. My stepfather leaned down and kissed my mother's forehead, the nurse pushed the morphine solution into her IV, and then my stepfather gently removed the oxygen mask.

"Remember me," she said.

Her grip slackened. My mother was still alive, in there somewhere, but beyond our reach. Was she in pain? We didn't know. She couldn't talk to us now, or focus on us, but she was awake, her eyes open. She gasped for breath, again and again, as we sat there waiting for her heart to stop, my sister and I both waiting for the very first sound that we ever heard—our mother's heartbeat—to go silent.

At that moment an orderly entered my mother's room. She walked up to the end of the bed and extended her arm. There was a menu in her hand—a menu she was trying to hand to my mother. "Time to pick your meals for tomorrow," the orderly announced. It was a staggering blow, this unwelcome reminder that "tomorrow" was coming and that, for the first time in my life and my sister's life, our mother would have no part in it. It felt like we had all just been punched in the stomach. My stepfather rose from his chair and howled so loudly that the orderly gasped, dropped the menu, and ran from the room. The menu fluttered to the floor, coming to rest under my mother's deathbed.

I still have that menu. It sits on the mantle in my living room under her bronzed baby shoes. I see them every day and I remember. My mother died on March 31, 2008. So the date on the menu?

April 1, 2008.

April Fool's Day. My mother was of Irish descent and imbued with her countrymen's dark wit. She would've appreciated the irony.

We must accept death "at the hour chosen by God," says Pope Benedict XVI, head of the Catholic Church, which poured millions of dollars into the campaign to defeat Washington State's Death with Dignity Act.

The hour chosen by God.

What does that even mean? Without the intervention of man—and medical science—my mother would have died years earlier. And even without physician-assisted suicide as an option, my mother had to make her own choices at the end. Another two days hooked up to machines? Six more hours with the mask on? Two with the mask off? Once things were hopeless, my mother chose the quickest, if not the easiest, death. Mask off, two hours. That was my mother's choice, not God's.

Was my mother a suicide? I wonder what the pope might say.

I know what my mother would say: The head of a church that can't manage to keep its priests from raping children isn't entitled to micro-manage the final moments of her life.

If religious people believe assisted suicide is wrong, they have an absolute right to say so. Same goes for gay marriage and abortion—think they're wrong? Preach it, brother. But somehow it's not enough for them to die "at the hour chosen by God," marry the person they think God wants them to marry, carry the fetuses they believe God wants them to carry. They feel they have a right to order everyone's intimate lives, to impose their choices on all of us, and they have somehow managed to convince themselves that your freedom to make your own choices—perhaps different choices—somehow op-presses them.

The proper response to religious opposition to choice or love or death can be reduced to a series of bumper stickers: Don't approve of abortion? Don't have one. Don't approve of gay marriage? Don't have one. Don't approve of physician-assisted suicide? For Christ's sake, *don't have one*. But don't tell me I can't have one—each and every one—because it offends your God.

My mother was given morphine—not enough to kill her, only enough to deaden the pain while her lungs finished her off. Still: *Was she in pain?* I will be forever haunted by the thought that she might have been in pain, pain we promised to spare her from, and she had no way to tell us, no way to ask for more or stronger painkillers, no way to let us know that she needed us, that she needed our help, or that she wanted us to hasten her inevitable death and put an end to her suffering.

I don't know what my mother would have done if she had had the choice to take a few pills and skip the last two hours of her life. She was a practicing Catholic. But she was also pro-choice, pro–gay marriage, pro–ordaining women. If she could've committed suicide, by her own hand, with a physician "assisting" only by providing her with drugs that she would administer to herself, I don't know that she would have done it. I do, however, know that the choice should have been hers to make. It wasn't a choice that the Catholic Church, Pope Benedict, or Joel Connelly had a right to make for her.

And I also know that if my mother had wanted to end her own life, if she had wanted to spare herself the terror of imminent suffocation, I would've held a glass of water to her lips, so she could swallow the pills that would've spared her the agony that uncertainty brought to her final conscious moments. And that shouldn't be a crime.

It isn't a crime anymore, not in Washington State. Voters overwhelmingly approved Washington's Death with Dignity Act in November of 2008, despite the objections of the Catholic Church (the six top donors to the campaign against the Death with Dignity Act were Catholic groups), and the opposition of the state's governor at the time, Democrat Christine Gregoire, ironically a pro-choice Catholic.

As of this writing, a total of 255 terminally ill adults have ended their lives with the assistance of a physician since the law came into force in 2009. The Washington State Department of Health is required to issue an annual report on the law, and the state has not documented a single case of the law being abused. Depressed and disabled people are not being put to death by incompetent or impatient doctors; sick people are not opting for physician-assisted suicide to avoid crushing medical bills.

A bill to legalize physician-assisted suicide in Massachusetts narrowly lost (49 percent to 51 percent) in the 2012 election. Despite its not passing, the bill's popularity in the state is significant. Massachusetts is home to some of the nation's leading medical schools, medical journals, and hospitals. In addition, 42 percent of the state's residents are Catholic, and as in Washington State, the Church's hierarchy fervently opposed the bill. In a *Slate* article about the bill, Lewis Cohen wrote, "Death with dignity is not incompatible with palliative care, and data show that 90 percent of Oregon patients who choose assisted dying are simultaneously enrolled in hospice, and 95 percent die at home. Death with dignity epitomizes self-determination at a moment when palliative medicine bumps up against its limits, when patients are undergoing irremediable existential suffering and are in the process of losing everything that is meaningful to them." In other words, it's not a choice between hospice and suicide, or loving care and suicide.

Votes for women, ending segregation, allowing gays to marry—conservatives invoke doomsday scenarios whenever people organize to demand justice or freedom. Washington has not become the "Las Vegas of suicide," as opponents of Washington State's Death with Dignity Act predicted, and no one who opposes physician-assisted suicide is being compelled to submit to it.

The residents of Washington, Oregon, and Montana—the only US states where the courts have legalized physician-assisted suicide—are simply free to make their own choices, and to end their own suffering, at the end of their lives. Everyone should have the right to make that choice for themselves.

14. Rick and Me

My last chance to get the picture—*the picture*—may have been the 2011 Conservative Political Action Conference (CPAC) in Washington, DC.

Ana Marie Cox may have dropped *assfucking* from her vocabulary after she left Wonkette.com—the political blog where she made her name—to write for *The Guardian,* but Cox will always be Wonkette to me. I ran into Cox when I arrived at CPAC, and I immediately asked for her help: I had to get my picture with that man. Hours later, standing near a booth manned by pro-gun nuts or anti-gay closet cases—I can't remember which—Cox flagged me down.

"He was *just* here! He went *that* way!"

I went that way. But by the time I got where he was going, he'd already left.

The 2011 CPAC was a frustrating repeat of the 2008 Republican National Convention.

Real Time with Bill Maher sent me to the Republican National Convention with a camera crew and a team of producers. Everyone was under orders to keep their eyes peeled for him. But he somehow managed to leave every place we went the moment before we arrived and arrive every place we left the moment after we departed.

It was almost as if Rick Santorum were avoiding me.

I'll probably slip into CPAC again this year—I can't help myself—and I hope to attend the Republican National Convention in 2016. (Because that one's gonna be a hugely entertaining shit show.) But I won't be chasing after Rick Santorum at either event. I would still love to get close enough to Rick Santorum to have my picture taken with him, of course, but getting close enough to Rick Santorum to get the picture I want means handing Santorum the opportunity to get the video he wants.

Chris Christie, the current Republican governor of New Jersey, and the man Rick Santorum will likely have to beat if he wants to be his party's nominee in 2016 (and Santorum very much wants to be his party's nominee in 2016), came to national attention when he started posting videos of himself to YouTube giving verbal beat downs to teachers, union members, small children, and little old ladies. At this point it's probably occurred to Santorum—or someone advising Santorum—that a video of him beating me up Christie-style would play well with the right-wing Christian nuts he needs to win the Iowa caucuses in 2016.

"Rick Santorum would very much like to be president," Stephanie Mencimer wrote in the September 2010 issue of *Mother Jones,* nine months before Rick Santorum announced what would be his first, but certainly not his last, run at the White House.

"For the past few years, he has been diligently appearing at the sorts of conservative events—the Values Voters Summit, the Conservative Political Action Conference—where aspiring Republican candidates are expected to show up," Mencimer continued. "But before he starts printing 'Santorum 2012' bumper stickers, there's one issue the former GOP senator and his strategists need to address. You see, Santorum has what you might call a Google problem. For voters who decide to look him up online, one of the top three search results is usually the site SpreadingSantorum.com, which explains that Santorum's last name is a sexual neologism for . . ."

I'm going to hold back the new definition of Rick Santorum's last name, a neologism created and promoted by Savage Love readers. Most readers of this book probably already know it—most of you can probably recite the definition from memory—but the few of you who don't know the meaning of *santorum* can enjoy your innocence for a few more minutes. I would like to clarify one thing right now, though: SpreadingSantorum.com, a website I launched in 2003, was the *top* search result, not "one of the top three search results," when a person googled "Rick Santorum" for nearly a decade. And the new definition— the sexual neologism in question—popped right up on the top of the search page in all its stomach-churning glory.

That was Santorum's Google problem.

And it wasn't just lefty publications like *Mother Jones* that wrote stories about Santorum's Google problem, as the former senator from Pennsylvania prepared to run for the 2012 Republican nomination. ABC News, *The New Republic*, CNN, *The Christian Science Monitor*, and numerous mainstream daily newspapers all wrote about it. *Roll Call*— "The Source for News on Capitol Hill Since 1955"—published a long and detailed investigation into Rick Santorum's Google problem in February of 2011.

"It would be among the first 'Google bombs' in the modern political era," *Roll Call* staff reporter Steve Peoples wrote. "The nationally syndicated [Dan] Savage inspired a coalition of gay activists and liberals from across the country to spread the term as widely as possible, creating a meme that helped now-Sen. Bob Casey (Pa.) unseat Santorum in 2006, and, ultimately, one that makes Santorum's presidential hopes laughable in some circles."

Peoples discovered that Santorum allies, contrary to statements made by Santorum himself, had consulted with "technology experts" about how to make the new definition of Santorum's last name go away.

"Ultimately," Peoples continued, "they found there was little they could do. 'You can bury anything on the Internet,' said David Urban, a Santorum ally and former chief of staff for former Sen. Arlen Specter (Pa.) 'But at what financial cost and at what political cost? You can bury a bad story. But how do you bury your own name?' "

As more and more stories were written about Santorum's Google problem in 2011 and 2012, angry e-mails started popping into my in-box from furious conservative supporters of Rick Santorum. The funniest letter I got was from a person who accused me of—actually it's a pretty short letter, so I'm going to reproduce it here in its entirety:

> Dan Savage is a sick, pathetic excuse for a human being. Truly a sad piece of shit. Especially now that he's trying to insert himself into the GOP presidential race.

It would be more accurate to say that the 2012 GOP presidential race inserted itself into me, seeing as the campaign to redefine *santorum* was launched a decade before Rick Santorum ran for president.

Santorum officially got into the race on June 6, 2011. And he did much better than anyone expected. What looked like a vanity campaign at the outset—or an effort to secure a lucrative contract with Fox News—turned into a real campaign at the eleventh hour. Because as either luck or divine intervention would have it, Rick Santorum wound up being the last Not Romney standing, just as frustrated (and prescient) GOP primary voters went to the polls. Rick Perry surged and flopped too soon, as did Michele Bachmann, Herman Cain, and Newt Gingrich. (Poor Jon Huntsman, of course, only flopped. But the most spectacular flop of all was Minnesota governor Tim Pawlenty—I had forgotten he was even in the race until I went back and reread a news report about the first GOP primary debate.) After scraping along in the polls at less than 1 percent for more than a year, Rick Santorum wound up winning the Republican primaries in eleven states. No one saw that coming. Santorum's breakout led to headlines like SANTORUM SURGES

FROM BEHIND IN NORTH TEXAS, ROMNEY HOPES TO HOLD OFF RISING SANTORUM, and my personal favorite, SANTORUM COMES FROM BEHIND IN ALABAMA THREE-WAY.

Those headlines won't be funny to anyone who doesn't know the new definition of Rick Santorum's last name. So here it is:

> **santorum** (san-TOR-um) n. the frothy mixture of lube and fecal matter that is sometimes the by-product of anal sex.

Now reread those headlines and try not to laugh.

Do you know who else won primaries in eleven states, lost the GOP nomination to a stiff who went on to lose the general election, and then came back four years later to win both the Republican nomination and the general election, and serve two terms in the White House? Ronald Reagan. (Reagan lost the nomination to Gerald Ford in 1976; Ford lost the election to Jimmy Carter; Reagan came back to beat Carter in 1980.) Rick Santorum is going to spend the next three years reminding every Republican in the country that, *just like Ronald Reagan,* he won eleven GOP primaries.

Rick Santorum is *definitely* running for president again in 2016, which means we'll be treated to another round of "Google problem" stories about two years from now. So I want to set the record straight about something before those stories are written: exactly why we—me and my readers—redefined Rick Santorum's last name in the first place. Because some folks keep getting it wrong.

"In what has been a long-running burden for Mr. Santorum, his online identity has been pranked—given a meaning involving bodily fluids, *meant to ridicule him for his strong criticism of same-sex marriage,*" Noam Cohen wrote on *The New York Times Media Decoder* blog on January 4, 2012. [Emphasis added.]

Jon Stewart, who made roughly one hundred "ass juice" jokes during the 2012 primaries, stated repeatedly on the *The Daily Show* that Santorum's last name was synonymous with "ass juice" because some gay people were angry about Senator Ass Juice's opposition to same-sex marriage.

Stewart and Cohen were misinformed. And to Cohen and *The New York Times*'s credit, the paper issued a prim correction when the paper's readers—myself included—pointed out the error.

But there are some who are actively trying to mislead people about why Rick Santorum's last name is synonymous with ass juice. The conservative writer Mark Judge, to take one example, wrote a column for *Real Clear Religion* in January of 2012 in which he attempted to turn the whole "problem" meme around on me. "Dan Savage has a santorum problem. Yes, santorum with a small s," Judge wrote. Judge went on to call me an "angry sexual zealot" (am *not*) and dismissed my column as "demented and dehumanizing" (is *not*). After a lengthy discussion of the new meaning of *santorum,* Judge wrote, "Savage wanted to attack Rick Santorum because Santorum is pro-life and *opposes gay marriage*."[1] [Emphasis added.]

The effort to redefine Rick Santorum's last name was not motivated by Santorum's opposition to same-sex marriage. Barack Obama opposed same-sex marriage in 2008, and he justified his opposition in patently offensive terms. "I believe that marriage is the union between a man and a woman," Obama said in an interview with Rick Warren, the anti-gay pastor of Saddleback Church. "Now, for me as a Christian," Obama added, "it is also a sacred union. God's in the mix." No one had to ask Warren or his congregation who they believed was in the mix when two men married. I didn't respond to Obama's opposi-

---

1 Judge also wrote this: "In the last 30 years or so, gay people have gained wide acceptance in society. . . . Savage's santorum prank sets all of that progress back." Voters in three states, including my own, would approve same-sex marriage at the ballot box ten short months later. And Judge accuses me of living in a "state of free-floating apoplexy"?

tion to gay marriage by attempting to redefine his last name. I sent Obama a check in 2008—a big one—and voted for him. Two years before sending a check to Barack Obama, I sent one to Bob Casey, the Pennsylvania Democrat who ran against Rick Santorum in 2006. Casey is a conservative Catholic Democrat who opposes same-sex marriage and abortion. I encouraged my readers in Pennsylvania to hold their noses and vote for Casey because the lesser of two evils is *less* evil. Casey would beat Santorum by eighteen points, turfing him out of the US Senate in "the largest defeat by a Republican United States senator seeking election or re-election in modern Pennsylvania history," G. Terry Madonna, professor of public affairs at Franklin & Marshall College, told Bloomberg News.

Clearly, mere opposition to same-sex marriage isn't enough to bring my meme-creating wrath down on a politician's head. So why would a writer like Judge want to mislead his readers on this point? Because he wants his readers to believe that supporters of marriage equality are angry and vindictive shits who will unfairly attack and malign "honest" opponents of marriage equality for sport. My support for Bob Casey in 2006 and Barack Obama in 2008 disproves that charge.

So if it wasn't Santorum's opposition to same-sex marriage that led to the creation of the world's filthiest sexual neologism, what was it?

Andrew Marantz of *The New Yorker* got it right and offers this succinct recap:

> In April of 2003, Santorum, then a senator from Pennsylvania, sat for an interview with the Associated Press. The discussion turned to *Lawrence v. Texas*, a case before the Supreme Court, in which the plaintiff argued that antisodomy laws were unconstitutional, on the ground that adults have a right to privacy. Santorum disagreed. "If the Supreme Court says that you have the right to consensual

sex within your home," he said, then "you have the right to anything. Does that undermine the fabric of our society? I would argue yes, it does." A healthy society, Santorum continued, would not condone sodomy or "man on child, man on dog, or whatever the case may be."

"I'm sorry," the reporter said. "I didn't think I was going to talk about 'man on dog' with a United States senator. It's sort of freaking me out."

Santorum's comments caused a minor stir. President George W. Bush defended him; Howard Dean attacked him. Then everyone seemed to forget about it.

Dan Savage's readers did not forget.

They most certainly did not.

Remember that drunken crowd in a bar talking about sex that I mention in the chapter "Mistakes Were Made"? They're the ones who created Rick Santorum's Google problem back in 2003. And they didn't do it because Rick Santorum, like every national politician in the country at the time, opposed marriage rights for same-sex couples. My readers made a vile and disgusting joke at Rick Santorum's expense to retaliate against the vile and disgusting comments he made about gays and lesbians. Santorum, then the third most powerful person in the United States Senate, equated gay people to child rapists and dog fuckers. That didn't sit well with my readers—gay and straight.

Oh, sure, I certainly helped to redefine Santorum's last name.[2] But I don't deserve all of the credit—or all of the blame—for launching "the frothy mixture of lube and fecal matter that is sometimes the by-product of anal sex" into American public life. ("It's one guy," Santorum himself told *Roll Call*, "you know who it is.") In May of 2003, just

---

2 My readers' efforts to redefine Rick Santorum's last name weren't even the first. Former Nebraska senator Bob Kerrey remarked, shortly after meeting Santorum in 1995, "Santorum? That's Latin for asshole."

as everyone seemed to be forgetting about Rick Santorum's man-on-dog comments—just as the minor stir was dying down—this letter arrived at Savage Love world headquarters, aka my laptop:

> I'm a 23-year-old gay male who's been following the Rick Santorum scandal, and I have a proposal. Washington and the press seem content to let Santorum's comments fade into political oblivion, so I say the gay community should welcome this "inclusive" man with open arms. That's right; if Rick Santorum wants to invite himself into the bedrooms of gays and lesbians (and their dogs), I say we "include" him in our sex lives—by naming a gay sex act after him. Here's where you come in, Dan. Ask your readers to write in and vote on which gay sex act is worthy of the Rick Santorum moniker. It could be all forms of gay sex ("I pulled a Rick Santorum with my straight roommate in college"), or orgasm in a gay context ("We fooled around, and then I Rick Santorumed all over his face"), or maybe something weirder ("We've bought some broom handles, and we'll be Rick Santoruming all night"). You pick the best suggestions, and we all get to vote! And then, voilà! This episode will never be forgotten!

I thought that was a great idea. So I ran the letter in my nationally syndicated column, asked my readers to send in proposed new definitions, selected the ten best, and then asked these same readers to vote for the best one. But I didn't limit the proposed new definitions to gay sex acts. Santorum wasn't arguing that the government had the right to regulate the private and consensual sexual conduct of gay and lesbian adults alone. He believed—and still believes—that the government should be able to regulate the private and consensual sexual conduct of all Americans, from the gayest gays to the straightest straights. Rick Santorum doesn't believe a right to privacy—or bodily integrity—exists in the US Constitution. Who you sleep with, whether you can use birth control, whether you can obtain an abortion: Santorum told the Associated Press in 2003 that he wanted the Supreme Court to uphold state sodomy laws, some of which regulated straight sodomy, because he believed the state should be able to regulate all of our sex lives. (Yes, Virginia, straight people can be sodomites too.)[3] Because Rick Santorum believes in small government: He believes government should be so small it can fit inside your vagina.

Santorum believed this in 2003, when he was urging the Supreme Court to uphold state sodomy laws, and he believed it in 2012, when he was running for president.

In October of 2011, while campaigning in Iowa, Santorum pledged that he would, if elected president, wage war on contraceptives.

"One of the things I will talk about, that no president has talked about before, is I think the dangers of contraception," Santorum said in a videotaped interview for the Christian news and commentary blog *Caffeinated Thoughts*. "Many of the Christian faith have said, well, that's okay, contraception is okay. It's not okay. It's a license to do things in a sexual realm that is counter to how things are supposed to be."

Santorum made these comments after telling ABC News that the Supreme Court's 1965 *Griswold v. Connecticut* decision was incorrect. Griswold, *Salon*'s Irin Carmon points out, "struck down a ban on dis-

---

3 "It's worth noting, then, that from the very beginning sodomy and homosexuality were two categorically separate things," Andrew Sullivan wrote in *The New Republic* in March 2003. "The correct definition of sodomy—then and now—is simply non-procreative sex, whether practiced by heterosexuals or homosexuals. It includes oral sex, masturbation, mutual masturbation, contraceptive sex, coitus interruptus, and anal sex—any sex in which semen does not find its way into a uterus. . . . As a simple empirical matter, we are all sodomites now, but only homosexuals bear the burden of the legal and social stigma."

cussing or providing contraception to *married couples,* and established a right to privacy that would later be integral to *Roe v. Wade* and *Lawrence v. Texas.* . . . [Griswold] would be the case where the majority asked, 'Would we allow the police to search the sacred precincts of marital bedrooms for telltale signs of the use of contraceptives? The very idea is repulsive to the notions of privacy surrounding the marriage relationship.' Rick Santorum disagrees. He thinks, using the currently popular states' rights parlance, that 'the state has a right to do that.' "

So I opened the contest up to gay and straight sex acts because, legally speaking, Rick Santorum doesn't distinguish between them: He would like the government to regulate all sex. And there really is no such thing as a gay or a straight sex act; straight people can do pretty much everything gay people can do and vice versa. And the winning entry wound up not being a sex act at all, as you already know, but a sexual by-product. Here's the letter that created Santorum's Google problem:

> While I agree with the spirit of naming something objectionable (to him) after Rick Santorum, I think it should be a substance, not an act. I would never want to "santorum" anyone I liked. What a turnoff. Instead, I think it would be better to name some kind of sexual byproduct after him. After all, ending up with idiots like Santorum in elected office is a byproduct of the otherwise desirable practice of letting any old yokel vote. Specifically, I nominate the frothy mixture of lube and fecal matter that is sometimes the byproduct of anal sex. As in, "We had a great time, but we got santorum all over the sheets." Or better yet, "Before I sodomize my gay, unmarried dog, I like to give him an enema so there won't be any santorum."

The "frothy mixture" definition won by a landslide, beating the nearest runner up—"farting in the face of someone who's rimming you"—by a three-to-one margin.

I've kept in touch with the person who came up with the winning definition for *santorum* over the last decade. He's debated coming forward and claiming his share of the credit—and he deserves the lion's share—but he fears potential personal and professional repercussions. Since I can't use his name, let's call him Frothy Mix.

"The entire definition, including frothy, came to me at once," Frothy Mix said. "I also kind of knew that it would win and become a big enough deal that Rick Santorum himself would hear about it."

It might surprise some people to know that Frothy Mix is straight—and that he grew up in a deep red state. "Otherwise I am probably basically who people think I am," says Frothy Mix. "An atheist progressive in a big liberal city who went to impressive-sounding schools and has held some of the kinds of jobs right-wingers might associate with a vast liberal conspiracy. In terms of my personal life, though, I'm not a swinger or particularly kinky."

But unlike far too many of his fellow straights, Frothy Mix recognizes that politicians like Rick Santorum threaten his freedom too.

"Santorum didn't just say that gay people don't have a right to have sex, though that's bad enough," Frothy Mix told me. "He's on record basically saying that no one has a right to sexual privacy. We should keep in mind that it hasn't been that long since we've had the right to have a sexual relationship outside of marriage or with a person of another race."

And Frothy Mix didn't decide to "punk Rick Santorum" simply for laughs. He was genuinely outraged by Santorum's remarks. "What really got me was the way he used such dehumanizing language so casually," Frothy Mix said. "I wanted to make it harder for a sitting US senator to feel like he could say something like that in the future."

Why was he so sure his definition would win?

"First of all, I knew most people were going with a verb," said Frothy Mix, "and I'd have the noun category basically to myself. It is about the worst thing you could call Mr. Santorum, but there's nothing inherently gay about it. I knew 'frothy' would work sort of like the hook in a pop song. It would make people think of lattes and beer, which just makes it that much more gross. Still, I've been continually surprised that it took off the way it did, then has stuck around for so long."

I want to break in here for a moment to unpack the genius of Frothy Mix's definition for *santorum,* and why I think it's stuck around for so long. While Frothy Mix viewed the word *frothy* as crucial, for my money—and in my particular area of expertise—the word *sometimes* is crucial. Lowercase *santorum* is only the by-product of anal sex *sometimes.* If you're doing anal sex right, if you're assfucking correctly, *there will be no santorum.* If there is *santorum*—if fecal matter intrudes on your assfucking—the anal sex is ruined. The same can be said of Rick Santorum. He would like to intrude on your sex life and would ruin it if he could. Santorum, like so many religious conservatives, is obsessed with anal intercourse, and Frothy Mix's definition offered sweet poetic justice, forever linking Santorum to anal sex and its unpleasant potential by-product.

And you could say that the winning definition—once again: "the frothy mixture of lube and fecal matter that is sometimes the byproduct of anal sex"—managed to do something that Rick Santorum hasn't managed to pull off and hopefully never will: It won a free and fair national election.

"You can say I'm a hater," Rick Santorum said during a 2004 Senate debate—at the height of the Iraq War—about putting an amendment into the United States Constitution that would ban same-sex marriage. "I would argue I'm a lover. I'm a lover of traditional families and of the right of children to have a mother and father. I would argue that the future of America hangs in the balance, because the future of the family hangs in the balance. Isn't that the ultimate homeland security? Standing up and defending marriage?"

Santorum was responding to California senator Barbara Boxer, who earlier in the debate had asked, "What is more of a threat? Al-Qaida or gay marriage?"

You might think that a man who described banning same-sex marriage as the "ultimate homeland security" measure—because the threat gay families pose is on par with the threat that Al-Qaida posed—doesn't have many gay friends or supporters. But Elizabeth Santorum, Rick Santorum's adult daughter and his chief campaign staffer during his 2012 campaign, would have you believe that he does.

"It is tough, after all, being a young surrogate for a candidate and father clinging to an older worldview," Elise Foley wrote in a fawning profile of Elizabeth Santorum that appeared on the *The Huffington Post* just before the 2012 Iowa caucuses. "Her father's stance on same-sex marriage and gay rights, in particular, has caused some friction. . . . Opposed to same-sex marriage herself, Elizabeth said she has gay friends who support her father's candidacy based on his economic and family platforms."

So . . .

Elizabeth Santorum, who doesn't support marriage rights for gay people, has gay friends. And Elizabeth's gay friends support her father's candidacy "based on his . . . family platforms."

Right.

To Ms. Foley and all the other political reporters out there who will write puff pieces about Rick and Elizabeth Santorum in 2016: When Elizabeth Santorum tells you that she has gay friends and that her gay friends support her dad . . . how can I put this? Your interview subject has made an astonishing claim, a claim that must be verified before you publish it. Your response should be a demand for the names and phone numbers of these "gay friends." You can offer to quote them anonymously to protect their privacy and to shield them from the social consequences of their stupidity. (No gay person who goes on the record supporting Rick Santorum will get laid ever again.) But you need to verify the existence of these gay friends because you're a journalist, not a stenographer.

In fairness to Elizabeth Santorum, she's not the only anti-gay bigot who has been allowed to make the "I have gay friends!" claim unchallenged. Rick Warren, Sarah Palin, Joel Osteen, Donny Osmond, Pat Boone—all the biggest homophobes tell reporters that they can't be bigots because they have gay friends. (My personal favorite: the Reverend Peter Mullen, an Anglican priest in London, who got in trouble for writing this on his personal blog: "Let us make it obligatory for homosexuals to have their backsides tattooed with the slogan SODOMY CAN SERIOUSLY DAMAGE YOUR HEALTH." After he got in trouble, he defended himself by saying he had "nothing against homosexuals," and he couldn't be a bigot because, "many of my dear friends have been and are of that persuasion.")

If I told a reporter from *The New York Times* or *The Huffington Post* that I had the Hope Diamond in my pocket—if I told a reporter from the *Thrifty Nickel* that I had the Hope Diamond in my front pocket—the reporter would ask me to *present the diamond* before publishing my claim. It's not impossible for me to have the Hope Diamond in my pocket, of course, but it is extraordinarily unlikely. A good reporter would check my Hope Diamond claim out before publishing it.

But never once, in the short and sordid history of anti-gay bigots claiming to have gay friends, has a political reporter asked the obvious follow-up question: "Can I have your gay friends' phone numbers, please?" I can't understand why. Political reporters: If Elizabeth or Rick or Joel or Sarah or Rev. Peter can't produce their gay friends, you will have caught a public figure telling a very revealing lie. Isn't that what you live for? And if Elizabeth or Rick or Joel or Sarah or Rev. Peter *can* produce a gay friend, you'll be able to treat your readers to an entertaining interview with a deranged homo.

Elizabeth Santorum is about as likely to have gay friends who support her father as I am to have the Hope Diamond in my pocket.

So, political reporters, when the time comes to write puff pieces about Elizabeth Santorum in 2016, ask her for proof about her gay friends, the same way you would ask for proof from any other nut making an extraordinary claim.

I'd ask her myself but she blocked me on Twitter.

"Sen. Rick Santorum may have lost the presidential primaries in Arizona and Michigan, but there's at least one thing he can celebrate: His Google problem appears to be subsiding," *The Wall Street Journal* reported on February 29, 2012. "Following a surge of interest in Santorum's presidential campaign, as of late Tuesday Savage's webpage had fallen down the list."

A triumphant Santorum staffer claimed that his Google problem wasn't just subsiding: "Rick Santorum's presidential campaign says his 'Google problem' has been solved. Until recently, the top result for users who typed Santorum's name in the search engine was a crude sexual term devised by gay columnist Dan Savage to attack Santorum," Alex Pappas wrote on Tucker Carlson's conservative news/alternative universe site *The Daily Caller*. "Peter Pasi, a digital consultant to the Santorum campaign, said that they were finally able to overcome this problem as Santorum has risen in the presidential race. Santorum's campaign website now ranks higher in Google."

It's true that the link to SpreadingSantorum.com, which included the definition (you didn't have to click through to read it), did drop down to eighth place in February of 2012, before creeping slowly back up to third place on most searches. "The most horrific filth that you ever want to see," as Santorum himself described Spreading

Santorum.com, was no longer the first search result. (Rick apparently hasn't seen the viral video *Two Girls, One Cup*, which is much more horrifying than SpreadingSantorum.com, which is just a blog.) But the site was still among the top returns—and it remained among the top returns—for the remaining four weeks of Santorum's campaign for the GOP nomination. Anyone who googled Santorum would still see the "frothy mixture" definition for *santorum* created and promoted by my readers.

And just now, when I googled Santorum in a restaurant in Portland, Oregon, in early 2013, SpreadingSantorum.com was still on the first page. Not the top return, sadly, but the top return wasn't Santorum's official website either, or a news story about Santorum's desperate efforts to keep himself in the news. (Hey, did you know that Ronald Reagan won eleven primaries in 1976?) What comes up first is a *Wiki* page titled "Campaign for 'Santorum' Neologism." And here's the first paragraph of that page:

> In May 2003, the columnist and gay rights activist Dan Savage held a contest among his readers to create a definition for the word "santorum" as a response to comments by then-U.S. Senator Rick Santorum that had been criticized as anti-gay. Savage announced the winning entry, which defined "santorum" as "the frothy mixture of lube and fecal matter that is sometimes the byproduct of anal sex."

Rick Santorum still has a Google problem.

And he always will. Because Santorum's problem ultimately isn't Google, or me, or my readers, or Frothy Mix.

Rick Santorum's problem is Rick Santorum.

15. Still Evil. Less Evil. But Still Evil.

Peter LaBarbera, whom you met in an earlier chapter, is a right-wing evangelical Christian, the head of an anti-gay hate group, and someone I follow (and occasionally bait) on Twitter. I just can't quit him. In addition to opposing the gay agenda, because it opens the door to man-on-manatee marriage, LaBarbera opposes the Patient Protection and Affordable Care Act, aka Obamacare, because it opens the door to socialism.

No, wait: Obamacare *is* socialism, according to LaBarbera—and Michele Bachmann and Rick Santorum and Tony Perkins and every other spokesperson for the highly politicized (and, after the last election, extremely butt-sore) conservative Christian movement in the United States. And while we Americans are fond of our socialized police forces, fire departments, interstate highways, and public universities (LaBarbera got his publicly subsidized degree in political science from the University of Michigan), conservative Christians like Peter and Michele and Rick and Tony draw the line at socialized medicine because . . . well, I'm not exactly sure.

Jesus commanded his followers to clothe the naked, shelter the homeless, and care for the sick. Making health care available to all seems like a no-brainer, Jesus-wise, among the most Christian projects a president, or a nation, could possibly undertake. Speaking as someone who was raised in a Christian home and who has actually read the Gospels (and recently, at that), I have to say that such fierce opposition to Obamacare by conservative Christian activists and politicians doesn't make sense. (It doesn't make sense to many Christians either. I'm no fan of Pope Benedict XVI—and he's no fan of mine—but I have to give credit where credit is due: In November of 2010, the pope weighed in on the debate, calling health care an "inalienable right," and stating that all nations had a "moral responsibility" to "guarantee access to health care for all of their citizens, regardless of social and economic status or their ability to pay.")

You know what else doesn't make sense? Opposing Obamacare on the grounds that it's socialism.

Obamacare is socialism? "Bitch, *please,*" as Vladimir Lenin once said to no one. Obamacare isn't even the weak tea of "socialized medicine."

The Patient Protection and Affordable Care Act (PPACA), which Barack Obama signed into law in March of 2010, overhauled our hugely inefficient employer-provided health insurance system but otherwise left it in place—even as fewer and fewer employers offer health insurance. The PPACA pushes millions of uninsured Americans into the arms of private insurance companies (by providing tax credits to companies that offer their employees health care coverage through private insurance companies, and by imposing fines on uninsured individuals who fail to purchase health insurance from private insurance companies); it provides subsidies to poor and low-income workers so that they can buy health insurance from private insurance companies; and much to the consternation of some corporate CEOs, it levies fines on large companies that fail to provide health insurance (yes, again from private insurance companies) for their employees. Once Obamacare is fully implemented, the government plans to make health insurance even more widely available by handing the money it collects in fines over to—can you guess?—*private insurance companies.*

Obamacare bears about as much resemblance to socialism as the "Springtime for Hitler" number in *The Producers* bears to fascism. The

PPACA rains billions of dollars on private insurance companies, privately owned hospitals, and doctors in private practice, making it possible—in theory, at least—for all Americans who aren't old or poor enough to qualify for Medicare or Medicaid to acquire health insurance from private insurance companies. Obamacare does all of this without raising costs; it won't technically lower overall costs, either, but it does make the costs lower than they would have been (something poetically dubbed "bending the cost curve" by policy wonks). It also won't end private, for-profit health care in the United States. By putting an end to some of the worst abuses perpetrated by the private insurance industry (the denial of coverage based on preexisting conditions, lifetime limits on coverage, the routine practice of canceling people's insurance policies the minute they get sick), and by extending private health insurance to millions of previously uninsured Americans, Obamacare may have extended the life of our private health insurance system indefinitely.

Don't get me wrong: Obamacare is good; it's a start; it's better than what we had—millions of Americans who didn't have health insurance soon will—and Obamacare is now the "law of the land," as House Speaker John Boehner said after Barack Obama's reelection, and access to health care will only grow as more aspects of the law come into effect.

But Obamacare is *not* the health care system preferred by sensible socialists.

"The United States is the only major nation in the industrialized world that does not guarantee health care as a right to its people," Vermont senator Bernie Sanders, the only actual socialist in Congress, said as the Affordable Care Act was making its torturous way through Congress. "Meanwhile, we spend about twice as much per capita on health care with worse results than others that spend far less. It is time that we bring about a fundamental transformation of the American health care system. It is time for us to end private, for-profit participation in delivering basic coverage. It is time for the United States to provide a Medicare-for-all single-payer health coverage program."

A single-payer health care system would cut out the middleman—the private insurance companies that will continue to skim billions off the top under Obamacare—and deliver care to all Americans with less overhead, less waste, and considerably less stress for individuals. Canada, Germany, France, Sweden, Denmark, the United Kingdom, the Netherlands, and every other Western industrialized nation have national health care systems that are more efficient and humane than our system *and* provide better health outcomes. Even Israel, which can do no wrong in the eyes of the Christian fundamentalist right, has a single-payer health care system.[1]

---

1 Nations with generous, single-payer health care systems also have lower abortion rates, something that should prompt conservative Christians to embrace health care for all. This little truism, which clocks in at exactly 140 characters, regularly makes the rounds on Twitter: "If you want to prevent abortions, you make sure everyone has health care, a high school education, and birth control. Not the exact opposite." It turns out that women with access to primary health care *and* contraceptives are less likely to experience an unplanned pregnancy that ends in abortion. (I know, right? No one could've predicted.) And a woman with access to health care and contraceptives who *does* experience an unplanned pregnancy—which is not, as social conservatives frequently assume, due to carelessness (condoms sometimes break, hormonal birth control can fail)—is less likely to abort if having the baby doesn't mean racking up medical bills she could never hope to pay. Some conservatives see the link: "As a general rule, societies that do the most to support mothers and child-bearing have the fewest abortions," rogue conservative pundit David Frum wrote in the fall of 2012 in an opinion piece on CNN's website ("Let's Get Real About Abortions," CNN.com, October 29, 2012). "Societies that do the least to support mothers and child-bearing have more abortions."

Frum, who grew up in Canada, is too polite to mention it—Canadians are like that—but the United States is one of those societies that "do the least" to support mothers. "Germany, for example, operates perhaps the world's plushest welfare state," Frum continues. "Working women receive 14 weeks of maternity leave, during which time they receive pay from the state. The state pays a child allowance to the parents of every German child for potentially as many as 25 years, depending on how long the child remains in school. Women who leave the work force after giving birth receive a replacement wage from the state for up to 14 months. Maybe not coincidentally, Germany has one of the lowest abortion rates, about one-third that of the United States. Yet German abortion laws are not especially restrictive."

Frum neglects to mention that Germany also has a universal health care system (the oldest in the world), a pillar of its welfare state.

"Abortion is a product of poverty and maternal distress," Frum concludes. "A woman who enjoys the most emotional and financial security and who has chosen the timing of her pregnancy will not choose abortion, even when abortion laws are liberal."

But we don't have to look to Europe or Israel for examples of government-run health care systems that work.

"All, and I mean all, the evidence says that public systems like Medicare and Medicaid, which have less bureaucracy than private insurers (if you can't believe this, you've never had to deal with an insurance company) and greater bargaining power, are better than the private sector at controlling costs," writes Paul Krugman, the Nobel Prize–winning Princeton economist and columnist for *The New York Times*. "I know this flies in the face of free-market dogma, but it's just a fact. . . . You can see it from comparisons between Medicaid and private insurance: Medicaid costs much less."

Medicare and Medicaid are hugely popular government programs—so popular, in fact, that millions of Americans aren't even aware that they are government programs. An entire wing of the Internet is dedicated to photographs of senior citizens waving signs at Tea Party rallies that read KEEP GOVERNMENT OUT OF MY MEDICARE!, DON'T STEAL FROM MEDICARE TO SUPPORT SOCIALIZED MEDICINE!, and SAVE MEDICARE! SAY NO TO GOVERNMENT HEALTH CARE! How is it possible that senior citizens on Medicare don't know that the program is a government-run, socialized medicine program for seniors? I credit thirty years of Republican antigovernment demagoguery. (Ronald Reagan at his first inaugural address in 1981: "Government is not the solution to our problem. Government is the problem.") If government is bad and Medicare is good, then government must not have anything to do with Medicare, right? And if socialism is bad and Medicare is good, then Medicare can't be socialism.

See how that works?

You know what else is bad? Barack Obama is bad. He runs the *government* (bad) and he's a *socialist* (bad). And if a government-running socialist is for something, well, then that thing must be *very* bad. Obamacare is so bad they named it after him! (I suggested, when the law first passed, that the White House should embrace the term

Obamacare, which it eventually did during Obama's reelection campaign. I'm sure I don't deserve credit, but I'm happy to claim it.)

"The stupid," as the bloggers say, "*it burns.*" Not only isn't Obamacare socialism, the final version of the bill didn't include a "public option," that is, an opt-in, government-run insurance plan for Americans who don't want to deal with private insurance companies. An early version of Obamacare included a public option, but it was dropped to appease the insurance industry, which feared competing with a more efficiently run government health care program, as well as Republicans, who feared that Americans would opt for socialized medicine en masse. (Even worse: They might realize one day that they had!)

For a measure of just how big a disappointment Obamacare is to progressives, just peruse the liberal blogosphere.

"The shabby and compromised health care bill . . . ended poorly for not just liberals, but all Americans, [and] left me wondering what, exactly, we 'won' in 2008," the anonymous blogger Cocktailhag wrote at the left-wing blog *Firedoglake* in 2012. Far from reforming our health care system, Obamacare "[leaves] us all to the tender mercies of larcenous and immoral insurance companies."

The failure to institute a single-payer system or, at the very least, the failure to include a public option (the unseemly rush to scrap the public option!)—that's what liberals hate about Obamacare. (It should be noted, by liberals particularly, that about half of the coverage expansion under Obamacare comes through Medicaid, a single-payer program.) So what do conservatives hate about it?

For many the most controversial aspect of Obamacare is the *individual mandate,* a requirement that all Americans purchase health insurance. This mandate is the engine that will drive down the cost of health insurance over time by spreading the risk around. We need healthy people paying into our private insurance system so that insurance companies—which can no longer refuse to cover people with preexisting conditions, or cancel people's policies once they get sick, or impose lifetime limits on coverage—can actually afford to, you know, *pay for people's health care* while at the same time continuing to skim billions of dollars off the top. And who came up with this idea? Why, that pack of dirty hippies at the Heritage Foundation, a conservative think tank based in Washington, DC.[2] The Heritage Foundation is dedicated to promoting "public policies based on the principles of free enterprise, limited government, [and] individual freedom."

"The core drivers of the [PPACA] are market principles formulated by conservative economists," J. D. Kleinke wrote in *The New York Times*. Kleinke is a resident fellow at yet another conservative think tank, the American Enterprise Institute. "The president's program extends the current health care system—mostly employer-based coverage, administered by commercial health insurers, with care delivered by fee-for-service doctors and hospitals—by removing the biggest obstacles to that system's functioning like a competitive marketplace. Chief among these obstacles are market limitations imposed by the problematic nature of health insurance, which requires that younger, healthier people subsidize older, sicker ones. Because such participation is often expensive and always voluntary, millions have simply opted out, a risky bet emboldened by the 24/7 presence of the heavily subsidized emergency room down the street. The health care law forcibly repatriates these gamblers. . . . This explains why the health insurance industry has been quietly supporting the plan all along. It levels the playing field and expands the potential market by tens of millions of new customers."

---

2 This just in: The most conservative, tea-party-hardiest member of the Senate—the guy who hates Obamacare harder than anyone else—South Carolina's Jim DeMint—just resigned to head . . . the Heritage Foundation, which cooked up Obamacare to begin with. DeMint, in the words of Dana Milbank, a columnist for *The Washington Post*, "is, arguably, the perfect candidate to run a post-thought think tank." On the subject of Obamacare, the good senator remarked, "If we're able to stop Obama on this, it will be his Waterloo. It will break him." How's that working for you, Jim? And on the president in general, DeMint offered these words in the run-up to the 2012 election: "Just because you are good on TV doesn't mean you can sell socialism to freedom-loving Americans."

If a Republican president had signed the Patient Protection and Affordable Care Act into law—crafted by a conservative think tank, beta-tested by a Republican governor, backed by the health insurance industry—the GOP would be crowing about how it represented a triumph for conservative thought and governance. They would claim the PPACA as a right-wing *twofer:* It's a free-market solution to our health care crisis (just look at all the money pouring into the bank accounts of private insurance companies!) *and* it forces Americans to take personal responsibility for their health care needs (no more moochers showing up at emergency rooms demanding "free" chemotherapy!). That's what conservatives said after Mitt Romney signed nearly identical reforms into law in 2006, when Romney was the governor of Massachusetts. That's what *Mitt Romney* said in 2006—the same Mitt Romney who pledged to repeal Obamacare on his first day as president—when he described the individual mandate in his health care bill as "essential for bringing health-care costs down for everyone, and to getting everyone the health insurance they deserve and need."

But it's difficult to give a Democratic president credit for maneuvering a conservative health reform package through a Democratic-controlled Congress after you've accused him of being the love child of Joseph Stalin and the Antichrist. (The *adopted* love child of Stalin and the Antichrist, obviously, since Stalin and the Antichrist are both men, and two men can't make a baby. Get Michele Bachmann drunk and she'll tell you that preventing Stalin and the Antichrist from raising a love child together is one of the reasons she opposes adoptions by same-sex couples.) So what was promoted as a conservative solution to our health care crisis in 2006—the individual mandate—was redefined as a socialist assault on every American's sacred freedom to die an early, preventable death from a treatable disease by 2012.

The GOP turned the 2012 election into a referendum on Obamacare *and* socialism. If you want to see Obamacare repealed, vote Barack

Obama out; if you oppose socialism, vote Mitt Romney in. A majority of Americans voted to reelect Barack Obama.

And while some Republicans made conciliatory noises about Obamacare after the election, and while the percentage of Americans who tell pollsters they want to see Obamacare repealed dropped into the thirties for the first time, no one should expect that Obama's victory will either shut Republicans up or prevent them from undermining Obamacare in the future. Medicare is hugely popular and Republicans have been trying to destroy it for decades. (We haven't heard the last of Paul Ryan and his vouchers.) And Republicans will continue to argue that Obamacare is socialism—Republicans will continue to lie—and they will continue to argue that it is unnecessary. They will continue to insist that our health care system didn't need to be reformed.

"People have access to health care in America," George W. Bush said in 2007. "After all, you just go to an emergency room."

Five years later Mitt Romney would make the same claim: "We do provide care for people who don't have insurance. If someone has a heart attack, they don't sit in their apartment and die. We pick them up in an ambulance, and take them to the hospital, and give them care."

"No Americans have died for lack of health care coverage" will take its place beside "tax cuts raise revenue," "Saddam Hussein had weapons of mass destruction," and "Social Security is going bankrupt" on the ever-expanding list of right-wing zombie lies that refuse to die.

Thousands of Americans did die every year for lack of access to health insurance, pre-Obamacare. According to a study conducted by the Harvard Medical School and Cambridge Health Alliance, which was published in the *American Journal of Public Health* in 2009, an estimated 44,789 Americans were dying *every year* for lack of health insurance. Mitt Romney knew this in 2006, when he was the moderate governor of Massachusetts, but he had forgotten it by 2012, when he was the "severely conservative" GOP nominee for president. Mitt Romney, in another 2012 interview: "We don't have a setting across this country where if you don't have insurance, we just say to you, 'Tough luck, you're going to die when you have your heart attack.' No, you go to the hospital, you get treated, you get care, and it's paid for, either by charity, the government, or by the hospital."

Hospitals were required to provide *emergency* care to the uninsured (and they still are) if they wanted to participate in the Medicare program (which all of them do, though in theory they could say no to Medicare patients and the uninsured), costs that were passed on to the insured in the form of jacked-up prices that led to jacked-up insurance rates (and they still are). But hospitals could refuse to treat the uninsured, and many of the uninsured didn't seek treatment for fear of being bankrupted. Thousands of Americans died annually as a result—including children (and they still do).

"Lack of health insurance might have led or contributed to nearly 17,000 deaths among hospitalized children in the United States in the span of less than two decades," according to research from the Johns Hopkins Children's Center. The study—published on October 29, 2009, in the *Journal of Public Health,* which reviewed more than twenty-three million hospital records in thirty-seven states—is one of the largest to look at the impact of insurance on the number of preventable deaths among sick children in the United States. "If you are a child without insurance, if you're seriously ill and end up in the hospital, you are 60 percent more likely to die than the sick child in the next room who has insurance," lead investigator Fizan Abdullah, MD, PhD, a pediatric surgeon at the Johns Hopkins Children's Center, wrote in the report's conclusion.

This is the sort of thing that happened to children—routinely—under the health care status quo that candidate Mitt Romney defended:

> Twelve-year-old Deamonte Driver died of a toothache Sunday. A routine, $80 tooth extraction might have saved him. If his mother had been insured. . . . By the time Deamonte's own aching tooth got any attention, the bacteria from the abscess had spread to his brain, doctors said. After two operations and more than six weeks of hospital care, the Prince George's County boy died.

Yes, if someone without insurance had a heart attack or was in a car accident, an ambulance would deliver that person to an emergency room, and the doctors in the ER would have to treat him. But he would still be billed—and he could still be bankrupted—for the treatment he received, and that includes a bill that can run into the thousands of dollars for the ambulance ride alone. But if someone who didn't have health insurance needed a heart transplant, or had a chronic condition, or was a twelve-year-old boy with a *fucking toothache,* that person could not simply stroll into an emergency room and demand treatment—not until it was an actual emergency. Deamonte Driver couldn't get a tooth pulled, because he didn't have insurance. Only when his condition worsened to the point where he needed emergency care was he admitted to a hospital. But it was too late to save his life.

A few years ago an emergency room doctor—a friend of a friend—told me that she saw people every day who had diabetes but couldn't afford their insulin. They didn't show up in the emergency room until they were very, very sick, and many wound up losing limbs because they couldn't afford medication or preventive treatment. An emergency amputation costing thousands of dollars and requiring an extended hospital stay? Yes, you could get *that.* But the insulin and regular checkups that would've kept you from losing that limb in the first place? No, you couldn't get *that.*

This was the system—the pre-Obamacare system, approximately

fifty million Americans uninsured, tens of thousands of men, women, and children dying every year for lack of access to care—that Romney was fighting to protect.

Justin Bieber said it best in a 2011 interview with *Rolling Stone*. Asked if he thought about becoming an American citizen, the Canadian-born pop star flatly refused, citing Canada's system of socialized medicine as the chief reason. (A recent poll by the Association for Canadian Studies found that 94 percent of the Canadian citizens surveyed said their universal health care system was a source of collective pride.)

"You guys are evil," Bieber said. "Canada's the best country in the world. We go to the doctor and we don't need to worry about paying him, but here, your whole life, you're broke because of medical bills. My bodyguard's baby was premature, and now he has to pay for it. In Canada, if your baby's premature, he stays in the hospital as long as he needs to, and then you go home."

But now that Barack Obama has been reelected, now that Obamacare is safe for at least the next four years, it's time for liberals and progressives to come out of our defensive crouches and admit that Obamacare—as good as it is, as much of an improvement as it is—is still kinda evil. It's the lesser evil, sure. But it's still evil.

Obamacare is still health insurance. It's not single-payer, it's not socialized medicine. People can still lose their health insurance, or risk going without it, or wind up bankrupted even if they have health insurance, or wind up dead if they don't. Fewer American children will die of toothaches, it's true, but American children—unlike, say, Canadian children or German children—will still die of toothaches.

Obamacare—which is good, which is a start—isn't universal health care. "Rather than simply providing health insurance to everyone by extending Medicare to cover the whole population," Paul Krugman wrote of Obamacare after Obama was reelected, "we've constructed a Rube Goldberg device of regulations and subsidies that will cost more than single-payer and have many more cracks for people to fall through."

Obamacare will leave millions of Americans uninsured. Some will be uninsured by choice—foolish choice—but millions of other Americans will be uninsured because they cannot afford to purchase health insurance even with subsidies. So even with Obamacare, we will still see flyers taped to windows in small-town diners announcing spaghetti feeds to raise money for an uninsured child's medical bills. We will still get e-mails from those in need, like the one I got last month asking me to donate money to help pay for the medical expenses of an uninsured dancer who broke both her legs in a car accident.

And we will still be reading headlines like this one from the Associated Press: BARTENDERS RALLY TO HELP FAMOUS SEATTLE BARMAN. Murray Stenson, an internationally known and much-loved Seattle bartender, was diagnosed with a defective heart valve after blacking out and breaking his arm on his walk home from work one night in the fall of 2012. Like most in the restaurant industry, Stenson does not have health insurance. When word got out, fund-raising efforts began in earnest in bars all over Seattle, and as far away as Singapore and Australia, to raise money to pay for the heart surgery that Stenson needs to live.

"What's amazing is that I don't know half the people who have donated," the sixty-three-year-old bartender told the Associated Press.

When these kinds of stories are reported—and they will continue to be reported under Obamacare—they are packaged as "feel-good" human-interest stories. Isn't it wonderful how this man's friends, and even perfect strangers, rallied to his side, from all over the world, to raise the money he needs for his heart surgery? After the mass shooting in Aurora, Colorado, we were supposed to be delighted when three of the four hospitals where the victims were rushed elected not to bill the uninsured victims for the care they received. (Don't feel bad if you can't remember exactly what shooting I'm talking about. There are so many, after all, that it's easy to lose track. The Aurora, Colorado, mass shooting was the one at the late-night screening of the newest Batman film. That one.) Some of the victims, however, still face a long recovery ahead and the associated medical costs—all without health insurance. But, hey, a feel-good story: Three hospitals declined to bankrupt the Aurora shooting victims, and yes, that's good news for the uninsured victims of the Aurora movie-theater shooting. Uninsured shooting victims who weren't fortunate enough to get shot in a particular movie theater on a particular night are out of luck, however, as are the Aurora victims who had the misfortune of being rushed to the one hospital that did decide to bill—and likely bankrupt—the uninsured victims.

And it's not like the insured are safe from bankruptcy.

The insured and uninsured alike will continue to go bankrupt even after Obamacare is fully enacted because, even as good as Obamacare is (and it's good; it's better than what we had before!), it isn't single-payer; it isn't universal health care. It's health *insurance*. And, yes, while some of the worst abuses of the health insurance industry have been banned, does anyone really think that the health insurance industry—where the practice of canceling the health insurance policies of the sick was so routine that it had a name (*rescission*)—isn't capable of coming up with brand-new abuses?

The story of the Colorado shooting victims, the story of the Seattle bartender, stories about spaghetti feeds for sick children—these are not feel-good stories. They are feel-bad stories. Or, more to the point, they are we-ought-to-be-ashamed-of-ourselves stories.

A single-payer system means not having to worry about medical bills, or going bankrupt, or losing your home, if you or your child should get sick or injured, or if your baby is born prematurely. And, again, it's not just the uninsured who are one tumor or broken bone from financial ruin. According to a 2009 Harvard University study, roughly nine hundred thousand Americans go bankrupt each year due to medical bills.

"Unless you're a Warren Buffett or Bill Gates, you're one illness away from financial ruin in this country," said Steffie Woolhandler, MD, lead author of the report. "If an illness is long enough and expensive enough, *private insurance offers very little protection against medical bankruptcy,* and that's the major finding in our study." [Emphasis added.]

Woolhandler noted that of the 2,314 bankruptcies they investigated, three-quarters of those who had medically related bankruptcies had health insurance.

"That was actually the predominant problem in patients in our study—78 percent of them had health insurance, but many of them were bankrupted anyway because there were gaps in their coverage like co-payments and deductibles and uncovered services," Woolhandler noted. "Other people had private insurance but got so sick that they lost their job and lost their insurance."

Obamacare is good. It's better than what we had. But it's not universal care. Even after Obamacare is fully implemented, millions of Americans will fall through the cracks. Millions will remain uninsured; millions with insurance will still be ruined; millions will find themselves without insurance—by choice or by circumstance—at the precise moment they need it most, and the larcenous and immoral insurance companies will still come up with new abuses.

Our health care system is less evil than it used to be.

But it's still evil.

And speaking of evil . . .

During one of the 2012 GOP nomination debates, the candidates were asked to share a story about an event that shaped their religious convictions. Rick Santorum spoke about his youngest child, Bella, and Newt Gingrich spoke about the child of a friend. The lives of both of these children were saved after extraordinary medical interventions: weeks in neonatal ICUs, round-the-clock care, heart transplants, multiple brain surgeries. Both of these children were expected to die at birth and both survived. In Santorum's case, doctors had all but declared his newborn daughter dead; the doctors, according to Santorum, coldly advised him and his wife to "accept the inevitable" death of their newborn daughter. (No one ever got the doctors' side of the story.) But both children deserved a chance at life, and by God, Rick Santorum and Newt Gingrich made sure they got their chance—even if it meant defying their doctors and the odds. Santorum and Gingrich pledged that, should either be elected president, no child would ever be denied a chance at life because every single life is precious.

Anyone who hadn't been paying attention during the fight over the Affordable Care Act, which was signed into law six months before this particular debate, would have come away with the impression that Rick Santorum and Newt Gingrich supported the PPACA and that Barack Obama opposed it. Hell, if all you had to go on was what both men said during this debate, you might've gotten the impression that the Obama administration had issued new regulations requiring hospitals to pull sick infants out of incubators and toss them out windows.

But both Rick Santorum and Newt Gingrich opposed Obamacare. And both men, in the very next breath, at the very same debate, pledged to repeal Obamacare if they were elected. (Every Republican at every debate pledged to repeal Obamacare.) Gingrich and Santorum are both Roman Catholics who say they oppose abortion, access to contraception, and gay marriage because their faith demands it. Yet both men oppose the Affordable Care Act despite Pope Benedict's rather unambiguous statement about health care: Governments have a "moral responsibility" to "guarantee access to health care for all of their citizens, regardless of social and economic status or their ability to pay." And both men would regard the creation of a single-payer health care system—like the one Justin Bieber enjoys—as an unacceptable socialist assault on freedom. Because letting other people's children die of toothaches while his own enjoy access to every available medical treatment is a price that Rick Santorum is willing to pay for freedom.

A little more credit for Pope Benedict: He doesn't just talk the talk when it comes to states guaranteeing access to health care for all citizens. He walks the walk. The pope is a head of state, and the state that Benedict heads provides universal, single-payer health care for all its citizens. (Vatican City's health plan doesn't mandate birth control coverage—one controversial aspect of Obamacare—but altar boys don't get pregnant).

Santorum is planning a second run for president in 2016. Maybe we should ask the pope to moderate one of the GOP debates. Because I'd like to see Rick Santorum tell the pope that the Vatican's single-payer health care system is socialism and that it oppresses people of faith. It would make for great television.

Anyway, what was I talking about again? Oh, right—Peter LaBarbera and conservative Christian opposition to Obamacare. (Kind of lost track of Peter. Sorry about that. It's just that, well, you know what else happened on election night 2012? Washington State legalized marijuana for recreational use. Just sayin'.) Shortly before the 2012 presidential election—while Mitt Romney was running around the country promising to repeal Obamacare—LaBarbera sent this tweet to his followers:

Jimmy John's is a chain of sandwich shops owned by Jimmy John Liautaud, a Republican businessman who enjoys going on safari and shooting endangered animals. (Pictures of Liautaud posing with a dead elephant and a dead cheetah—and the gun he used to kill both—were posted online in 2010.) Like a lot of wealthy business owners, Liautaud, a major donor to Mitt Romney's presidential campaign, issued threats in the run up to the 2012 election. While some right-wing businessmen threatened to lay off employees if Barack Obama was reelected, and others threatened to cut their employees' wages, Liautaud wasn't in a good position to threaten his employees. He doesn't pay his workers much more than minimum wage, so he can't cut their wages; and those sandwiches aren't going to make themselves, so he couldn't threaten layoffs. In addition, Liautaud and his franchisees don't provide health insurance to the men and women who make his sandwiches—the men and women at corporate HQ are a different story—so he couldn't threaten his employees with health benefit cuts. So Liautaud threatened his customers instead: If Obama was reelected—if Obamacare wasn't repealed—the price of a Jimmy John's sandwich would probably go up.[3]

Okay, we have to get into the weeds here for a moment: Under the Affordable Care Act, a business (with fifty employees or more) that doesn't provide health insurance coverage for a full-time employee will have to pay a 2,000-dollar fine per employee to the federal government. Rather than pay that fine, Liautaud threatened to cut all of his employees down to part-time.

"Yes, we have to do that," Liautaud said on Fox News in October of 2012. "There's no other way we can survive it, because we think it will cost us 50 cents a sandwich. That's just the actual cost."

---

3 Jimmy John's employees in Minneapolis waged a yearlong battle to unionize. One of their key concerns was lack of health care benefits. Workers do not get paid sick days and can't miss work without a note from their doctor. If they can afford to go to one that is. "Since most of the workers don't have health insurance, most employees work through their health problems," reports *City Pages* (Minneapolis). "Mike Wilklow, a long-time employee who has worked at Jimmy John's across the city, says he worked bicycle delivery shifts with a broken clavicle. Jared Ingebretson, a 24-year-old who works at the Riverside store, recalls working shifts with colleagues so sick they had to periodically duck into the bathroom to vomit. 'If someone's that sick, we try to keep them on the register and away from the sandwiches, but still, it's not how you want to be working,' Wilklow says." Even if you don't find Jimmy John Liautaud's actions offensive enough to stop eating at his sandwich shops altogether, you might want to avoid the place during flu season at least.

Faced with a choice between cutting his employees' hours—cutting the hours of people who are already struggling to get by on minimum-wage jobs—or charging fifty cents more per sandwich and providing his employees with health insurance, Jimmy John's is going to cut the hours of all of his employees. The meanness, the pettiness, is staggering.

Liautaud isn't the only founder of a fast-food chain to sound alarm bells about Obamacare driving up the cost of fast food. In August of 2012, John Schnatter, the founder and CEO of Papa John's Pizza, warned his customers that Obamacare, when fully implemented, would raise the price of a Papa John's pizza by upward of fourteen *cents*.[4]

Jon Stewart took John Schnatter and other fast-food CEOs to task in a postelection installment of *The Daily Show* after Schnatter threatened to cut the hours of his employees to avoid having to pay for their health care (costs he could've covered, again, by raising the price of his pizzas by fourteen cents): "Not that you guys don't have a legitimate gripe against this president. If Obama had fought harder for single-payer health care, business owners like you would never have to pay another premium in your lives. You could stuff your pizza crusts with money and still sell them for ten dollars."

Grumbling from right-wing Republican business owners I can understand. They are simply wealthy businessmen who want to keep their taxes low, and defending our broken employer-provided health

---

4 This just in (well, at the time of writing) from *The Huffington Post*: Seems math is hard for John Schnatter, who argues that Obamacare is forcing him to raise the cost of the pizza he sells you by up to fourteen cents, as well as cut back workers' hours so he doesn't have to provide health care to them. "Caleb Melby of *Forbes* has graciously done the math on Obamacare's cost to Papa John's and according to his analysis, to cover the cost of Obamacare, the pizza chain would have to raise prices by 3.4 to 4.6 cents per *pie*—way less than the 11 to 14 cents Schnatter claims he needs. And there are other changes the chain could make to save some money, Melby notes, like not giving away 2 million pizzas for free at a cost of between $24 and $32 million to the company, for example." It's a safe bet that Jimmy John Liautaud is similarly math challenged, and that providing health insurance for his sixty thousand workers would not translate into a full fifty cents a sandwich. . . . Or if it does, maybe Liautaud could cut back on the African safaris so his employees can have a sick day, afford to see a doctor, and don't have to vomit in the chain's bathrooms whilst making those economical sandwiches.

insurance system is one way to do it. (Proof that our employer-provided health insurance model is really and truly broken? As noted, neither Liautaud nor Schnatter, brave defenders of the employer-provided health insurance model, actually provides health insurance to their employees. After all, safaris are expensive, to say nothing of having the elephant you shot in Africa stuffed, mounted, and shipped back to your home in Illinois. How can poor Mr. Liautaud afford these small pleasures if he has to extend health care coverage to the freeloading 47 percent who make his sandwiches?)

But, like I said, I can understand grumbling about Obamacare when it comes from right-wing business owners. I don't like the grumbling; I think Liautaud and Schnatter are complete shits for grumbling (if Starbucks can provide health insurance—and stock options!—to their employees, so can Jimmy John's and Papa John's), but I can certainly understand the grumbling. And I certainly understand the grumbling from left-wingers who would've preferred the more humane, more efficient single-payer system. What I can't understand is the outrage from fundamentalist American evangelical Christians. Their grumbling baffles me.[5]

---

5 In fairness, it's not just conservatives who oppose Obamacare or—God forbid—a single-payer health care system. Libertarians oppose it on principle because they believe in principle that the government should be as small as possible, and they're willing to sacrifice their lives—and your life, and your spouse's life, and your kids' lives—in defense of their principles.

And I personally know some contrarian progressives who don't want to pay the higher taxes that a single-payer health care system would require because they've never been sick a day in their lives and they never intend to get sick. (Unlike your aunt who died of breast cancer on purpose.) These healthy anti-single-payer progressives are, it seems, immune to all known human diseases, they have unbreakable bones, and they have jobs that include health insurance that they're never going to need to use and they're never going to lose their jobs and their employers are never going to stop offering health insurance. So what's in a single-payer system for them?

Not much, I'll concede. There's really not much in a single-payer health care system for immortals with titanium bones and lifetime job security at companies that offer generous benefits. But for the rest of us—for those of us who are lucky to be healthy but know that we could get sick or injured at any time, for those of us with children who could get sick or injured at any time, for those of us who have health insurance through our employers but know that we could, like so many other Americans, lose our jobs and our health insurance

Here's an interesting statistic: the more religious a state, the greater the opposition to Obamacare.

Christians—America's loudest, if not America's best—are up in arms about the new law that makes health insurance available to millions of previously uninsured Americans. Somehow more people with access to health care is an affront to Jesus and everything he stood for. The advent of Barack Obama's reelection inspired a crisis of faith of sorts for many right-wing Christians. It seems God either didn't hear or chose to ignore the messages emanating from the 40 Days of Prayer campaign (praying for the election of Mitt Romney, that is).[6]

After warning that the reelection of Obama will bring God's judg-

---

at any time—here's what's in a single-payer system for us: *peace of mind*. Even if we never get sick, even if we never have to spend a day in a hospital in our lives, we get peace of mind. We don't have to worry about being bankrupted if we get sick, and we don't have to worry about what will happen to our family members, friends, coworkers, and neighbors if they get sick.

Knowing that you're covered, not having to worry about health insurance, not having to worry about losing your health insurance, not having to worry about your children or your friends losing their health insurance, not having to worry about being crushed by medical bills even if you do have health insurance—all of that peace of mind, being relieved of all of those worries, *that has to be worth something*.

After all, people insure homes that never burn down. They get car insurance and never get into accidents. You get insurance *in case* something bad happens. My house is one hundred years old; we pay homeowners insurance, as did the previous owners. And the house has—as of this writing—never burned down. Does that mean we wasted our money? No. Because you insure your home in case it burns down. For the *peace of mind*. You don't think you've been cheated if you pay car and house insurance and never get in an accident nor lose everything in a fire. And here's the thing: Your home may never burn down, and you may never get in a car accident. But you will one day sicken and die. That's absolutely, positively going to happen. Why wouldn't you want to be insured for that?

6 Focus on the Family founder James Dobson released this statement in regards to God's apparent denial of the urgent prayers for the defeat of Barack Obama sent forth by the National Day of Prayer Task Force. "Many, many, many Christians were praying and we really need to address that issue first: Where was God? Because there were these '40 Days of Prayer,' there were several of those that took place, where people fasted and prayed for forty days asking the Lord for His intervention on Election Day. We did a program last week where my wife Shirley came in with her vice-chairman John Bornschein and told how three hundred Gideon prayer warriors came to Washington, went to every single office of the House of Representatives and the Senate and prayed for the occupant, prayed for our representatives, went to the White House, went in a vigil to the Supreme Court, which is now at great risk, and went to the Pentagon. People like that were praying all over this country and the Lord said no."

ment and ultimate destruction, Franklin Graham, while speaking to David Brody of the Christian Broadcasting Network, asserted that Obama's second term will "usher in the largest changes in our society since the Civil War." He later maintained that Obama's reelection is proof that we Americans have "turned our back on God," and said that "we need someone like a Jerry Falwell to come back and resurrect the Moral Majority movement."

They prayed and prayed and the Lord said no. Or maybe the Lord said yes to health care? Maybe that's what the Lord said?

Whether the Lord approves of Obamacare or not, we know it doesn't do away with those larcenous and immoral health insurance companies, but it will save tens of thousands of lives every year. Indeed, with full implementation still years away (some Obamacare provisions don't go into effect until *2020*), Obamacare is *already* saving lives.

Stacey Lihn, to give one example, has a daughter who was born with a congenital heart defect. Unlike Rick Santorum, Lihn isn't a wealthy and well-connected politician who can afford to pay out-of-pocket for the medical care her daughter needs. Lihn spoke at the Democratic National Convention about the three open-heart surgeries her daughter, Zoe, needed to survive and the fear that her insurance company would refuse to cover any more of her daughter's medical expenses due to a "lifetime cap" set by the insurer. But the Affordable Care Act made those caps illegal, and Lihn's daughter got the care she needed. ("Governor Romney says people like me were the most excited about President Obama the day we voted for him," Lihn told the crowd at the DNC. "But that's not true. Not even close. For me, there was the day the Affordable Care Act passed and I no longer had to worry about Zoe getting the care she needed. There was the day the letter arrived from the insurance company, saying that our daughter's lifetime cap had been lifted.")

Curious as to why Christians would oppose Obamacare, I typed

"Why would a Christian oppose Obamacare?" into Google. A Yahoo! Answers page was the first search result. There I found a dozen self-identified Christians weighing in on why Jesus Christ believes Stacey Lihn's daughter should die.

"Christ believed in people giving out of the goodness of their own hearts," GOZ2FAST writes, "not through government control and taxation."

"Jesus said we should help the poor," writes crash.override, "but he didn't say that we should pay the GOVERNMENT to help the poor."

"Jesus wasn't a big government coercion dude," writes Shovel Ready.

These "government control" and "coercion" themes aren't just popular with anonymous Internet trolls. The Catholic author Greg Stone writes of the Affordable Care Act: "Only a despot seeking to dominate others could love such legislation; the legislation contradicts [St.] Francis' advice to avoid the desire to dominate and coerce others."

I had actually heard these arguments against Obamacare before. Whenever I blog about health care—particularly when I say something in support of a single-payer system—people who claim to be Christian turn up in the comments thread to insist that, yes, while access to health care is *good,* and while it would be nice if all sick children could see doctors, Obamacare isn't Christian because Jesus Christ wants each of us to make an individual choice to be charitable. Collective acts of charity—a society coming together to make sure all citizens have access to health care—isn't Christian because Jesus wants us to *choose* to be charitable. Coerced acts of charity aren't charity. You're not doing good if the government is forcing you to do good.

Oddly enough, the very same Christians who oppose collective, coerced, society-wide action to provide health care to all—health care the way those socialists do it in Vatican City—turn around and argue that we must take collective, coercive action as a nation to prevent women from having abortions—even in cases of rape or incest. A society that allows children to die of toothaches isn't an affront to God, but one that allows women to terminate an unplanned pregnancy is. We can, they argue, employ the coercive powers of the state to close women's clinics, arrest doctors who perform abortions, imprison women who obtain abortions. Using the coercive powers of the state to force a rape victim to carry her rapist's baby to term? That's the right thing to do, Jesus-wise. Using the coercive powers of the state to collect taxes so that the women you're forcing to give birth to their rapists' babies can get prenatal care? That's an outrage, Jesus-wise.

This is Christianity? A collective action taken by a society that alleviates suffering—creating a health care system that extends coverage to millions of Americans—is un-Christian because it doesn't allow for individual agency. But collective action that heaps misery on top of someone who has already suffered—forcing a woman to give birth to her rapist's child—is just what Jesus would do. An isolated, terrified, and impregnated rape victim should be forced to give birth to her rapist's baby because Jesus loves babies. But *you* shouldn't be forced to pay taxes to support a health care system that could save that child's life if it's born with a life-threatening medical condition, because that's a coercive abuse of state power and Jesus hates that shit.

The mind boggles.

Listening to conservative Christians condemn Obamacare makes you wonder what Jesus would say if he could have a short conversation with one of his followers—particularly one like Peter LaBarbera. Peter's panicked tweet about the impact of Obamacare on the price of a Jimmy John's sandwich inspired me to write a one-act play. There are only two roles in this play: Jesus Christ and Peter LaBarbera. Imagine a ripped, bearded Jake Gyllenhaal in the role of Jesus and twitchy, sweaty Jeffrey Jones (the bug-eyed character actor who played the principal in *Ferris Bueller's Day Off*) in the role of Peter.

Jesus And The Huge Asshole

A one-act play by Dan Savage

Curtain. Jesus Christ is sitting in a garden in quiet contemplation.

One of Jesus's followers, Peter LaBarbera, approaches Jesus.

PETER: Jesus?

JESUS: Yes, Peter?

PETER: I want a Jimmy John's sandwich and a bag of chips.

JESUS: Okay, Peter. So go get a sandwich and a bag of chips.

PETER: I can't, Jesus.

JESUS: [*After a long pause.*] Why not, Peter?

PETER: Because, Jesus, the price of a Jimmy John's sandwich just went up fifty cents thanks to Obamacare, and now I can't afford to get a sandwich *and* a bag of chips. I can only afford a sandwich.

JESUS: You are an asshole.

PETER: Excuse me, Jesus?

JESUS: Are you deaf? I said, YOU ARE AN ASSHOLE. You're seriously standing there bitching about having to pay a little more for a sandwich?

PETER: You don't understand, Jesus, the *government* is forcing me to pay more—

JESUS: Shut the fuck up. I was crucified for your sins and all I asked in return was for you people to be nice to each other—

PETER: But the government—

JESUS: *Shut the fuck up, Peter.* All I asked was for you people to be nice to each other. And you're telling me that you're not willing to pay fifty cents more for a fucking sandwich so that the guy who made it for you can go see a doctor when he's sick? You're not a Christian.

PETER: But I go to church, Jesus, and I hate gay people so hard!

JESUS: Not good enough, Peter. Stop bothering me and go worship Thor or Quetzalcoatl or Isis instead, okay? I don't want you calling yourself a Christian anymore. You're a dick.

PETER: I can't believe Jesus just called me a dick.

JESUS: Yeah, well, you are a dick. I sacrificed my *life* for you, and you can't sacrifice a bag of chips for the sandwich guy? Or scrounge up the extra fifty fucking cents? Dick.

PETER: With all due respect, Jesus, I don't think you fully appreciate the implications of the Affordable Care Act. The state is using its coercive authority to collect taxes in order to provide health care to the poor in what amounts to a massive redistributionist welfare scheme that, yes, in the final accounting makes health care more available to *some,* Jesus, but it does so while driving up the cost of Jimmy John's sandwiches for *all.* And this is not the kind of private charity that you encouraged your followers to engage in. This is socialism, Jesus. Socialism!

JESUS: Do you remember that render-unto-Caesar shit I talked about in the Bible? When I said, basically, "Pay your fucking taxes and don't bitch about it." Remember that?

PETER: Yes, of course, but—

JESUS: Shut up, Peter. When I said, "Render unto Caesar," I was talking to *Jews* about paying taxes to *Romans*. Romans who turned around and spent the tax money they collected from Jews on swords and armor for Roman soldiers who they sent to Israel to *oppress the Jews*. The Romans were coercing the living shit out of the Jews, Peter, and I told them to shut up and pay up. And here you are bitching about the Caesar Obamulus using a few of your precious tax dollars to provide people with health insurance—people including you, members of your own family, other Christians, the guy who made your lousy sandwich, the kids of the guy who made your lousy sandwich. You have got to be fucking kidding me.

PETER: But Jesus! It's socialism!

JESUS: Love one another as I have loved you, the Greatest Commandment, do unto others as you would have them do unto you, take care of the poor, take care of the sick, give away all that you have and follow me—does any of this shit ring a bell? Any of it, you stupid asshole?

PETER: Okay, Jesus! Okay! I'm sorry! I'll go worship Quetzalcoatl instead!

The End.

16. It's Happened Again

Wednesday night, the door to our garage was open. And the last time either one of us remembered checking, it was shut. And padlocked. It wasn't hanging wide open, either, just cracked open a few inches. "Suspiciously ajar," you might call it. We couldn't see in, but the door was open just enough for someone inside the garage, if someone was standing inside the garage, to see us standing on the back porch, about twenty feet away, looking concerned about our open garage door.

With three news choppers thumping overhead, cop cars tearing up and down the street, and our then-twenty-month-old son pulling newspapers out of the recycling bin, Terry turned to me and said, "Go shut the garage door."

Earlier in the day a white guy walked into the office of a shipyard on Seattle's Lake Union, about eight blocks from our house, pulled out a semiautomatic handgun, and shot four people. Two men died; two men ended up in the hospital. And by dusk, the shooter was still at large, believed to be hiding somewhere in our neighborhood. Streets were blocked off, schools were locked down, and police were everywhere checking cars, houses, trees, basements—and garages. Seattle's police chief went on television to warn area residents to use caution when returning home from work.

Guns are everywhere in the United States, and I don't need to tell you that a week hardly goes by without someone walking into a school or an office building or a church or a day care center and opening fire. When any of the evening news anchors begin their broadcasts with the words "It's happened again," they don't even have to tell us what they mean by "it" anymore. Despite a comparatively piddling body count, the shooting in Seattle managed to knock the previous day's shooting in Hawaii off the top spot on every network news website. But I suspect that without the subsequent manhunt and school lockdowns, Seattle's shooting wouldn't have captured the attention of national evening news anchors. Only four shot? Two dead? That's local news, "routine" gun violence. Manhunts, school lockdowns? That's sexy.

Now, the next time "it" happens, Seattle will be added to the list of cities that have hosted a mass shooting. Seattle is on the map now—literally. After the next big mass shooting, Seattle will have the honor of appearing on one of those four-color "mass shooting" maps on the cover of *USA Today*.

There's no question that shutting the garage door was my job—all the dirty work is my job. When a rat died in the crawl space under the living room, Terry handed me a flashlight and a pair of rubber gloves. This time, Terry handed me a flashlight, picked up D.J., and—using caution—returned to the living room. Dead rats and live murderers are my job, Terry feels.

As I approached the garage, I thought to myself, "We should really call the cops." What kind of idiot points a flashlight into a dark garage and says "Hello?" when there's an armed murderer somewhere in the neighborhood? But I calmed myself and kept walking, telling myself that (A) nothing interesting ever happens to me, so I'm unlikely to be victim No. 5; and (B) since it's already occurred to me that the shooter could be in our garage, he won't be in our garage.

There are only ten steps from the back porch of our house to the garage door, but I took the scenic route, circling around to the side of the garage with a broken window. If the shooter wanted to run away, I didn't want to be blocking the door.

Standing to the side, I reached up and pointed the flashlight into the garage.

"Anybody in there?" I called out, trying to sound tough without sounding cop-tough. There was no sound, though, and no shots. I walked around to the door, slowly opened it with my foot, and stepped inside. Nothing. Only when the garage door was padlocked and I was heading back to the house did I realize how fast my heart was beating.

Later that night, with the shooter still at large, a local TV anchor-woman clucked her tongue, shook her empty head, and said, "Who would have thought something like this could happen right here, in Seattle?" I wanted to shoot my television set. How could it *not* happen here?

With so many guns, so many nuts, and so many spineless politicians taking orders from the National Rifle Association, it's really only a matter of time before "it" will happen in every city in the United States. So common is gun violence that "routine" shootings don't even make the news anymore. Terry has been robbed at gunpoint, so has my older brother; a good friend of my sister's was standing on a street corner in Chicago with his fiancée when he was shot dead by gang-bangers; a friend of my family was shot and killed on a subway platform. None of these events made the news.

Sadly, when the latest mass shooting is pointed to as evidence that we need tough national gun control laws, professional gun huggers and their congressional apologists cry foul, accusing gun control advocates of exploiting a tragedy. There's a difference, however, between exploiting a tragedy and learning from it.

When a plane drops out of the sky, we search for the cause and pass laws, if needed, to prevent similar tragedies in the future. Why have we not done the same with guns? To declare the scalding proof that we need tough gun control laws off-limits when discussing gun control—and the evidence builds with each new mass shooting—makes about as much sense as declaring the crash of EgyptAir's Flight 990 off-limits during a discussion of airline safety.

So, another day, another mass shooting. It's happened again. And it's going to keep happening until we work up the courage to do something about it.

Here's the sad truth. I wrote that piece, the one you just read, thirteen years ago, in November of 1999. Our country has experienced a deadly mass shooting every year—scratch that: nearly every fiscal quarter—since then. The most recent, most deadly, and perhaps most tragic (if there's a contest for things like that) took place late last year, in Newtown, Connecticut, where a twenty-year-old walked into an elementary school and killed twenty first graders and six adults. As a nation, we hadn't even recovered from the shock of a mass shooting in a mall outside of Portland, Oregon, packed with Christmas shoppers, when the Newtown shooting occurred. And as I write this the trial of another mass shooter is playing out in a Denver courtroom, that of James Holmes, the Aurora movie-theater killer.

Shortly after Newtown, Newark mayor Cory Booker called the gun control argument raging in the country (yet again) "a false debate," arguing that there are provisions we can put in place right now, provisions we can *all* agree on, to make the nation safer. "Most of us in America, including gun owners, agree on things that would stop the kind of carnage that's going on in cities all over America," Booker stated, adding, "I'm tired of the political debates. They're not necessary. I'm tired of the ideological positions. We don't even need to visit them. Let's stick to the pragmatic center where all Americans believe the same thing and let's pass legislation that would make America safer."

Booker's "pragmatic center" consists of background checks and closing down secondary gun markets, a common means for illegally acquiring firearms. But the guy who killed all those kids in Newtown used his mother's gun, which his mother acquired legally, and the guy who shot the holiday shoppers in Clackamas Town Center outside of Portland, Oregon, stole the gun from someone he knew who had apparently acquired it legally. The guy on trial now for killing all of those people in a movie theater in Aurora, Colorado, bought his small arsenal (four guns, thousands of bullets, and explosive chemicals) legally from three different stores in the Denver area.

Mandating background checks and shutting down secondary gun markets won't solve the problem.

So what is the problem? The defunded mental health system in the United States? The culture of violence so prevalent in the digital media targeted at young boys and men? The fact that on any given day you can buy a small arsenal legally in most places in America? A paranoid, gun-crazed country, hell-bent on protecting itself from invisible dangers lurking around every corner or garage door? (What if I owned a gun? What if there was someone in our garage that day—not the killer, but maybe a homeless person who'd ducked in to get out of the rain or a couple of high school students who needed a private place to get high? What if they had come toward the door, in the dark, and I shot them in a moment of panic?)

Scholars, gun advocates, and gun control advocates have argued for decades about what the founding fathers had in mind when they wrote the Second Amendment. A citizen army—the number of professional soldiers in 1791 was not large—that could come to the aid of the government? Or an armed citizenry empowered to protect itself from a tyrannical government? Or was it simply an American extension of English law at the time, where gun ownership was viewed as a natural right?

In a *New Yorker* blog post three months before the Aurora shooting, in April of 2012, Jill Lepore, writing about the history of the Second Amendment, quoted a response to a 2008 Supreme Court case (*District of Columbia et al. v. Heller*) signed by fifteen eminent university professors of early American history:

Historians are often asked what the Founders would think about various aspects of contemporary life. Such questions can be tricky to answer. But as historians of the Revolutionary era we are confident at least of this: that the authors of the Second Amendment would be flabbergasted to learn that in endorsing the republican principle of a well-regulated militia, they were also precluding restrictions on such potentially dangerous property as firearms, which governments had always regulated when there was "real danger of public injury from individuals."

I'm not a Revolutionary-era historian, but I don't think what we have today is what the founding fathers had in mind either. I don't think they believed Americans should have essentially unregulated access to military-grade weaponry. Lepore writes, "The United States has the highest rate of civilian gun ownership in the world, twice that of the country with the second highest rate, which is Yemen. The United States also has the highest homicide rate of any affluent democracy, nearly four times higher than France or the United Kingdom, six times higher than Germany. In the United States in 2008, guns were involved in two-thirds of all murders. Of interest to many people concerned about these matters, then, is when the debate over the Second Amendment will yield to a debate about violence."

But every time there's a shooting—every time the debate begins—the NRA and gun nuts in private and public life tell us that now is not the time to have a debate about guns or the violence guns facilitate.[1]

"If roads were collapsing all across the United States, killing dozens

---

1 One of the arguments that gun nuts make: There are too many guns out there already—more than three hundred million in private hands in the United States—so there's no point enacting gun control regulations now. New regulations won't stop the violence. It's like an arsonist telling you not to bother calling the fire department. It's too late—he already set your house on fire, there's nothing you can do about it now.

of drivers, we would surely see that as a moment to talk about what we could do to keep roads from collapsing," Ezra Klein wrote for *The Washington Post* after the Newtown shooting. "If terrorists were detonating bombs in port after port, you can be sure Congress would be working to upgrade the nation's security measures. . . . Only with gun violence do we respond to repeated tragedies by saying that mourning is acceptable but discussing how to prevent more tragedies is not. 'Too soon,' howl supporters of loose gun laws. But as others have observed, talking about how to stop mass shootings in the aftermath of a string of mass shootings isn't 'too soon.' It's much too late."

So let's talk about guns.

But for starters, how about a few precautions from America's "pragmatic center," as Mayor Booker calls it. How about an assault weapons ban? How about a ban on high-capacity ammunition magazines? How about a ban on unrestricted and unregulated gun-show purchases? How about some more money for mental health services? How about that for a start?

And that's basically what the White House, in the wake of the most recent mass shooting, proposed while they still had the national will on their side. Of course, the House of Representatives is still held hostage by the NRA, so the chances of any of these pragmatic ideas making it through the congressional gauntlet are slim.

Vice President Biden "is seriously considering measures backed by key law enforcement leaders that would require universal background checks for firearm buyers, track the movement and sale of weapons through a national database, strengthen mental health checks, and stiffen penalties for carrying guns near schools or giving them to minors," *The Washington Post* reported in January of 2013.

Isn't it ironic that the one group who has control over our nation's gun laws and refuses to make any provisions to potentially make its citizens safer is the one group that enjoys the benefits of unqualified gun control?

You can't carry a gun into the US Capitol—and there are metal detectors and guards at every entrance to make sure you don't try. Your congressperson enjoys a safe workplace. Yet members of Congress in both parties have worked hard to make sure your workplace is more dangerous. The Second Amendment—the NRA and its elected accomplices insist—gives people a constitutional right to carry guns into *your* workplace but not *their* workplace. It seems to me that members of Congress should have to live and work under the same threat of random gun violence that the rest of us do. If our elected officials believe it should be legal for Americans to carry concealed weapons into schools, churches, shopping malls, and offices buildings, it should be legal for Americans to carry concealed weapons into the US Capitol Building.

Fair is fair.

Or, on second thought, maybe we should just do what comedian Chris Rock proposes: Let's raise the price of bullets. If every bullet costs 5,000 dollars, we'd surely eliminate a lot of innocent bystander deaths, and probably the demand for high-capacity magazines and automatic weapons as well.

Until we do that—until we do something—it will keep happening.

17. Bigot Christmas

It's Christmas in August."

Terry was standing in our dining room, glaring at me as he wrapped the cord around the vacuum cleaner. He had just finished vacuuming the intricately carved legs of our massive old dining room table, a chore normally performed once a year, right before Christmas. But from the look on his face I could tell he wasn't feeling festive. He looked like he'd rather be wrapping that cord around my neck.

"You owe me for this," he said. "A week in Hawaii. Two weeks in Hawaii."

We were cleaning the house like Christmas was coming. We were cleaning the house like family and friends were about to arrive.[1] Every square inch of carpet had been vacuumed; every last tchotchke had

---

1 Pat Robertson wants you to believe that we atheists hate Christmastime. Robertson recently said this on his television show: "The Grinch is trying to steal our holiday. It's been so beautiful, the nation comes together, we sing Christmas carols, we give gifts to each other, we have lighted trees and it's just a beautiful thing. Atheists don't like our happiness. They don't want you to be happy. They want you to be miserable. They're miserable, so they want you to be miserable. So they want to steal your holiday away from you." Well, these particular atheists—Terry and D.J. and I—pull out all the stops at Christmas. We have a beautiful tree; we have presents; we have lights. We even have a crèche. We have a sit-down Christmas Eve dinner for some dear friends and their children, and on Christmas Day we host an open house for our neighbors. It's always a treat to see our friend Zach, a gorgeous porn star and a personal trainer, tossing children into the air while our very Catholic next-door neighbor chats amiably with our friend the professional dominatrix over champagne cocktails and Christmas cookies.

been dusted. Mail that had stacked up on the kitchen counter over the summer had been sorted and either recycled or filed; the books and musical instruments and board games that accumulate on and around every piece of furniture in our house had been returned to the shelves and closets they were pulled from days, weeks, or months before. But Santa Claus wasn't coming to town.

Brian Brown was coming to dinner.

Brown is the head of the National Organization for Marriage (NOM), the most prominent, most militant, and most malignant organization fighting marriage equality in the United States. NOM, like the Family Research Council and Americans for Truth About Homosexuality, was designated an anti-gay group by the Southern Poverty Law Center in 2010. Cofounded by Maggie Gallagher in 2007, NOM fights against equal marriage rights for same-sex couples. That's all NOM does. Its sole purpose is to make sure that fewer couples marry. While Gallagher and Brown argue that they oppose same-sex marriage because "every child deserves a mother and a father," and while they claim to be concerned about fatherlessness, and while they cite studies that demonstrate the vulnerability of children from broken homes to justify their opposition to same-sex marriage, NOM doesn't work to strengthen existing marriages; it doesn't fight no-fault divorce laws; it hasn't proposed a lifetime limit on the numbers of marriages a straight person can have. (Hasn't Newt Gingrich done enough damage to the institution?)

No, NOM fights same-sex marriage. Period.[2]

---

2 "Suppose you were interested in promoting children's well-being, and in particular, in addressing the problem of fatherlessness," John Corvino writes in *Debating Same-Sex Marriage*. "What could you do? You could work on comprehensive sex-education programs, including accurate information about both abstinence and contraception. You could aim at some of the purported root causes, including poverty, lack of educational and employment opportunities, and incarceration policy. You could tighten up divorce laws, given the documented effect of divorce on children's well-being. You could promote relationship counseling. You could do all of these things, and a hundred more. Or you could do what the National Organization for Marriage does."

Brown is NOM's second president, after Gallagher, and he earns more than 500,000 dollars a year defending "traditional marriage."[3] Born and raised in California, Brown got his undergraduate degree at Whittier College, and then went on to study philosophy at Oxford. While at Oxford, Brown, who had been raised a Quaker, converted to Catholicism. In a blowjob in *The Washington Post*—excuse me, in a profile in *The Washington Post* in August of 2009—Brown claimed that he was attracted to "Catholicism's traditions of social justice and work for the poor." (Quakers, as everyone knows, roam the streets after their meetings setting homeless people on fire.) Despite his stated reasons for converting, Brown has never worked to advance social justice or alleviate the suffering of the poor. He's held just one job prior to taking a position with NOM: at the Family Institute of Connecticut, where Brown fought to keep condoms out of schools. (Working to drive up the rate of sexually transmitted infections among teenagers ≠ social justice.)

Brown has a stocky build and a large, square head. He has a vulpine smile and tends to shout when he speaks. After making a bigoted statement, Brown has a revealing habit of shifting his gaze to the left and then the right with a look on his face that is equal parts aggression and insecurity.

"You know I'm right about this," the look on his face says. "And I am right about this—right?"

Brown's demagoguery on the issue of marriage equality is some-

---

3 By "traditional marriage," Brian Brown and his organization merely mean "opposite-sex marriage." A marriage can take any form whatsoever and still be seen as "traditional," at least to NOM, so long as it involves one man and one woman. Take a married straight couple that lives a hardcore Femdom lifestyle (i.e., the husband wears a male chastity belt, spends most of his time in a cage, and submits to sexual torture at the hands of his wife. Maybe his testicles are crushed in a vise when he displeases his wife; maybe she shoves needles through the head of his penis when he really displeases her). That's a "traditional" marriage, according to NOM, because penis + vagina + wedding = traditional marriage. A couple of lesbians with two or three kids, one partner works, the other stays home. For kicks they sometimes get a babysitter and go to the movies. That's a radical redefinition of marriage because vagina + vagina + wedding = END OF THE WORLD!

times breathtaking. Under Brown's leadership, NOM has linked—or has attempted to link—marriage rights for same-sex couples to child rape and crafted a plan to "drive a wedge between gays and blacks," according to internal NOM memos obtained by the Human Rights Campaign (HRC). ("One of NOM's goals is 'fanning the hostility' between the LGBT community and the black community," HRC's report on the memos read.) NOM under Brown has skirted campaign finance disclosure laws, misrepresented attendance at their rallies (the organization got caught claiming that a photo of a 2008 Obama rally was a photo of a 2011 NOM rally), and—discredit where discredit is due—led successful campaigns to ban same-sex marriage in numerous states. A NOM-backed organization recently warned parents against allowing their college-age children to have gay friends.

Brown may be the most loathed anti-gay activist in the United States. Not for nothing did prominent gay blogger Joe Jervis dub him "Brian Brownshirt."

Even John Corvino, perhaps the nicest, calmest, and most measured advocate of marriage equality in the United States, has a hard time concealing his dislike of Brown. Corvino, a gay man in a long-term relationship (and a professor of philosophy at Wayne State University), coauthored the book *Debating Same-Sex Marriage* with NOM's Maggie Gallagher. Corvino tells me he likes Gallagher personally, even if he finds her political views objectionable. He can't say the same about Brown.

"I have a kind of visceral negative reaction to Brian Brown that I don't have to Maggie," Corvino wrote in an e-mail. "Of course, I have a personal relationship with Maggie, whereas I hardly know Brian. But something about him just rubs me the wrong way, beyond the fact that I sharply disagree with his moral stance and his politics."

So, yeah, Brian Brown isn't exactly a friend of the family. So how did he wind up coming to our house for dinner, along with a four-person camera crew and Mark Oppenheimer, the religion columnist for *The New York Times*?

It's a long story.

In October of 2011 the local chair of the Washington Journalism Education Association sent me an e-mail begging me to give the keynote speech at the 2012 National High School Journalism Convention. (I'm not going to give his name here, as he's doubtless suffered enough, so I'll just use his initials.) S.M. had e-mailed me three times already, and left a couple of phone messages, yet I had somehow missed his earlier e-mails and calls. But I got his third e-mail and it worked like a charm: "I feel like we are on a first-name basis already since, starting last August, I have sent you three e-mails and made two phone calls to get in touch with you," S.M. wrote. "In a few days I need to sign a keynote speaker for our high school journalism convention. I had hoped that speaking to 4,000 teenagers might interest you, given your awesome work with the It Gets Better Project. Maybe not. After all, the pay stinks—it's all but a volunteer gig. It probably won't get a lot of national attention."

Here's a tip: Want me to show up at your event and give a speech? Insinuate that I'm only interested in money ("the pay stinks"), lay a guilt trip on me ("I had hoped that speaking to 4,000 teenagers might interest you"), and suggest that I'm a media whore ("probably won't get a lot of national attention"), and I am so there. I wrote S.M. back and told him I'd give the keynote—and hey, the convention was taking place in Seattle, just a few blocks from my office, so no need to send a car, much less pay me. I offered to walk down.

But the speech I gave before four thousand high school journalists at the Washington State Convention Center on Friday, April 13, wound up getting a little national attention.

ANTI-BULLYING SPEAKER CURSES CHRISTIAN TEENS (Fox News)

DAN SAVAGE STANDS BY COMMENTS ON "BULLS**T IN THE BIBLE"
(CNN)

"IT GETS BETTER" CREATOR OFFENDS CHRISTIAN STUDENTS (*The Huffington Post*)

SPARKS FLY OVER DAN SAVAGE'S COMMENTS TO STUDENTS ABOUT
BIBLE (*The Seattle Times*)

DAN SAVAGE OFFENDS WITH COMMENTS ON CHRISTIANITY (*The Washington Post*)

DAN SAVAGE ACCUSED OF BULLYING (*New York Daily News*)

CHRISTIANS: SAVAGELY BULLIED (Townhall.com)

DAN SAVAGE VS. THE BIBLE (*The Atlantic*)

ANTI-BULLYING TZAR BULLIES CHRISTIANS (*The American Catholic*)

PARENT OF KIDS WHO WALKED OUT ON SAVAGE: "WHAT A PIG"
(Breitbart News)

DAN SAVAGE IS A BAD, BAD MAN (Wonkette.com)

Before I gave the speech, I asked my handlers from the National Scholastic Press Association and Journalism Education Association if they wanted me to pull my punches. Despite the It Gets Better Project's touchy-feely-up-with-people aura, the project is an act of cultural defiance. The It Gets Better Project is about LGBT adults talking to and talking with isolated and bullied LGBT youth—whether their parents, preachers, and teachers want us to or not. (Not all LGBT youth are bullied or isolated, for the record. The project, however, is targeted at LGBT youth who are bullied and isolated.) I warned the organizers that my remarks about the project can be confrontational, even aggressive—like the project itself. I don't just talk about how it gets better. I talk about who is making it worse and why they're making it worse. I was told not to dial it back for the students. They didn't want me to patronize their student journalists.

So I delivered my usual It Gets Better remarks. Those remarks include a section on the role religious bigotry plays—and the role certain passages from the Old and New Testaments play—in the bullying of LGBT children by their peers and, most destructively of all, by their own parents. When I first mentioned the Bible, a small number of students rose from their seats and started to walk out. When I got to the end of my remarks on religion, I invited the students who'd walked out to come back in. (Fun fact: The hall in which I was speaking was so large—there were four thousand students within its walls—that I had concluded my remarks on religion before anyone had managed to get all the way out of the room.)

More than a month after the event a video of my remarks was released. It wasn't the entire speech. Here's a complete transcript of the video:

> The Bible. We'll just talk about the Bible for a second. People often [claim] that they can't help it. They can't help with the anti-gay bullying because it says right there in Leviticus, it says right there in Timothy, it says right there in Romans that being gay is wrong. We can learn to ignore the bullshit in the Bible about gay people the same way we have learned to ignore the bullshit in the Bible about shellfish, about slavery, about dinner, about farming, about menstruation, about virginity, about masturbation. We ignore bullshit in the Bible about all sorts of things. The Bible is a radically pro-slavery document. Slave owners waved Bibles over their heads during the Civil War. And justified it. The shortest book in the New Testament is a letter from Paul to a Christian slave owner about owning his Christian slave. And Paul doesn't say, "Christians don't own people." Paul talks about *how* Christians own people. We ignore what the Bible says about slavery because the Bible got slavery

wrong. Sam Harris in his book *Letter to a Christian Nation* points out that the Bible got the easiest moral question that humanity has ever faced wrong: slavery. What are the odds that the Bible got something as complicated as human sexuality wrong? One hundred percent. The Bible says that if your daughter's not a virgin on her wedding night, if a woman isn't a virgin on her wedding night, she shall be dragged to her father's doorstep and stoned to death. Callista Gingrich lives. And there is no effort to amend state constitutions to make it legal to stone women to death on their wedding night if they're not virgins. [LGBT youth] are dying because people can't clear this one last hurdle. They can't get past this one last thing in the Bible: about homosexuality. One last thing I want to talk about is—so you can tell the Bible guys in the hall they can come back now because I'm done beating up the Bible. It's funny to me, as someone who is on the receiving end of beatings that are justified by the Bible, how pansy-ass some people react when you push back. I apologize if I hurt anyone's feelings, but I have a right to defend myself and to point out the hypocrisy of people who justify anti-gay bigotry by pointing to the Bible and insisting we must live by the code of Leviticus on this one issue and no other.

Okay, I could've said that better. I usually do say that better—I've given many talks about the It Gets Better Project—but I was honestly a little flummoxed when those students began to walk out. That had never happened before.

Presumably the person or group that taped my speech didn't just capture those remarks. They got the whole speech on tape. But for some reason they didn't release any of the other remarks I made about the Bible. So no one besides the four thousand students in the Washington State Convention Center that Friday the thirteenth got to hear me praise the activism of progressive and liberal Christians, or acknowledge the moral truths that can be found in the Bible. Nor did they hear me say that the Christian Bible can be read—and, in my opinion, should be read—as a journey from the harsher laws of the Old Testament (a proclivity for the stoning of disobedient children) to the more "Golden Rule" ethos of the New Testament. ("Do unto others as you would have them do unto you.") Though, it should be noted that the Golden Rule does appear in the Old Testament, in our old friend Leviticus, of all places.

If I may quickly dispose of a few falsehoods spread by Fox News and various right-wing blogs in the wake of Bullshitgate: I was speaking at a journalism conference, not a conference on bullying. (The theme of this conference? "Journalism on the Edge.")[4] I wasn't speaking at a high school. I wasn't speaking at a Christian high school. I've never met the president and I am not now, nor have I ever been, Barack Obama's "bullying tzar." I did not blindside the organizers. It wasn't a "mass walkout." (Unless a staged walkout by .0055 percent of an audience constitutes a "mass walkout.") I received a standing ovation from the nearly four thousand students who were left in the room, almost all of them Christian, when I finished. And while the organizers of the conference praised the speech at first, telling Fox News that they "appreciated the level of thoughtfulness and deliberation" that went into my speech, they backtracked when the right-wing blogs blew up. (Breitbart.com: JOURNALISM CONFERENCE ORGANIZERS REVERSE COURSE, APOLOGIZE FOR SAVAGE INVITE.) The National Scholastic Press Association and Journalism Education Association accused me of

---

4 From the promotional materials for the 2012 National High School Journalism Convention: "You are already on the Edge. Journalists have always lived on the edge. Deadlines, and the edge of time. Facts, and the edge of truth. Authority, and the edge of free expression. We balance on the edge of legitimate public interest and the interests of those who would rather we not publish." Forgive me for getting edgy at your "Journalism on the Edge" conference.

having "veered from the topic" of bullying (sorry, no: religious bigotry is relevant to the topic of anti-gay bullying), "and for this our organizations apologize." (Real profile in courage there, gang!)

Did I bully anyone? I certainly don't think so; no one who has ever been the victim of actual bullying would think so. But I'm not an impartial observer. So I'll let those left-wing radicals at *The Economist* defend me on that charge:

> Bullying is the strong picking on the weak, not the other way around (the other way around is satire). One could make the argument that in the case of Mr Savage's speech, he was the strong one, and the high-school students were "victims", but that would be weak tea indeed. Mr Savage is one person, not a movement, and of course those students whom he gave the vapours were free to leave. Not everyone has such freedom. Gay teens, not Christian teens, kill themselves at higher rates than the general populace. Nobody calls Christianity an abomination. One blogger accused Mr Savage of "Christian-bashing" for pointing out the Bible's position on slavery. A writer for a Focus on the Family site said that "using profanity to deride the Bible . . . is obviously a form of bullying and name-calling." In fact it is neither: Mr Savage, however intemperate his language, was arguing, not name-calling. That is a crucial distinction, and one that too often eludes the showily devout.

Whatever else Brian Brown is, he's a media-savvy guy. When Brown saw me being attacked on Fox News and right-wing blogs, he sensed an opportunity.

"Let me lay down a public challenge to Dan Savage right here and now: You want to savage the Bible? Christian morality? Traditional marriage? The Pope?"[5] Brown wrote in a post on NOM's blog. "You name the time and the place and let's see what a big man you are in a debate with someone who can talk back!"

Debate Brian Brown? And I get to name the time and place?

Well, that was a tempting offer—in fact, it seemed like an offer that was designed to tempt.

It didn't take me long to figure out what Brown was tempting me to do: He wanted me to accept his offer, pack an auditorium with angry gays and lesbians, and "debate" him in front of a booing, hissing crowd that wouldn't let him get a word in edgewise. Being silenced by a hostile crowd would play into the narrative being pushed by NOM and the rest of the anti-gay right: They're the real victims! By refusing to tolerate their intolerance, LGBT people are oppressing them. Because LGBT people refuse to tolerate being called sick and sinful and perverse, because we refuse to tolerate second-class citizenship, because we refuse to tolerate the bullying of LGBT children in their homes, schools, and churches, they're the real victims of intolerance! I don't think Brown really wanted to debate me. He wanted to stride into a coliseum filled with angry LGBT people. He wanted to be shouted down. Then Brown could upload the video of the aborted debate to

---

5 Brown is referring to some remarks I made about the pope that Peter LaBarbera caught on video and posted to YouTube. Here they are: "The pope recently said that gay marriage is a threat to the survival of the human race. Because once we can get gay married, once gay marriage is legal, everybody's gonna get gay married. The pope is saying that there's no such thing as a straight person. There are only people who wish they were gay, and would be gay, but they can't get married. What the pope is saying is that the only thing that stands between my dick and Brad Pitt's mouth is a piece of paper. . . . When the pope says these things, gay writers like me, we blow up on our blogs, we write about it. I don't understand why straight people don't get mad. The pope is projecting. . . . You would think straight people would feel insulted and aggrieved by this argument: The human race is going to go extinct if we can all get gay married! It's hilarious when you follow [the pope's argument] to its logical conclusion. What the pope is saying is that once we're all gay married, we're going to go extinct in a generation. Once we're all gay married, we're going to forget which hole shits babies. We won't do IVF, we won't take one for the team and have opposite-sex sex just every once in a while. We're all going to stand around going, 'Huh! I don't know what the problem is—I keep inseminating Terry and nothing!' "

YouTube and say, "See?!? They're the intolerant ones! We're the real victims!"

Yeah, right. Gay men are turned away from their partners' bedsides during medical emergencies as a direct result of Brown's activism, lesbian widows are losing their homes after losing their wives as a direct result of Brown's activism, but somehow Brian Brown is the one who's being persecuted. (It reminds me of a great political cartoon by Mike Ritter: A priest is nailing a young man wearing jeans and an "LGBT Civil Rights" T-shirt to a cross in front of an angry mob. "Quit squirming," the exasperated priest says. "You're oppressing our religious freedom!")

I can be stupid. I've certainly done stupid things. (Using the word *bullshit* at a high school journalism conference, even one "on the edge"? That was stupid.) And I'm probably going to get stupider now that marijuana is legal for recreational use in Washington State. But I'm not that stupid.

I responded to Brown's challenge on my podcast. "Sure, Brian, let's debate!"—and then I named the place and time: my house, after dinner.

> Here's the deal. We can fill a room with my screaming partisans . . . but that will create more heat than light. So what I'd like to do is challenge you to come to my house for dinner. Bring the wife. My husband will be there. I'll hire a video crew and we'll videotape an after-dinner debate and post the whole debate to YouTube. The trick here is you have to acknowledge my humanity by accepting my hospitality, and I have to acknowledge yours by extending my hospitality to you.

Honestly I thought Brown would view my counteroffer as a trap—which is exactly what it was—and back out. ("I challenged you to a debate, Dan Savage, not a double date!") Brown even had a perfectly legitimate reason to back out: His wife was pregnant with their eighth child, and the only date that worked for Brown's schedule and mine was close to his wife's due date. But Brown accepted and after a back-and-forth about details, the debate was on. (Those details: Brown, fearing "creative editing," wanted to bring his own camera crew. Savage, fearing NOM staffers roaming around his house while he was trapped at the dining room table, said no way. Brown dropped his demand for his own camera crew after our moderator—Mark Oppenheimer of *The New York Times,* who had written profiles of me for the paper's magazine and of Maggie Gallagher for *Salon*—offered to hire the video crew, oversee the edit, and upload the video himself.) We both agreed to keep the date of the debate secret to prevent protesters—pro-gay or anti-gay—from turning up at my house on the day of the debate: August 15, 2012. There was just one last detail to attend to . . .

Someone needed to tell Terry that Brian Brown was coming to dinner.

The Dinner Table Debate, as it was dubbed by bloggers on both sides, was something I should've cleared with Terry first, seeing as it's his dinner table too. But I honestly didn't think Brown would accept and so, you know, why make Terry mad and have a big fight about something that probably wasn't going to happen anyway?

And I knew Terry would explode when I told him the news. And my husband—like a lot of people's husbands (including my husband's husband [follow that?])—is scary when he's mad. And if there's one thing Terry hates, it's having to be civil to people who view him as sick and sinful and perverted and covered with poop.[6] While I enjoy argu-

---

6 My friend and colleague Dominic Holden did a story for *The Stranger* on donors who contributed large sums of money to fund an anti-gay ballot initiative in Washington State backed in part by NOM. He called these donors and asked them what was so awful about gay partnerships.

"A penis does not belong in someone's anus," donor James McFadden told Holden. Esther Mayoh also opposed gay partnership rights because of butt sex: "My main reason is

ing with anti-gay bigots, Terry, who grew up in Spokane, Washington, has a low threshold for hatred in faith drag. He had his fill of anti-gay bigots—and black eyes—as a teenager. He would sooner jump in a swimming pool filled with stale piss than attend CPAC (the Conservative Political Action Conference), the annual meeting of far-right-wing political hacks, religious fascists, and Republican presidential hopefuls. Me? I've been to CPAC twice and I would go every year if we lived in Washington, DC. (I'm surprised more Democrats don't go to CPAC. It's like watching the Republican Party lie down in a bathtub, slice open a vein, and drain itself of whatever support it might have among women, gays, Jews, immigrants, Hispanics, and scientists.)

The conversation went like this:

"Guess who's coming to dinner?" (Because how often do you get to say that?)

"Tell me." (Terry doesn't play games, guessing or otherwise.)

"Brian Brown from the National Organization for Marr—"

BOOM.

Now some reading this are probably thinking, "I would've liked to have been a fly on the wall when Dan told Terry that Brian Brown was coming to dinner!" No, you wouldn't have. My eardrums barely survived the volume at which Terry screamed, "WHO?!? WHY?!?

---

that I don't want our state to, well, to put it bluntly, I don't want our state to legalize sodomy," she said (never mind, Holden pointed out, that sodomy was already legal). He then asked donor Paul Henry point-blank if he thought gay people were gross. "I would say even more than gross," Henry said. "I think they are major incubators of a lot of the bacteria." Three years later, when NOM was the leading force to overturn a marriage equality law in Washington State, Holden heard similar statements when he again called the top individual donors. "Penetration of the rectum is bad for them," Curtiss Wikstrom, who gave 2,500 dollars, explained.

Holden's analysis: "A lot of their opposition just came down to the fear of nasty, no-good, dirty gay poop sex. They're obsessed with poopy, poopy gay sex. And all that poop sex results in gay people being, well, smeared with poop. AND THEY MIGHT TOUCH YOU WITH THEIR POOPY, DISEASE-RIDDEN SKIN. So when they say gay folks are 'sick, sinful, or perverse' or that gay parents are unfit to raise kids, what many of them are actually thinking is that gay people are smeared with shit. (Never mind that lots of straight men in 'traditional marriages' penetrate their wives' rectums. But when straight couples do it, that's not poop sex—that's *love*.)"

WHEN?!?" If there were any flies on our walls—if there were any flies within earshot—the shock wave struck them dead.

Breaking the news to D.J. was a little easier. When our son—adopted at birth by two gay men—was informed that the nation's most prominent anti-gay activist was coming to dinner, D.J. shrugged and said, "Whatever." (A three-syllable response from our teenage son? A small triumph.) D.J.'s only objection: The Dinner Table Debate doubled the number of times he would have to wear a collared shirt in a single calendar year—once for his annual picture with Santa, and once during dinner with Brian Brown. (IT WASN'T FAIR! STOMP! STOMP! STOMP! SLAM!)

It was Terry who recognized that our preparations for Brown's arrival mirrored our Christmas routine. We were stocking up on wine, planning out a menu, and cleaning the house from top to bottom. In addition to the film crew, a photographer from *The New York Times* was coming. We dusted the fucking baseboards.

"Worst Christmas ever," Terry said, as I was mopping the kitchen floor the morning of the debate. "Ho, ho, ho. It's Bigot Christmas."[7]

---

7 Is it fair to label Brian Brown a bigot? "Brian Brown runs a website with a page called 'SAME-SEX MARRIAGE: Answering the Toughest Questions,'" writes the gay blogger Rob Tisinai. If you oppose gay marriage and someone asks you why do "you want to interfere with love?" Brown and NOM suggest you reply: "Love is a great thing. But marriage isn't just any kind of love; it's the special love of husband and wife for each other and their children."

So "gay and lesbian couples aren't capable of feeling the same sort of love that straight couples can?" writes Tisinai. "Even more outrageously . . . we can't feel the same love *for our children* that straight couples can? . . . It's literally dehumanizing to claim such a thing—to argue that we're missing some essential component of what makes people human." If that's not bigotry, what is?

"Homosexuality is the only 'sin' toward which straight people literally cannot be tempted and, not unsurprisingly, homosexuality is the only 'sin' listed in the Bible that Christians treat as an absolute sin," writes John Shore, a progressive evangelical Christian, author, and blogger. "Murder can be heroic or a travesty depending on its context. Lying can be heroic. ('Do you have any Jews hiding in your attic?') Most Christians drink. Everyone is at times profoundly greedy. Homosexuality is the only sin for which Christians wholly and consistently reject any and all relative and/or contextual considerations," such as hot, sweaty gay sex taking place in the context of a loving, committed relationship. "And

Since Brown uses the Bible to defend his opposition to marriage equality, and since it was my remarks about the Bible that led Brown to challenge me to debate the Bible with him, let's go back to the high school journalism conference for a second—the walkout and the fallout.

After watching the video I apologized for describing the walkout as a "pansy-ass" move. I wasn't calling the handful of students who walked out pansies; I was describing the walkout itself as a pansy-assed thing to do. But that's a distinction without a difference—like that "love the sinner, hate the sin" line. Fundamentalist Christians who don't enjoy being thought of as hateful are often shocked when their gay friends and family members are upset by their "compassionate" attempt to make a distinction between a gay person (lovable!) and a gay person's emotional and sexual connection with another human being (hateful!). But gay people feel insulted by "love the sinner, hate the sin" because it is insulting. Likewise, I recognize that my use of "pansy-ass" to describe the walkout was insulting. And I apologized for it. But I didn't apologize for saying that there was "bullshit in the Bible" then, and I'm not going to apologize now. Because guess what? There's bullshit in the Bible.

Merriam-Webster defines "bullshit" as "untrue words or ideas." And I'm sorry to say—no, wait: I'm not sorry to say—there are untrue words or ideas in the Bible.

The bullshit artists on Fox News accused me of saying that Christianity itself was bullshit. But I didn't attack Christianity, the faith in which I

---

why do Christians treat this *one* 'sin' so differently than they do virtually all the others? It cannot be because of Biblical 'reasoning'; it can only be bigotry."

And here's what I don't understand about rabidly anti-gay Christian activists: They don't like it when you call them "bigots"—and they really don't like it when you call them "haters"—but they run around claiming that LGBT people are sick and sinful, that we want to "normalize" pedophilia, that our relationships are a threat to the family, the nation, the species, and the planet (and they do make all of those claims), and that those of us who are parents are a threat to our own children. If someone believes all of that . . . why wouldn't they hate us? I'd hate me if all or any of that were true.

was raised. I attacked the argument that gay people must be discriminated against because it says *right here* in the Bible that homosexuality is an abomination. I attacked the argument that efforts to address anti-gay bullying in schools must be blocked, or exceptions must be made for teenage bullies who are "motivated by faith," as lawmakers have proposed in numerous Southern states, because it says *right here* in the Bible that homosexuality is an abomination. I used colorful and, yes, inappropriate language to point out that the same people who claim they can't ignore what the Bible says about homosexuality—or what the Bible seems to say[8]—somehow manage to ignore what the Bible says about a great deal else, from menstruation to masturbation, from circumcision to slavery. I was not attacking Christianity. I was attacking hypocrisy.

Here's a much more famous—and, yes, much more talented—American writer on the subject of the Bible:

> It is full of interest. It has noble poetry in it; and some clever fables; and some blood-drenched history; and some good morals; and a wealth of obscenity; and upwards of a thousand lies.

---

8 Not all Christians—liberal ones, progressive ones, gay ones, informed ones—believe that the New Testament is anti-gay. "The interpretation of the New Testament passages is of particular importance for determining what most churches actually teach—not just for sloganeering—and gay rights supporters shouldn't concede that they are 'anti-gay' in any sense that we understand that term," says Matthew Vines. "Here's why: By far, the most common form of same-sex union in antiquity was pederasty (man/boy relationships), which is the most likely referent in 1 Corinthians 6:9 and 1 Timothy 1:10; and to the extent that adult same-sex relations were visible in the biblical world, they tended to be viewed as the product of 'normal' sexual desire having been overindulged, not of a different sexual orientation. Thus, Paul's condemnation of 'homosexuality' in Romans 1:26–27 is better understood simply as a condemnation of excess passion, of which same-sex relations were a mere symbol—and a symbol that in no sense transfers to modern discourse about LGBT identity. None of the three NT verses have anything to do with people having or expressing a same-sex orientation, so in that core sense, the NT doesn't contain anti-gay passages at all." Vines is a gay man who grew up in an evangelical home in Kansas. He took a yearlong leave from Harvard to research homosexuality and the Bible. An hour-long lecture on his research, which Vines delivered at a church in Wichita, Kansas, was uploaded to YouTube ("The Gay Debate: The Bible and Homosexuality") and quickly went viral. Vines's upcoming book—tentatively titled *The Bible and the Gay Christian*—will be published in February 2014.

I'm not guilty of saying anything that Mark Twain didn't say a hundred years earlier and a hundred times better. For what, in contemporary vernacular, is "bullshit" but "upwards of a thousand lies"?

I'll give this to Fox News: They sure know how to blow up a guy's Twitter feed and e-mail in-box.[9] Elderly people who enjoy feeling outraged tune in to Fox News for stuff to feel outraged about—it's that or get a pacemaker installed (average age of Fox News viewer: sixty-five)—and I heard from thousands of them over the course of a couple days.

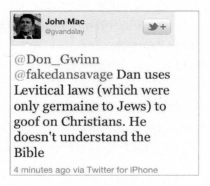

John "Reagan Conservative" Mac isn't someone I know personally; he's just another TCOT—"True Conservative on Twitter"—bravely battling the forces of liberalism and secularism. I don't usually get into arguments with Twitter trolls. But Mac sent me that tweet two minutes before this e-mail popped into my in-box: "God is not mocked! So mock on. You will soon see Who has the last laugh. Hear the Word of the Lord: Leviticus 20:13: 'If a man also lie with mankind, as he lieth

---

9 Quick bit of advice for anyone who ever finds himself under attack by Fox News and its viewers: Their anger burns hot but it burns fast. Turn off your computer, go to the movies, and before you know it the gang at Fox is back to the War on Christmas or the New Black Panthers. Then, when it is safe to turn your computer back on, you can count all the e-mail addresses that are from AOL accounts and have a laugh at the olds.

with a woman, both of them have committed an abomination: they shall surely be put to death; their blood shall be upon them.' Mock on, pervert. This is your time. Enjoy it. It is brief."

So you see, John Mac, the Old Testament *is* germane.

Anti-gay Christian hypocrites—for the record: Not all Christians are anti-gay, not all Christians are hypocrites—are constantly citing passages from the Old Testament to justify their hatred of LGBT people. We are far likelier to hear about Leviticus 20:13 or Sodom and Gomorrah from an anti-gay bigot than we are to hear about Corinthians or Timothy or Romans. It doesn't matter if the anti-gay bigot is ranting on the subway, on a "Christian" television network, or during a GOP presidential debate: They're all citin' the Old Testament. Even those ADAM AND EVE, NOT ADAM AND STEVE! signs the haters like to wave at anti-gay demonstrations—and I've seen plenty of 'em at NOM demonstrations—are a reference to the Old Testament.[10]

Baptist minister Louie Giglio was invited to give the benediction at Barack Obama's second inauguration and then quickly dropped from the program after numerous news reports about an anti-gay sermon Giglio delivered in the mid-nineties and still stood by. In the sermon Giglio described gay people as "haters of God," said that people who engage in gay sex are "worthy of death," and—inevitably—Giglio cited Leviticus 20:13. Evangelical Christians were outraged, of course, but not at Giglio for citing Leviticus. They were outraged that Giglio would be dropped from the inauguration for calling for the deaths of Neil Patrick Harris, Ellen DeGeneres, and Chris Colfer, among others.

But let a gay person bring up Deuteronomy 22:20–21 and the same people who were citing Leviticus 20:13 a minute ago, or standing si-

---

10 As my much-missed friend David Rakoff once said: "Well, of course not Adam and Steve. Never Adam and Steve. It's Adam and *Steven*."

lently by while others cited Leviticus 20:13, are suddenly up on their feet, loudly objecting to this spurious reference to the Old Testament. (For those of you who have yet committed the Pentateuch to memory—for shame—Deuteronomy 22:20–21 goes a little something like this: "If there is no proof that his bride was a virgin, the men of the town will take the woman to the door of her father's house and stone her to death. This woman brought evil into your community by sleeping with someone before she got married, and you must get rid of that evil by killing her.") Every time a gay person brings up a verse from the Old Testament in self-defense, the John Macs of the world start shouting, "Silly faggot! That stuff about girls being stoned to death on their wedding nights is in the Old Testament! That's not in the New Testament!"

Neither is the book of Leviticus. So if it isn't kosher for LGBT people to bring up what the Old Testament says about shellfish or personal grooming or tattoos or menstruation or slavery or stoning women to death for the crime of premarital sex, then it's not kosher for Christian conservatives to bring up Leviticus or Sodom and Gomorrah or Adam and Eve. But they do bring it up.

All. The. Fucking. Time. They. Bring. It. Up.

And it's not like they need to. There's no shortage of anti-gay passages in the New Testament, courtesy of Paul, but no one ever flings Timothy in our faces. And why is that? I have a theory. It's not because we might like the idea of having Timothy—any Timothy—thrown in our faces. It's because what the New Testament has to say about homosexuality ("abusers of themselves with mankind will not inherit the Kingdom of God") isn't nearly as violent as what the Old Testament has to say about homosexuality ("they shall surely be put to death"). For anti-gay bigots it's not enough to let God punish us in the afterlife. Many long to murder us here on earth. (Anyone who thinks I'm exaggerating hasn't been following the news about Uganda's proposed "kill the gays" law. In December of 2012, the pope granted an audience to

Rebecca Kadaga, the Ugandan lawmaker pushing the bill, and offered her his blessing.)

Sorry, John Mac, but people waving Bibles around point to Leviticus every day to justify their hatred of LGBT people. And we have a right to crack open that same Bible and ask . . . what else is in here?

We have a right to point out the hypocrisy.

And do you know what they call "pointing out the hypocrisy" where I come from?

Calling bullshit.

On the day of the debate—was Bigot Christmas really here at last?—the camera crew showed up first. While the three-person crew rearranged the furniture, set up the lights, and tested the sound equipment, Terry slipped out of the house and went across the street to check on dinner preparations.

Here's another funny detail about the Dinner Table Debate: One of our neighbors—a straight married guy named John—knew that Brian Brown was coming to dinner before a gay married guy named Terry did.

John Colwell is a stay-at-home dad to four wonderful kids, an absolutely amazing cook, and we count John and his wife Mishy among our best friends. Before I responded to Brown's debate challenge, I walked across the street and asked John if he would cook dinner if Brown accepted my invitation. John immediately agreed. The only thing John loves more than a dinner party is a good argument—and the only thing he loves more than a good argument is a good shit show.

Now Terry is a great cook—let the record show—but I know my husband. There was no way in hell that he would agree to cook for Brian Brown. In fact, the second fly-on-the-wall-flattening thing Terry shouted after I told him that Brown was coming to dinner was this: "I am NOT cooking for that bastard!"

"You don't have to," I said. "John said he would cook."

"JOHN KNEW ABOUT THIS BEFORE I DID?!?"

Birds fell dead from the sky.

Asking John to cook wasn't just about sparing Terry from the nightmare of preparing a meal for Brian Brown. The onus was on me to reassure Brown that there would be no shenanigans with the food, and I hoped that knowing the food was being prepared by a fellow traditionally married straight man would calm any fears Brown might have. (Google "Dan Savage" and "Gary Bauer" if you're curious about why Brown might need a little reassurance on this point. Mea culpa: I behaved terribly in 2000—but, you know, so did the national press corps, George W. Bush, Maureen Dowd, Nader voters, Joe Lieberman during his debate with Dick Cheney, Jeb Bush, Katherine Harris, the Brooks Brothers rioters . . .)

Mark Oppenheimer showed up next, about an hour before Brown was scheduled to arrive. Mark is an upbeat guy, and he did his best to lighten the mood. But Terry was tense and even I confessed to Mark that I was nervous—and pretty seriously jet-lagged too. Terry and I spent the previous two weeks in Munich and Stockholm, on a long-overdue vacation, and we hadn't readjusted to Seattle time.

John came over with trays of appetizers and laid them out on the kitchen counter. Terry laid out cocktail fixings. The film crew tested the equipment. The photographer from *The New York Times* lurked by the living room window, keeping a lookout for Brown.

"Here he comes!"

Brian Brown had arrived. I opened the front door and invited our guest in. Brian handed me a bottle of wine, and we shook hands. I showed Brown to the kitchen and introduced him to Terry and D.J.

Terry made mai tais for everyone—he even made one for Brown, a major concession on Terry's part—and Mark and Brian and I all carried our drinks out to the backyard, where we sat under an ancient apple tree and made small talk. All of this was less awkward, somehow, than any of us expected it to be. (Credit for that goes to Terry: He makes a wicked mai tai.) Brown was his usual blustery self, but with the debate topic off-limits until after dinner—those were Mark's rules—we had no choice but to find something else to talk about. Brown and I stumbled, again and again, onto things we had in common: activism, Catholicism, parentism.

John leaned out the back door and announced that dinner was on the table: local wild salmon with sweet corn, heirloom tomatoes, and new-potato gnocchi, followed by roasted peaches with an oat-and-almond crumble for dessert.

The first thing Brown saw when we walked into the dining room was a six-foot-tall plaster statue of Christ. There's a lot of Catholic kitsch in our dining room—there's a lot of Catholic kitsch in our living room, kitchen, bathrooms, and bedrooms. Most of the statues, crucifixes, rosaries, saint cards, and hymnals strewn all over our house belonged to my parents, grandparents, great-grandparents. Terry and I briefly debated moving all the Catholic kitsch to the basement. We didn't want Brown to score points by accusing us of being disrespectful. But we decided that while we would clean the house, we weren't going to scrub it. So instead, I explained to Brown, as he took in one of our larger pieces of kitsch, how I had stepped in to prevent my grandfather's Giant Plaster Jesus from going to a landfill.

We had agreed that there would be no discussion about the Bible—or about precisely how sinful and perverse gay people are—while D.J., in his collared shirt, sat with us during dinner. So the small talk continued through the meal. We talked about snowboarding (Terry, D.J., and I all snowboard); we talked about surfing (Brown grew up surfing; Terry and D.J. had just learned); we talked about schools and summer vacations.

The dinner dishes were cleared away and Mark reminded us of the rules: I would have twelve uninterrupted minutes to make my case;

Brian would have twelve uninterrupted minutes to make his. Then we could argue with each other, with Mark moderating to keep things focused and fair. The cameras would roll for one hour and only one hour.

Terry got up and walked out before the debate started. He had no intention of sitting at the table, or standing in our kitchen, and listening to Brown—or to me, for that matter. Terry doesn't see his equality—he doesn't see his humanity—as something that should be up for debate. Not anymore. For Terry, and for millions of other Americans, the debate is over: Human rights are universal, LGBT people are humans, we exist in this universe, and marriage is a human right. The end. Terry waited just long enough for D.J. to get out of his collared shirt, and then bolted from the house. He would pass the hour across the street, at John and Mishy's house, playing video games with their kids.

If you agree with Terry—the debate is over, LGBT people won, and you can't stand hearing from bigots—you can skip the debate, just like Terry did, by jumping ahead to page 266.

If you're the type of person who might enjoy attending CPAC, however, you should definitely keep reading.

Anyone who's been following the debate over marriage equality closely can predict how things unfolded. When I talked about "freedom," "equality," and "justice," Brown heard "moral chaos," "persecuting Christians," and "butt sex." When Brown talked about "tradition," "religious freedom," and "Natural Law," I heard "anachronism," "religious bigotry," and "double standards."

The formal topic of the debate, which was selected by Mark, was this: "Christianity is bad for LGBT Americans?"

The debate topic implicitly endorsed one of the two big lies pushed by NOM: There are Christians over here and the gays over there, they are two warring tribes, and a victory for the Gays is a defeat for the Christians and vice versa. In reality most LGBT Americans are Christians, many Christians are gay (Episcopalian Bishop Eugene Robinson comes immediately to mind), and not all straight Christians are anti-gay.

Christianity doesn't have to be bad for LGBT Americans. But many American Christians choose to be bad for and bad to their fellow citizens who happen to be LGBT. The existence of gay Christians and progressive and tolerant Christians, however, demonstrates that being anti-gay is a choice. No one is born that way. (NOM's other big lie: You can be for traditional marriage or you can be for gay marriage but you can't be for both. I'm a big supporter of "traditional" marriage, in the sense that I love and support my friends and family members who are in opposite-sex marriages. There's nothing Terry and I wouldn't do for John and Mishy, for example, or our married siblings. If they were in trouble—if their marriages were in trouble—and there was anything we could do to help, we would do it.)

Brown advanced the Natural Law argument against marriage equality again and again during our debate. The argument boils down to essentially this: Marriage is about—marriage is only about—male and female coming together, becoming one flesh, and making babies. Marriage bonds male and female together for life in recognition of this basic biological fact: man + woman = baby. Since two men can't make a baby, they can never become one flesh, so obviously two men shouldn't be allowed to marry.

And yet we allow infertile couples, elderly couples, and couples that don't want to have babies to marry. No one checks to make sure that married opposite-sex couples are consummating their marriages— there are more happy and purely companionate marriages out there than anyone realizes—and no one tells married straight couples who adopt, either by choice or necessity, that their marriages aren't real. We allow murderers on death row to marry, people who are physically incapable of engaging in sex to marry—so long as they're straight.[11]

The Natural Law argument isn't an argument at all. It's a head fake.

It's not NOM's only anti-marriage equality argument that's grounded in a ridiculous double standard. According to NOM, marriage isn't about the needs of adults, or the rights of adults, it's about the needs of children.[12] Marriage is about a child's right to his or her biological mother and father, married to one another, for life. Yet children—biological children, adopted children (who are also biological)—aren't mentioned in standard-issue marriage vows. The only time we're told that children define marriage is when same-sex couples want to marry. Never mind that many gay couples—a third of all gay couples—are raising children.

The double standards don't stop with children. Opponents of marriage equality tell us that marriage is defined not just by children, but by monogamy and faith—but, again, only when gay couples want to marry. Straight couples, married or not, can have children or not have children. Straight couples can be married without being monogamous and monogamous without being married. Straight couples can marry in church or they can marry at city hall. No one tells childless married couples that they aren't really married. No one tells nonmonogamous

---

11 Whatever happened to "anything is possible with God"? If an all-powerful God wanted Terry to have a baby, by God, Terry would have a baby.

12 A child needs a mother and a father, according to NOM, so gay marriage must be banned. But how does banning gay marriage provide children with mothers and fathers? Terry and I became parents long before gay marriage became legal in Washington State. John Corvino has fun with this argument in his book: Banning gay marriage will not prompt lesbian mothers to leave their same-sex partners and marry their sperm donors. And, as Corvino points out, if children need mothers and fathers, why isn't NOM campaigning against single parenthood? Or working to make it illegal for straight married couples to divorce after they've had children? If children "do best with their own married biological parents," as NOM argues, "what would follow? To put it bluntly, what would follow is that gay and lesbian couples should not kidnap children from their married biological parents. Back on Planet Earth, where gay men and lesbians are not involved in a mass-kidnapping scheme, it's less clear what would follow. Same-sex marriage never—and I mean *never*—takes children away from competent biological parents who want them."

married straight couples that they aren't really married. (There have certainly been no attempts to ban nonmonogamous heterosexual marriages!) And no one is attempting to ban atheists from marrying.

Hands down my favorite moment during the debate—the whole left-wing blogosphere's favorite—was a brief exchange about divorce. Brown repeatedly cited his Catholic faith as a reason why marriage should be restricted to opposite-sex couples only. The Catholic Church condemns gay sex and gay relationships, so same-sex couples—Catholic or not—should not be allowed to marry, according to Brown. But the Catholic Church regards divorce as sinful and Jesus explicitly condemns divorce. Would Brown support a ban on divorce?[13] For Catholics and non-Catholics alike?

> BROWN: No, because you believe something is wrong, doesn't mean you make it illegal.
> SAVAGE: Then why not the same policy toward civil gay marriage?
> BROWN: But that is—but again, there's a misunderstanding here. Gay marriage cannot exist. There cannot be a marriage of two men or two women. Just because the state—
> SAVAGE: It exists in Canada and Spain . . .
> BROWN: Just because the state says it's so, this is not based upon reality.

---

13 And, really, why isn't NOM—which gets its money from the Catholic Church—trying to ban divorce? Because that would touch on the rights of 95 percent of voters who happen to be straight. And while no one likes to think about getting divorced, most people can imagine what it must be like to be in a situation where they might want to avail themselves of the right to divorce. Few straight voters have ever imagined marrying someone of the same sex. And if all you have to do to be a "good" Christian—if all you have to do to be right with God and the pope and Brian Brown—is vote to deny others (same-sex couples) something you will never need (a license to marry someone of the same sex), why not vote against marriage rights for same-sex couples? That vote allows shallow people to demonstrate their "moral superiority" (and their lack of empathy) without requiring them to make a personal sacrifice. Like Bristol Palin, a straight person can go on having premarital sex and babies out of wedlock while considering herself a good Christian—so long as she opposes gay marriage. You wonder how Christ would feel about straight Christians setting the bar so low for themselves.

You can't argue with that kind of logic—because it's not logic. It's circular reasoning. And along with double standards and a set of goalposts on wheels, circular reasoning is all Brown's got.

Days later, on his blog, Brown wrote this about the Dinner Table Debate: "I took the opportunity to defend the Bible from the most radical charge Dan Savage hurled—that the Bible is a radically pro-slavery document. He uses that charge to undermine the moral authority of the Bible as the word of God. If it got slavery wrong, Dan maintains, what are the odds it gets human sexuality right? Zero, according to Dan Savage."

It annoys people who believe that the Bible is without error when you bring up slavery. The people it annoys most, of course, are the ones who insist that the Bible—which got something as easy and obvious as slavery wrong—somehow managed to get something as complicated as human sexuality right.

Here's what Brian said about slavery during our debate:

> As far as slavery goes, again, you're just completely wrong. Your interpretation of Scripture, Sam Harris's interpretation of Scripture, is completely wrong. If you look at the societies and cultures in which Jews lived, if you look at the Code of Hammurabi, for example, you see that a master over a slave had total control of life and death, could do anything at will, essentially. That is not the case in Judaism. Is a certain form of slavery accepted? Yes. But if you move to the New Testament, this is much more like indentured servitude. People would sell themselves essentially into a period of indentured servitude, usually between six and seven years, and then they could be released, and they could get money for that.

Hard to square Brown's claims about slavery with this from the Old Testament (Leviticus 25:44–46):

> As for your male and female slaves whom you may have: You may buy male and female slaves from the nations that are round about you . . . they may be your property. You may bequeath them to your sons after you, to inherit as a possession forever.

And it's even harder to square Brown's claims about slavery with this from the New Testament (Timothy 6:1–4):

> Let all who are under the yoke of slavery regard their masters as worthy of all honor, so that the name of God and the teaching may not be defamed. Those who have believing masters must not be disrespectful on the grounds that they are brethren; rather they must serve all the better since those who benefit from their services are believers and beloved. . . . If anyone teaches otherwise and does not agree with the sound words of our Lord Jesus Christ and the teaching which accords with Godliness, he is puffed up with conceit, he knows nothing.

But I let it go during the debate. There was so much else to argue about, so many double standards to point out, so much dizzying circular logic to chase after. But others quickly called bullshit on Brown's effort to exonerate the Bible.

"It is a routine lie of Christian apologetics that slavery in the Roman imperial period (in the first and second centuries CE, when the New Testament was being written) was largely indentured servitude of a temporary nature," Don M. Burrows, a scholar at the University of Minnesota wrote on his blog after watching the Dinner Table Debate.

"This is a flat-out lie. No scholar of antiquity that I am aware of would make such a claim, because all of our evidence says otherwise.

"In the Roman period," Burrows continues, "the period when the New Testament was actually written, slavery was largely the product of war. Captives were made slaves, and when they reproduced, those slaves belonged to the master. While it's true that slaves were freed in large numbers and could even go on to vote and have successful careers, that doesn't mean the institution itself was any less brutal or wrong, or that it was merely a temporary station used to make money. It was not."

In the Bible, Paul failed to make a distinction between "good" slavery (voluntary or involuntary servitude) and "bad" slavery (American-style slavery, a kind of slavery that existed at the time Paul was writing but that Paul—and Jesus and John the Baptist and the rest of the gang—failed to condemn). Pious Christian slave owners in the Civil War era certainly didn't regard slavery in any way as anti-Christian. Slave owners and their apologists leaned on the Bible.

"Slaveholding theologians had little trouble in demonstrating that the Bible did sanction slavery and that, specifically, God had sanctioned slaveholding among His chosen people of Israel," Elizabeth Fox-Genovese and Eugene D. Genovese wrote in the *Journal of the American Academy of Religion*. The abolitionists, they continue, "lost the battle of scholarly inquiry into the nature of the Israelite social system. The slaveholders' version stood up during the antebellum debates and has been overwhelmingly confirmed by modern scholarship. The abolitionists found themselves driven to argue that slavery contradicted the spirit of the Bible, especially of the New Testament, even though Jesus and the Apostles, who denounced every possible sin, nowhere spoke against it."

In fairness, as these scholars noted, the Christian opponents of slavery in the United States also cited the Bible. Modern Christians who are uncomfortable with the Bible's clear and unambiguous support for and acceptance of slavery—or those who aren't aware of it (because they're incapable of googling New Testament and *slavery* for themselves)—will sometimes toss this fact down like a trump card. But while the actions of Christians who fought slavery speaks well of them, their actions do not exonerate the Bible or erase "slaves, obey your earthly masters" from the New Testament.

The Bible got slavery wrong. It got other things right—the Golden Rule, the Greatest Commandment—and yes, some people were inspired to combat what the Bible got wrong ("slaves, obey your earthly masters") with what the Bible managed to get right. (Galatians 3:28: "There is neither Jew nor Greek, there is neither slave nor free, there is no male and female, for you are all one in Christ Jesus.") The Bible is a sprawling and contradictory text and bad people have used the Bible to justify bigotry and oppression and good people have used the Bible to fight bigotry and oppression. That only shows that the Bible is only as good and decent as the person reading it.

But even if Brown were correct—even if they practiced a kinder, gentler form of slavery when the Bible was being assembled (and he is not correct)—there's no kinder, gentler way to stone your daughter to death for not being a virgin on her wedding night. (How many brides were stoned to death for failing to bleed when they lost their virginities to their husbands on their wedding nights?)

Even if the Bible got slavery right, it still got that—and a great deal else—tragically wrong.

If you watched the Dinner Table Debate on YouTube—http://www .youtube.com/watch?v=oG804t0WG-c—you only saw the first hour. Brian, Mark, and I continued to argue long after the cameras were turned off; the camera crew joined in after we stopped filming, and John, leaning against the counter in the kitchen, lobbed some questions our way. A second bottle of wine was opened.

Terry had returned after an hour, expecting that the debate would be over, and he was annoyed to find us still deep in discussion. After another hour passed, Terry began to get angry—with me and with Mark. The camera crew had packed up and left, but Mark and Brian and I were still sitting at the dining room table, still arguing, and, as far as Terry was concerned, enjoying ourselves far too much. At one point I looked up and Terry was standing in the door to the dining room, directly behind Brian Brown, making slicing motions across his neck and mouthing the word "ENOUGH."

With no sign that the debate would ever stop—Mark kept peppering Brown with questions—Terry finally marched into the dining room, walked around the table, faced Brian Brown, and said that he had one question for him.

"Do you think our son should be taken away from us?"

Brian made an effort to look pained. He almost pulled it off.

"You shouldn't ask me a question when you know you won't like the answer," Brown said.

Terry took a breath, shot a look at me that said "three weeks in Hawaii," then turned to Brown, raised his arm, and pointed a finger at the front door.

"Get the fuck out of my house," Terry said.

Brown got his moment of intolerance. I'm sure he was disappointed that it wasn't captured on film, but here it is in print, as a consolation prize. Terry refused to tolerate Brown's intolerance—well, that's not entirely fair. Terry had tolerated Brian's intolerance for nearly four hours. But he had reached his limit and he couldn't tolerate Brown's intolerance for another minute longer. It's too bad the moment wasn't captured on film: If it had been, Terry wouldn't have to pay for a drink in a gay bar ever again.

Brown didn't respond to Terry. He looked at Mark and said, "Well, I guess it's time to go then."

Terry crossed through the living room and opened the front door as Mark and Brian rose from the table and made their way to the foyer.

They were standing by the door facing me, their backs to Terry, as I shook Brown's hand one last time. Terry was standing behind Mark, quietly seething, holding the door open. When Mark said he had just one more question for us—just one more—Terry picked up an imaginary knife and started stabbing Mark in the back.

"Who do you think is winning?" Mark asked. "Your side, Dan? Or yours, Brian?"

Our side was winning, I said: An unbroken series of polls showed that a majority of Americans now supported marriage equality. Brian said his side was winning: An unbroken string of victories at the ballot box—thirty-two in a row—showed that majorities of Americans, whenever they are given a chance to vote, reject same-sex marriage. Every single time marriage equality had been on the ballot, Brown pointed out, voters had rejected it.

"We are on a winning streak that shows no signs of stopping," Brown said.

Three months later NOM's winning streak came to an abrupt end when majorities in Washington, Maine, and Maryland voted to legalize same-sex marriage, and voters in Minnesota declined to add an anti-gay-marriage amendment to their state constitution.

The tide is turning and we're winning.[14] But Brown isn't losing. This

---

14 As of this writing, the Supreme Court has taken up two cases challenging bans on gay marriage. Even if we lose there, as NOM predicts we will (the same NOM that predicted we would lose in Washington, Maryland, Maine, and Minnesota), we will eventually prevail. E. J. Graff, a scholar and writer on issues of social justice and human rights, reminded readers in a posting on the Supreme Court cases on *The American Prospect* blog of this: "The Court will not and cannot invalidate existing marriages between same-sex couples. Those have been upheld by courts and legislatures, and accepted by citizens. Nine states have decided to marry same-sex couples. That will remain. Four states voted on the side of marriage equality just over a month ago. Citizens of three of those states voted to let same-sex couples marry while one, Minnesota, voted against a gay-marriage ban. It wasn't 'far-left, activist courts' championing same-sex marriage. Those were activist voters. And the nine justices noticed. They know which way the wind is blowing. The justices might not like to admit it, but they know not to get far out ahead of—or behind—the prevailing politics. Within the next two years, several more states will join the marriage-equality column. Minnesota, Rhode Island, Delaware, Oregon, Illinois, and New Jersey all look very good. Every state we win influences the country and the states around it."

isn't a zero-sum game. Nothing has been taken from straight couples in states where all couples can marry. We all win when everyone is free. It's just that some of us, sadly, are incapable of seeing that.

So who won the debate?

Terry did, obviously. I mean, come on.[15]

"Let me pose a question to the Dan Savages of the world," Brown wrote on his blog after our dinner date. "Once gay people were a powerless and defenseless minority. Now, you have organized, protested, and become powerful through the use of democratic freedoms and intellectual debate, a powerful cultural force in our time. What use do you intend to make of your power?"

Well, Brian, I can't speak for all the Dan Savages of the world, and there are quite a few—sorry guys, when I am being attacked by Fox News and their devoted followers, I am sure you have to deal with a lot of misdirected anger too—but I'll take this question.

---

15 According to the commenters on YouTube and at *The New York Times*, I won the debate. A lot of people gave the win to Brown, of course, particularly his friends in the religious right. But at least one person in Brown's camp thought I had won: my ol' buddy Peter LaBarbera. Peter declared me the winner during an episode of *Americans for Truth Radio Hour*. (I challenge anyone to get through an entire hour of *that*.) I won the debate, Peter and his guest, Pastor John Kirkwood, agreed, before it had even begun. Here's a taste:

> KIRKWOOD: So [Brian Brown] shows up at the house. The moderator is a *New York Times*, the head of the belief column in *The New York Times*, who happens to be an agnostic! An agnostic, although he played the Jew card, he said, "I'm Jewish," at one point to try and disagree with Brian on the Bible and it made no sense but he wasn't called on it. So here's an agnostic from *The New York Times* as the moderator. He didn't do a bad . . . he didn't do a bad job. But basically the way it starts is like a Dan Savage infomercial. I mean you have this NOM-guy show up, right? Mr. Tough Talk. He shows up with a bottle of wine! Hands Dan Savage a bottle of wine! Dan Savage treats him to this famous chef who lives down the street from him, makes this incredible meal.
>
> LABARBERA: God help us!
>
> KIRKWOOD: So it opens up with Dan Savage introducing him to his partner, Terry. He said, "This is my husband, Terry. This is my son . . ." because they have an adopted son. And it looks pretty much like, you know, *Leave It to Beaver,* but the really, really sinister way. . . . It came out normalizing Dan Savage!

But before I respond to the question, Brian, let's get this out of the way: I can see what you're doing with that "You gays are *sooooo* politically powerful, Dan, such a powerful cultural force to be reckoned with!" stuff.

"The 'gays are politically powerful' theme is part of a long-standing effort to falsely paint lesbians and gay men as wealthy, privileged, sophisticated people who don't need legal protections against discrimination," Kate Kendell, the executive director of the National Center for Lesbian Rights, argues. "It is a dangerous idea, and totally false."

But on to your question, Brian. What do the Dan Savages of the world intend to do with our power?

Despite your claims that we're the intolerant ones, Brian, LGBT people are willing to tolerate people who dislike us. We're willing to tolerate your marriages and your churches. We're willing to tolerate your contempt. What we can't tolerate—what we will not tolerate—is the status quo. So long as gay people are not equal under the law, so long as organizations like NOM are working to deny us full equality, we're going to fight you.

What are our plans for after we achieve full equality?

You can rest assured, Brian, that we aren't planning to amend state constitutions to prevent straight people from marrying. We have no desire to pass laws blocking adoptions by straight couples. We will fight until we have secured equal protection under the law—for all LGBT people, not just those of us who wish to marry—and then, well, then we're done. We will remain vigilant, of course, to protect our rights, but there's no top-secret, post-equality gay agenda that you need to worry about. We have no plans to seize control of the gold supply. We are not going to force the National Institutes of Health to divert funds from cancer research to genetically engineered unicorns. Peter LaBarbera will not be kicked off Twitter. Tony Perkins will not be dragged to gay weddings in chains and forced to serve as flower girl.

Once we achieve equality under the law straight people still will be free to disapprove of our marriages—and priests and ministers and rabbis will be free to refuse to officiate at our weddings—just as straight people are free to disapprove of each other's marriages right now. Literally nothing will change. Just as people are still free to believe that Jews should have to live in walled ghettos, women shouldn't be allowed to vote, and black people shouldn't be able to sit at their lunch counters, the Brian Browns of the world will still be free to believe that gay people shouldn't be allowed to marry. The only difference will be this: You won't be free to prevent us from marrying, Brian, just as anti-Semites aren't free to compel Jews to live in ghettos, misogynists aren't free to stop women from voting, and racists aren't free to refuse service to black people.

And after we've secured equal protection under the law, Brian, we will struggle to get by, knowing that there are still people out there who hate us. We will pause now and then, at brunch or before the curtain goes up at a Broadway show, to silently reflect on the haters and bigots, and we will ache for the LGBT kids unlucky enough to be born into hateful and bigoted families. But we will not hound you or persecute you. And, no, expecting you to obey the law—expecting you to obey the same antidiscrimination laws that prevent your fellow bigots from discriminating against people based on their race, gender, and faith—is not persecution. A hotel owner doesn't have to approve of interracial marriage, but he can't refuse to rent a room to an interracial couple. A hotel owner may not approve of my marriage, but it is illegal in Washington State for him to refuse to rent a room to a gay couple just the same.

Don't get me wrong: It would be nice, of course, if you could get past your hatred and bigotry. Nice, but not necessary.

Do you mind if we touch on the slavery stuff for just another second, Brian?

A viewer of *The 700 Club* recently put this question to Pat Robertson: "If America was founded as a Christian nation, why did we allow slavery?"

"Like it or not, if you read the Bible, in the Old Testament, slavery was permitted," Robertson responded. "We have moved in our conception of the value of human beings until we realized that slavery was terribly wrong." (Pat was half-right: Slavery was permitted—slavery was endorsed—in the Old Testament and the New Testament.)

LGBT Americans aren't asking Christians to do anything that Christians haven't done before. Christians are simply being asked to, once again, "move in [their] conception of the value of human beings"—in this instance, human beings who happen to be gay, lesbian, bisexual, or transgender.

We know you can do it. You've done it before, on race and other issues, and millions of American Christians have already moved in their conception of the value of LGBT human beings. We wouldn't be seeing the polling data or election night returns we're seeing, without the support of millions of Christian Americans.

But if you can't move in your conception of our value as human beings, well, we'll settle for your grudging tolerance. And frankly, Brian, you don't have much of a choice. Your efforts and the efforts of other conservative Christians to force us back into the closet by breathing new life into the old stigmas and hatreds aren't working. We're not going anywhere. Just look at the polls. Just look at the gay and lesbian couples marrying in Washington, Maryland, Maine, and the other six states where same-sex marriage is legal. It's over, Brian. You've already lost. The only question that remains is how much time and money you intend to waste between now and the advent of full civil equality for LGBT people.

You anti-gay bigots will have to adjust, just as anti-Semites, sexists, and racists have had to adjust before you. But, again, you will still be free—completely free—to be privately bigoted. You won't have to welcome us into your homes or your hearts. But you can no longer demand that the government persecute us and warp our lives to pander to your bigotry, soothe your insecurities, or give your religious beliefs preference over others. Your biases should not, and one day soon they will not, have the force of law.

Your biases will continue to warp lives, Brian, but only yours. You will stew in them and grow to be an embarrassment to your children and grandchildren. Because you are on the wrong side of history.

Or, hey, here's a better idea: Join us here in the twenty-first century. Come to brunch. Have you seen *The Book of Mormon*, Brian? I know a couple of guys in the show. I can get you a pair of tickets. You should take the wife.

Epilogue

Four months after Brian Brown came to dinner, I was standing on the steps of Seattle's city hall hoping that someone I'd met in a Seattle park a decade earlier was alive to see this day.

Kerry Park is one of Seattle's smaller parks. It perches on the south slope of Queen Anne Hill, just northwest of downtown, and boasts sweeping views—parks can be *such* braggarts—of the Space Needle, Elliott Bay, Mount Rainier, and downtown Seattle. (Frasier Crane's condo would have been located just behind Kerry Park, if Frasier Crane's condo had existed in Seattle and not on a soundstage in Los Angeles.) Locals and tourists crowd the park at all hours, day and night, all year long, to admire the view. (Or to take pictures of the view, which they upload to Instagram, so that they—the people taking the photographs—can be admired by their friends.)

I was in Kerry Park on a clear winter day, years ago, in the pre-Instagram era, when a limo pulled up. A wedding party spilled out. The photographer positioned the bride and the groom on the grass near the edge of the park. The newlyweds posed for a wedding portrait with the city and Space Needle behind them. As the bride and groom stood holding each other, with the photographer snapping away, the small crowd in the park began to applaud. Everyone was beaming. People shouted, "Congratulations!" as the newlywed couple climbed back into their limo.

I was standing on the sidewalk, at the edge of the park, near a couple of guys that I knew.

Well, I didn't *know* them. I didn't know them *personally*. (And, no, I didn't know them *biblically*.) But I knew them and they knew me. They were a couple of late-middle-aged gay men, a decade or two older than I was at the time, out for a walk with their dogs. I caught the eye of one of the guys while we were clapping for the straight couple getting in the limo. He shook his head, smiled wanly, and shrugged.

"We're always happy for *them*," he said. "Would it kill them to be happy for *us*?"

Terry and I got married at Seattle's city hall on December 9, 2012, the first day that same-sex marriage was legal in Washington State. We had married in Vancouver, British Columbia, in 2005, on our tenth anniversary. Our Canadian marriage was legally recognized by the state of Washington on December 6, the first day same-sex couples could apply for marriage licenses, so our city hall wedding was more of a renewal of vows. But we had fought long and hard for the right to marry in the state in which we lived, and we wanted that piece of paper. We slipped off our wedding rings—a pair of silver rings with skulls on them that D.J. picked out when he was six years old (he wanted us to remember that it's "until death do you part" every time we looked at our left hands)—a moment before our ceremony, quickly exchanged them, and then put them back on each other's fingers.

When Brian Brown came to dinner, Terry and I weren't legally married in Washington State. We are now, thanks to the voters here. (I'm proud to say that same-sex marriage passed by a wider margin in Washington than in the other two states that legalized same-sex marriage on Election Day of 2012.) Terry and I have gained something— the rights and protections of marriage that the state of Washington controls (I get to decide where Terry is buried if he dies before me); the federal Defense of Marriage Act (DOMA) still deprives us of the rights and protections of marriage controlled by the federal government

(Terry will not be able to collect my Social Security benefits if I die before him)—but Brian Brown and his wife lost nothing. Something was given to us but nothing was taken from them.

One hundred and forty-four other couples married at Seattle city hall on that rainy Sunday in early December. Five pop-up wedding chapels had been erected in the lobby of the building, and everywhere you looked you saw couples that had been together five, ten, twenty, even forty years exchanging vows in front of family members and friends. It was impossible to be at city hall that day and not be moved.

But for me the most moving moment came after our ceremony. A huge crowd had gathered on the steps outside city hall. All day long a brass band at the bottom of the steps played wedding marches. The names of each newly married couple were announced to the crowd as they exited the building. Each time the crowd burst into applause and cheers, throwing rice and flower petals. People shouted, "Congratulations!"

And almost all of the well-wishers gathered outside city hall on that glorious gray Sunday were straight people.

As Terry and I walked down the steps—moments after we were married by a straight judge, our marriage officially witnessed by two straight men we both admire (my brother Billy, who was the first person I came out to, and Seattle's mayor, Mike McGinn)—I thought of those guys in Kerry Park. On the steps of city hall, Terry's hand in mine, I quietly hoped that those guys were still around and that they were still together.

I hope they were one of the couples that married at city hall on December 9. I hope they got to walk down those steps. I hope they had lived long enough to see a crowd of straight people cheering for them. I hope they got to see it. *They* were happy for *us*.

Not all of them, of course, certainly not the Brian Browns and Rick Santorums and Maggie Gallaghers and Peter LaBarberas. But a growing majority of straight people are happy for us, just as we've always been happy for them. We felt it on election night, November 6, 2012, when marriage equality won in Washington, Maine, and Maryland, and we saw it—we saw it with our own eyes—on the steps outside of Seattle's city hall on Sunday, December 9, 2012.

Acknowledgments

I'd like to thank my superhumanly patient and always supportive literary agent, Elizabeth Wales, as well as my talented, organized, and insightful editor, and occasional schedule dominatrix, Ingrid Emerick, without whom this book would have been a lot later and a lot longer. I'd like to thank the smart and creative folks at Dutton, especially Brian Tart, Jessica Horvath, and Amanda Walker. I am deeply indebted to Ezra Klein and Mark Oppenheimer and Eli Sanders and John Corvino, all of who took the time to read certain chapters of this book and offer suggestions. I'd also like to thank Evan Wolfson, Kate Kendell, Alice Dreger, Rob Tisinai, Joe Jervis, John Aravosis, E. J. Graff, Jeremy Hooper, and Dominic Holden for their help. Thanks also to all of my bosses at *The Stranger*—Tim Keck, Nancy Hartunian, Christopher Frizzelle, Bethany Clement, Ira Glass, Lisa Pollak, Julie Snyder, and Nancy Updike—for giving me the time and space to work on this project.

I'm very grateful to my brother, Bill Savage, for giving the manuscript such a careful read and offering such invaluable comments. As a writer, it's a total bonus to have a brother who is a professor of English at Northwestern University, and even better to have said brother with a top-notch copy editor for a girlfriend. So thank you, Kelly, for putting our personal differences aside long enough to catch some potentially embarrassing mistakes. I promise to be nicer to you in the future.

Many thanks to Brian Pines, Seth Levy, Stephanie Laffin, and Brett

Peters for their support on this and every other project I work on. I'd like to thank Bethany Davis and Dave Valencia for helping to compile the excellent endnotes, a job I dreaded and in the end didn't have to do myself. A huge thanks to Seattle-based photographer and social-media innovator Larae Lobdell for allowing me to use the photograph that appears on the cover of the book. I'd like to thank the baristas at the Fourth and Union Starbucks in downtown Seattle, where I wrote massive chunks of this book, as well as the bartenders at Smith and Liberty. I'd like to thank Pope Benedict XVI for quitting, but I wished he'd done it sooner. I trust that my readers were nimble enough to read "retired pope" whenever "current pope" appeared in the text.

And last but certainly not least, many thanks and much love to my son, D.J., and my husband, Terry. You guys not only put up with the sleep-deprived, stressed-out jerk I become when I'm writing a book, but you graciously allow me to write about you. Here's hoping you're never in a position to return the favor.

Finally, I'd like to thank the person I forgot to thank. You were the best.

Notes

1. At a Loss

9   *Catholics have long realized that their own grasp of certain things, especially sex, has a validity that is lost on the celibate male hierarchy:* Garry Wills, "Contraception's Con Men," *The New York Review of Books*, February 15, 2012, http://www.nybooks.com/blogs/nyrblog/2012/feb/15/contraception -con-men/. Copyright © 2012 by Garry Wills, used by permission of The Wylie Agency, LLC.

13   *Ninety-eight percent of Catholic women use birth control:* Rachel K. Jones and Joerg Dreweke, *Countering Conventional Wisdom: New Evidence on Religion and Contraceptive Use* (New York: Guttmacher Institute, 2011), http://www .guttmacher.org/pubs/Religion-and-Contraceptive-Use.pdf.

13   *Ninety-three percent of Catholics support the use of condoms to prevent disease and HIV transmission:* Humphrey Taylor, *The Harris Poll* no. 78, 2005, http://www.harrisinteractive.com/vault/Harris-Interactive-Poll-Research -New-Finds-Different-Religious-Groups-H-2005-10.pdf.

13   *Seventy percent of American Catholics think abortion should be legal:* Catholics for Choice, "Catholic Voters' Presidential Preference, Issue Priorities, and Opinion of Certain Church Policies," survey, Belden Russonello Strategists, 2012, http://www.catholicsforchoice.org/news/pr/2012/documents/CFC -BRS_2012_Election_Study.pdf.

13   *Sixty-seven percent of Catholics believe premarital sex is morally acceptable:* David Morris, "U.S. Catholics Admire, Disagree with Pope," ABC News, October 15, 2012, http://abcnews.go.com/WNT/story?id=129364&page=1.

13   *Masturbation is an intrinsically and gravely disordered action:* Catholic Church, *Catechism of the Catholic Church* (Vatican City: Libreria Editrice Vaticana, 1993), 2352.

14   *The deliberate use of the sexual faculty, for whatever reason, outside of marriage is essentially contrary to its purpose:* Ibid.

14   *The natural purpose of sex is procreation:* Garry Wills, "Contraception's Con Men," *The New York Review of Books,* February 15, 2012, http://www.nybooks .com/blogs/nyrblog/2012/feb/15/contraception-con-men/. Copyright © 2012 by Garry Wills, used by permission of The Wylie Agency, LLC.

15   *For* Homo sapiens, *sex is primarily about establishing and maintaining relationships:* Christopher Ryan, "What Rick Santorum Doesn't Know About Sex,"

Psychology Today, January 6, 2012, http://www.psychologytoday.com/blog/sex
-dawn/201201/what-rick-santorum-doesn-t-know-about-sex.

15   *The vast majority of species have sex only to reproduce—a function reflected
      in a very low ratio of sex-acts-to-births:* Ibid.

2. It's Never Okay to Cheat (Except When It Is)

27   *A recent CNN story offering tips on how to save a "mediocre marriage" sug-
      gested divorce:* Pamela Haag, "Options for Your Mediocre Marriage," *CNN Liv-
      ing,* CNN, June 2, 2011, http://www.cnn.com/2011/LIVING/06/02/marriage
      .with.issues/index.html?iref=allsearch.

30   *According to anthropologists, only 1 in 6 societies enforces monogamy as a
      rule:* Daniel Engber, "Are Humans Monogamous or Polygamous: Archaeolo-
      gists, Anthropologists, and Biologists Agree: It's Complicated," Health & Sci-
      ence, *Slate,* October 9, 2012, http://www.slate.com/articles/health_and_science
      /human_evolution/2012/10/are_humans_monogamous_or_polygamous
      _the_evolution_of_human_mating_strategies_.html.

33   *Adultery has been documented in every human culture studied:* Christopher
      Ryan and Cacilda Jethá, *Sex at Dawn: How We Mate, Why We Stray, and What
      It Means for Modern Relationships* (New York: Harper, 2010).

33   *Defenders of "traditional marriage," circa 1750, not 1950, objected to anyone
      marrying for something so unstable as a feeling:* Stephanie Coontz, *Marriage,
      a History: From Obedience to Intimacy, or How Love Conquered Marriage* (New
      York: Viking, 2005).

35   *And the pressure to perfectly execute monogamy over the life of a marriage:*
      Meg Barker, *Rewriting the Rules: An Integrative Guide to Love, Sex and Relation-
      ships* (Oxford: Routledge, 2012).

38   *On our life together I want you to understand I shall not hold you to any medi-
      eval code of faithfulness:* Amelia Earhart, Letter to George Putnam, February
      7, 1931, quoted in Mary S. Lovell, *The Sound of Wings: The Life of Amelia Earhart*
      (New York: St. Martin's Press, 1989).

3. Sex Dread

42   *Taylor was "given no information" about contraception, condoms, or disease
      prevention in the abstinence-only sex-ed classes:* Teresa Watanabe, "Clovis
      Unified District Sued over Abstinence-Only Sex Education," *Los Angeles Times,*
      August 22, 2012, http://articles.latimes.com/2012/aug/22/local/la-me-sex-ed
      -20120822.

44   *While the teen pregnancy rate in the United States has been dropping for years
      (hitting a six-decade low in 2010):* Brady E. Hamilton and Stephanie J. Ventura,
      "Birth Rates for U.S. Teenagers Reach Historic Lows for All Age and Ethnic
      Groups," *NCHS Data Brief 89,* National Center for Health Statistics, 2012, http://
      www.cdc.gov/nchs/data/databriefs/db89.htm.

44   *The United States still has far and away the highest teen pregnancy rates in the
      industrialized world:* "Sexual Experience and Contraceptive Use Among Fe-
      male Teens—United States, 1995, 2002, and 2006–2010," *Morbidity and Mortal-
      ity Weekly Report (MMWR)* 61(17), Centers for Disease Control and Prevention,

May 4, 2012, http://www.cdc.gov/mmwr/preview/mmwrhtml/mm6117a1 .htm?s_cid=mm6117a1_e.

44   *The teen pregnancy rate in Mississippi, an abstinence-only state, is nearly four times higher than the teen pregnancy rate in New Hampshire:* Brady E. Hamilton and Stephanie J. Ventura, "Birth Rates for U.S. Teenagers Reach Historic Lows for All Age and Ethnic Groups," *NCHS Data Brief 89,* National Center for Health Statistics, 2012, http://www.cdc.gov/nchs/data/databriefs/db89.htm.

44   *Not only does Mississippi lead the country in teen births, but it takes first, second, and third place in reported cases of gonorrhea, chlamydia, and syphilis:* NCHHSTP State Profiles, National Center for HIV/AIDS, Viral Hepatitis, STD, and TB Prevention, Centers for Disease Control and Prevention, 2010, http:// www.cdc.gov/nchhstp/stateprofiles/usmap.htm.

44   *Teenagers who receive comprehensive sex ed are 60 percent less likely to get pregnant:* "Sex Ed Can Help Prevent Teen Pregnancy," *The Washington Post,* March 24, 2008, http://www.washingtonpost.com/wp-dyn/content/article /2008/03/24/AR2008032401515.html.

45   *The failure to provide young people with comprehensive sex education:* Naomi Cahn and June Carbone, "Did the Pro-Life Movement Lead to More Single Moms?," *Slate,* January 22, 2013, http://www.slate.com/articles/double_x /doublex/2013/01/did_the_pro_life_movement_lead_to_more_single_moms .html.

45   *In 2012 the governor of Tennessee signed into law an abstinence-only education bill that included a provision banning teachers:* Tim Ghianni, "Tennessee Governor Signs Controversial 'Gateway Sexual Activity' Bill," Reuters, May 11, 2012, http://www.reuters.com/article/2012/05/12/us-usa-politics-tennessee -idUSBRE84B00D20120512.

45   *There is abstinence-only sex education, and there's abstinence-based sex ed:* Laurie Abraham, "Teaching Good Sex," *The New York Times Magazine,* November 16, 2011.

46   *Researchers at York University in Toronto interviewed twelve hundred teenagers between the ages of thirteen and nineteen:* Sarah Flicker et al., *Sexpress: The Toronto Teen Survey Report* (Toronto, ON: Planned Parenthood Toronto, 2009), http://www.ppt.on.ca/teen_survey.asp.

46   *As fascinated as we all are with spermatogenesis and how egg meets sperm:* Zosia Bielski, "Teens Want to Learn About Healthy Sex, Not Just Sexual Health," *The Globe and Mail,* June 2, 2009.

4. The GGG Spot

54   *Savage, [for] all his experience, does not know what women are like:* Maggie Gallagher, "Dan Savage Educates Your Children?," *NOM* (blog), April 5, 2011, http://www.nomblog.com/7091/.

57   *[Sexual activity] was related to self-reported satisfaction for both sexes:* Pamela C. Regan et al., "Partner Preferences: What Characteristics Do Men and Women Desire in Their Short-Term Sexual and Long-Term Romantic Partners?," *Journal of Psychology & Human Sexuality* 12 (2000).

59   *Your letter is also eloquent counter-testimony to those who say loving partners should try to accommodate each other's sexual kinks:* Emily Yoffe, "Reign of

Terror," Dear Prudence, *Slate,* June 28, 2012, http://www.slate.com/articles
/life/dear_prudence/2012/06/dear_prudie_my_boss_pantsed_someone_at
_work_should_i_tattle_.html.

63   *Five years ago, sex columnist Dan Savage suggested that, when it comes to sex,
we should all aim to be GGG:* Debby Herbenick, "Science Proves it, Dan Savage
Is Right," *Salon,* September 11, 2012, http://www.salon.com/2012/09/12
/science_proves_it_dan_savage_is_right.

63   *The study Herbenick refers to was conducted by researchers at the University
of Arizona and Hanover College:* Tricia J. Burke and Valerie J. Young, "Sexual
Transformations and Intimate Behaviors in Romantic Relationships," *Journal
of Sex Research* 49 (2012).

64   *And this wasn't the only study that seems to prove the GGG concept:* A. Muise, E.
A. Impett, A. Kogan, and S. Desmarais, "Keeping the Spark Alive: Being Motivated to Meet a Partner's Sexual Needs Sustains Sexual Desire in Long-term Romantic Relationships," *Social Psychological and Personality Science* (2012), http://
spp.sagepub.com/content/early/2012/08/26/1948550612457185.abstract.

66   *Underlying all of Savage's principles, abbreviations, and maxims is a pragmatism:* Benjamin J. Dueholm, "Rules of Misbehavior," *Washington Monthly*,
March/April 2011, http://www.washingtonmonthly.com/features/2011/1103
.dueholm.html.

5. The Choicer Challenge

67–68 *On a subsequent appearance on CNN's* **Piers Morgan Tonight,** *Cain reiterated
his stand—he told Morgan that he believed being gay is a "personal choice":*
On Top Magazine staff, "Herman Cain Tells Piers Morgan That Being Gay Is
'Personal Choice,'" *On Top Magazine,* October 20, 2011, http://www.ontopmag
.com/article.aspx?id=9844.

69   *There's even a great, big book on the subject published by Oxford University
Press that has "science" in the title:* Simon LeVay, *Gay, Straight, and the Reason
Why: The Science of Sexual Orientation* (New York: Oxford University Press,
2010).

71   *Then in 2012 a groundbreaking study undertaken by the University of California, Santa Barbara:* "Study Finds Epigenetics, Not Genetics, Underlies Homosexuality," press release from the National Institute for Mathematical and
Biological Synthesis, December 11, 2012, http://www.nimbios.org/press/FS
_homosexuality.

71   *According to Jason Koebler of* **U.S. News & World Report,** *who reported on the
study:* Jason Koebler, "Scientists May Finally Have Unlocked the Puzzle of Why
People Are Gay," *U.S. News & World Report,* December, 11, 2012, http://www
.usnews.com/news/articles/2012/12/11/scientists-may-have-finally
-unlocked-puzzle-of-why-people-are-gay.

6. My Son Comes Out

76   *In 2000, the same year* The Kid *was published, there were sixty-five hundred
adoptions by gay American couples, according to a study by the Williams Institute:* Julie Bolcer, "Gay Adoptions Triple over Last Decade," *Advocate,* October

21, 2011, http://www.advocate.com/news/daily-news/2011/10/21/gay-adoptions
-triple-over-last-decade.

77 *A study by the Palm Center, formerly at the University of California and now independent, found that the repeal of the ban on openly gay soldiers has had "no overall negative impact":* Lila Shapiro, "Don't Ask Don't Tell Study Shows No Negative Effects on Military One Year After Repeal," *The Huffington Post,* September 10, 2012, http://www.huffingtonpost.com/2012/09/10/dont-ask -dont-tell-study_n_1868892.html.

77 *In 2012 the head of the largest "ex-gay" group in the country, Alan Chambers of Exodus International, admitted:* Andrew Potts, "Exodus International President Admits Sexual Orientation Change Impossible: Alan Chambers Becomes the Latest of a String of Senior Exodus International Leaders to Admit That People Cannot Change Their Sexuality Through Therapy," *Gay Star News,* July 7, 2012, http://www.gaystarnews.com/article/exodus-international-president -admits-sexual-orientation-change-impossible070712.

78 *And Fischer believes that children with gay parents should be* kidnapped *because:* "Bryan Fischer of American Family Association Slams Gay Marriage Victories, Same-Sex Parents," *The Huffington Post,* November 20, 2012, http:// www.huffingtonpost.com/2012/11/20/bryan-fischer-gay-marriage_n_2162477 .html.

78 *The study, authored by University of Texas sociologist Mark Regnerus, was funded by two anti-gay think tanks:* Brian Tashman, "Harry Jackson Cites Dubious Studies to Claim Gay Parents Harm Children," *Right Wing Watch,* September 24, 2012, http://www.rightwingwatch.org/content/harry-jackson-cites-dubious -studies-claim-gay-parents-harm-children.

78 *Among the problems is the paper's definition of 'lesbian mothers' and 'gay fathers':* Tom Bartlett, "Controversial Gay-Parenting Study is Severely Flawed, Journal's Audit Finds," *The Chronicle of Higher Education,* July 26, 2012, http:// chronicle.com/blogs/percolator/controversial-gay-parenting-study-is -severely-flawed-journals-audit-finds/30255.

79 *Case in point: UCLA released a study, published in October of 2012 in the* American Journal of Orthopsychiatry, *comparing (and tracking over time) children who were adopted:* Justin A. Lavner, Jill Waterman, Letitia Anne Peplau, "Can Gay and Lesbian Parents Promote Healthy Development in High-Risk Children Adopted from Foster Care?," *American Journal of Orthopsychiatry* 82, no. 4 (October 2012): 465–72, http://onlinelibrary.wiley.com/doi/10.1111/j.1939-0025.2012 .01176.x/abstract.

79 *The Academy supports the legal adoption of children by [same-sex] coparents:* American Academy of Pediatrics, "Coparent or Second-Parent Adoption by Same-Sex Parents," *Pediatrics: Official Journal of the American Academy of Pediatrics:* 338–41, http://pediatrics.aappublications.org/content/109/2/339.full .pdf.

82 *Marriage equality is socially liberal inasmuch:* Andrew Sullivan, "The Conservative Case for Gay Marriage (Again)," *The Daily Beast,* December 29, 2007, http://andrewsullivan.thedailybeast.com/2007/12/reihan-on-socia.html.

82 *We exist. We already exist. Our relationships exist, our children exist:* Mari Herreras, "Australian Labor Senator Louise Pratt: 'We Exist. . . . Stop Pretending That We Don't,'" *Tucson Weekly,* September 26, 2012, http://www.tucsonweekly.com

/TheRange/archives/2012/09/26/australian-labor-senator-louise-pratt-we-exist
-stop-pretending-that-we-dont.

83 *According to a Gallup poll conducted in 2011, the average American believes that 25 percent of the population is gay:* Lymari Morales, "U.S. Adults Estimate That 25% of Americans Are Gay or Lesbian: Those with Lower Incomes, the Less Educated, Women, and Young People Give the Highest Estimates," *Gallup Politics*, May 27, 2011, http://www.gallup.com/poll/147824/adults-estimate -americans-gay-lesbian.aspx.

90 *In January of 2011,* The New York Times *reported data that the Census Bureau had gathered on gay families:* Sabrina Tavernise, "Parenting by Gays More Common in the South, Census Shows," *The New York Times,* January 18, 2011, http://www.nytimes.com/2011/01/19/us/19gays.html?_r=1&pagewanted=all.

8. Folsom Prism Blues

101 *Loy Mauch, a Republican member of the Arkansas State House of Representatives, asked in a letter to the editor in the* Arkansas Democrat Gazette, *"If slavery were so God-awful":* Max Brantley, "Loy Mauch Update: The Republican Rep Is on Record on Slavery Too," *Arkansas Times,* October 6, 2012, http://www .arktimes.com/ArkansasBlog/archives/2012/10/06/loy-mauch-update-the -republican-rep-is-on-record-on-slavery-too.

101 *Terry England, a member of the Georgia State House of Representatives, compared women to farm animals:* Adam Peck, "Georgia Republican Compares Women to Cows, Pigs, And Chickens," *Think Progress,* March 12, 2012, http:// thinkprogress.org/health/2012/03/12/442637/georgia-rep-compares-women -to-animals/.

101–2 *I honestly think [homosexuality] is the biggest threat our nation has, even more so than terrorism:* Posted by I Want Democracy Now, "Oklahoma State Rep. Says Gays Biggest Threat to US," YouTube, March 11, 2008, http://www .youtube.com/watch?v=G_y3-ckuM3E.

102 *You know, I've done a lot of reading on this. I wish I could describe to you their behavior:* Kyle Mantyla, "Things That Make You Go 'Wow,'" *Right Wing Watch,* February 4, 2009, http://www.rightwingwatch.org/content/things-make-you -go-wow.

106 *Formed as a part-time venture in 1996 by long-time gay-basher Peter LaBarbera:* Evelyn Schlatter, "18 Anti-Gay Groups and Their Propaganda," Southern Poverty Law Center, http://www.splcenter.org/get-informed/intelligence -report/browse-all-issues/2010/winter/the-hard-liners.

107 *Would you want to sleep in the same bed where a homosexual orgy:* Peter LaBarbera, "AFTAH Writer Is Grossed Out by 'International Mr. Leather' Perversion-Fest Hosted by Hyatt Regency Chicago," *Americans for Truth About Homosexuality,* June 17, 2011, http://americansfortruth.com/issues/the-agenda -glbtq-activist-groups/gay-culture/homosexual-pride-parades-festivals /page/2/?googleb0t=true.

108 *LaBarbera's tongue hangs out as he details all of the various demos:* Joe Jervis, "Peter LaBarbera Hates Everybody Equally," *Joe.My.God.* (blog), February 6, 2009, http://joemygod.blogspot.com/2009/02/peter-labarbera-hates-everybody -equally.html.

108 *Straight people have anal sex too; in real numbers:* Noah Michelson, "Breaking: More Straight Americans Than Gay Americans Having 'Gay Sex,'" *The Huffington Post,* August 22, 2012, http://www.huffingtonpost.com/noah -michelson/gay-sex_b_1822137.html.

109 *Maybe it was the glowing feature about IML in the* Chicago Tribune *a few years ago:* Terry Wilson, "Leather Contest Seen as a Kind of Family Reunion," *Chicago Tribune,* May 22, 1998, http://articles.chicagotribune.com/1998-05-22 /features/9805220096_1_leather-community-contest-gay-community.

110 *Nothing screams 'Perversion!' like the annual Folsom Street Fair:* Peter LaBarbera, "Folsom Street Fair 2012 Poster Epitomizes San Francisco Homosexual Deviance and Folly of Liberal 'Tolerance,'" *Americans for Truth About Homosexuality,* August 13, 2012, http://americansfortruth.com/issues/folsom-street -fair-san-francisco/feed/.

110 *An Alabama minister who died in June of "accidental mechanical asphyxia" was found:* "Dead Reverend's Rubber Fetish: Autopsy: Pastor Found in Wet Suits After Autoerotic Mishap," *The Smoking Gun,* October 8, 2007, http://www .thesmokinggun.com/documents/crime/dead-reverends-rubber-fetish.

114 *Here's a Donohue classic: "Hollywood is controlled by secular Jews who hate Christianity":* "'Scarborough Country' for Dec. 8," MSNBC on NBC News, December 9, 2004, http://www.msnbc.msn.com/id/6685898/ns/msnbc-about _msnbc_tv/t/scarborough-country-dec/.

114 *Most 15-year-old teenage boys* **wouldn't allow themselves to be molested. So why did you?":** "Mark Foley Plays the Catholic Card," press release from the Catholic League for Religious and Civil Rights, October 4, 2006, http://media matters.org/research/2006/10/04/bill-donohue-to-foley-most-15-year-old -boys-wou/136833.

114 *Doing Donohue one better, Father Benedict Groeschel, of the conservative Franciscan Friars of the Renewal, told the* National Catholic Register: Annie-Rose Strasser, "Priest Blames Child Victims of Sex Abuse for Seducing Their Abusers," *Think Progress,* August 31, 2012, http://thinkprogress.org/politics /2012/08/31/785271/priest-blames-child-victims/.

116 *Last Sunday, homosexuals paraded around naked in the streets of San Francisco:* Bill Donohue, "Naked Gay Sadists Hit the Streets," Catholic League for Religious and Civil Rights, September 25, 2012, http://www.catholicleague .org/naked-gay-sadists-hit-the-streets/.

117 *This basic developmental system, one in which certain salient childhood events 'imprint' our psychosexuality:* Jesse Bering, "Oedipus Complex 2.0: Like It or Not, Parents Shape Their Children's Sexual Preferences," *Scientific American,* August 17, 2010, http://blogs.scientificamerican.com/bering-in-mind/2010/08 /17/oedipus-complex-2-0-like-it-or-not-parents-shape-their-childrens-sexual -preferences/.

118 [*The Passion*] *relies for its effect almost entirely on sadomasochistic male narcissism:* Christopher Hitchens, "Schlock, Yes; Awe, No; Fascism, Probably: The Flogging Mel Gibson Demands," *Slate,* February 27, 2004, http://www.slate .com/articles/news_and_politics/fighting_words/2004/02/schlock_yes_awe _no_fascism_probably.html.

9. The Straight Pride Parade

123 *The annual Halloween costume balls [were] run by the Mafia:* Eric Marcus, *Making Gay History: The Half-Century Fight for Lesbian and Gay Equal Rights* (New York: Harper, 2002).

124 *Americans spent 7 billion dollars on Halloween in 2011, and nearly 70 percent of adults now celebrate the holiday:* Martha C. White, "Now That's Creepy: Americans Will Blow $7 Billion on Halloween," Psychology of Money, *Time,* September 29, 2011, http://business.time.com/2011/09/29/now-thats-creepy -americans-will-blow-7-billion-on-halloween/.

125 *Daniels warns that Halloween . . . parties involve "sex with demons," "orgies," and "sacrificing babies.":* Kimberly Daniels, "The Danger of Celebrating Halloween," *Prophetic Insight* (blog), *Charisma Magazine,* October 27, 2009, http:// www.charismamag.com/blogs/prophetic-insight/7134-the-danger-of -celebrating-halloween.

125 *We all can see [that Halloween] is a huge celebration in the LGBT world, especially for the gender-confused folks. . . . The core of Halloween is glittering artificiality:* Linda Harvey, "Satan's Holiday: 10 Reasons to Fast from Halloween," WND.com, October 16, 2012, http://www.wnd.com/2012/10/10-reasons-to -fast-from-halloween/.

127 *When I see women dressed as sexualized fast-food sauces, I don't know whether to laugh or cry:* Amanda Hess, "Are Sexy Halloween Costumes Over?," *XX Factor* (blog), *Slate,* October 29, 2012, http://www.slate.com/blogs/xx_factor /2012/10/29/sexy_halloween_costumes_has_this_trend_come_to_an_end .html.

10. Four Closet Cases

134 *In May of 2005,* The Spokesman-Review *published a long story on West's secret double life:* Bill Morlin, "West Tied to Sex Abuse in '70s, Using Office to Lure Young Men: Allegations Shadow Politician Throughout His Career," *The Spokesman Review,* May 5, 2005, http://dlib.nyu.edu/undercover/west-tied-sex -abuse-70s-using-office-lure-young-men-bill-morlin-spokesman-review.

139 *Rekers was one of eight contributors to the* Handbook of Therapy for Unwanted Homosexual Attractions: Julie Harren Hamilton, PhD, Philip J. Henry, PhD, eds., *Handbook of Therapy for Unwanted Homosexual Attractions: A Guide to Treatment* (Maitland, FL: Xulon Press, 2009).

139 *The young man told reporters that he gave Rekers nude "sexual massages" during the trip:* CNN Wire Staff, "Anti-Gay Rights Activist Resigns After Trip with Male Escort," CNN, May 14, 2010, http://www.cnn.com/2010/US/05/12/anit .gay.activist.resigns/index.html.

11. Mistakes Were Made

147 *A new study casts doubt on whether true bisexuality exists, at least in men:* Benedict Carey, "Straight, Gay or Lying? Bisexuality Revisited," *The New York Times,* July 5, 2005, http://www.nytimes.com/2005/07/05/health/05sex.html ?pagewanted=all&_r=0.

150   *Three years later Mika told another interviewer that he had:* Instinct staff, "Exclusive Sneak Peek: Mika Tells Instinct, 'Yeah, I'm gay,'" *Instinct* magazine, August 3, 2012, http://instinctmagazine.com/blogs/blog/exclusive-sneak-peek-mika-tells -instinct-%E2%80%9Cyeah-i%E2%80%99m-gay-%E2%80%9D?directory=100011.

156   *Whenever, say, some prominent heterosexually married male public figure has a same-sex affair:* Tracy Clark-Flory, "The Invisible Bisexual Man," *Salon,* August 27, 2011, http://www.salon.com/2011/08/28/bisexuality_2/.

158   *However, I would be remiss to fail to acknowledge the fact that, on some level:* A. J. Walkley and Lauren Michelle Kinsey, "Bi the Bi: Are Closeted Bisexuals the Reason for Bi Invisibility?," *The Huffington Post,* December 28, 2012, http:// www.huffingtonpost.com/aj-walkley/bi-the-bi-are-closeted-bisexuals-the -reason-for-bi-invisibility_b_2365117.html.

159   *Some of the numbers that "Gary J. Gates, Williams Distinguished Scholar" came up with were disputed:* Gary J. Gates, "How Many People Are Lesbian, Gay, Bisexual and Transgender?," The Williams Institute, University of California, April, 2011, http://williamsinstitute.law.ucla.edu/research/census-lgbt -demographics-studies/how-many-people-are-lesbian-gay-bisexual-and -transgender/.

160   *In an unusual scientific about-face:* David Tuller, "No Surprise for Bisexual Men: Report Indicates They Exist," *The New York Times,* August 22, 2011, http:// www.nytimes.com/2011/08/23/health/23bisexual.html.

160   *Past research not finding bisexual genital arousal patterns among bisexual men may have been affected by recruitment techniques:* A. M. Rosenthal, "Sexual Arousal Patterns of Bisexual Men Revisited," *Biological Psychology,* September 2011, http://www.ncbi.nlm.nih.gov/pubmed/21763395.

12. On Being Different

163   *Miller came out in "What It Means to Be a Homosexual," which was published later that year in book form as* On Being Different: Merle Miller, *On Being Different: What It Means to Be a Homosexual* (New York: Penguin, 2012).

169   *Somewheres in Des Moines or San Antonio there is a young gay person who all of a sudden realizes:* Richard Metzger, "Christian Hate Group Protests 'Harvey Milk Day' in California," *Dangerous Minds,* May 19, 2011, http://dangerous -minds.net/comments/christian_hate_group_protests_harvey_milk_day_in _california.

172   *In the battle between reality and fundamentalism of all varieties:* Andrew Sullivan, "A Lot Better," *The Dish* (blog), October 10, 2012, dish.andrewsullivan .com/2012/10/10/better.

13. Extended Stay

175   *The purpose of a "democratic society," Connelly argued, was to "safeguard and enhance life":* Joel Connelly, "Assisted Suicide Gets Push from out of State," *Seattle Post-Intelligencer,* July 27, 2008, http://www.seattlepi.com/local /connelly/article/Assisted-suicide-gets-push-from-out-of-state-1280453.php.

182   *A total of 255 terminally ill adults have ended their lives with the assistance of a physician since the law came into force in 2009:* "Death with Dignity Data,"

2011 Death with Dignity Act Report, Washington State Department of Health, http://www.doh.wa.gov/DataandStatisticalReports/VitalStatisticsData /DeathwithDignityData.aspx.

183 **Death with dignity is not incompatible with palliative care, and data show that 90 percent of Oregon patients:** Lewis M. Cohen, "Massachusetts Vote May Change How the Nation Dies: Why It Matters That Death with Dignity Is Poised to Become the New Norm," Health and Medicine Explained, *Slate,* October 29, 2012, http://www.slate.com/articles/health_and_science/medical _examiner/2012/10/massachusetts_death_with_dignity_2012_kevorkian _and_humphry_started_the.html.

14. Rick and Me

186 **Rick Santorum would very much like to be president:** Stephanie Mencimer, "Rick Santorum's Anal Sex Problem," *Mother Jones,* September/October 2010, http://www.motherjones.com/politics/2010/08/rick-santorum-google -problem-dan-savage.

187 **It would be among the first 'Google bombs' in the modern political era:** Steve Peoples, "Santorum Talks About Longtime Google Problem," *Roll Call,* February 16, 2011, http://www.rollcall.com/issues/56_84/-203455-1.html.

189 **In what has been a long-running burden for Mr. Santorum:** Noam Cohen, "A Leader in Iowa, Santorum Still Has Trouble Online," *Media Decoder* (blog), *The New York Times,* January 4, 2012, http://mediadecoder.blogs.nytimes.com /2012/01/04/a-leader-in-iowa-santorum-still-has-trouble-online/.

190 **Dan Savage has a santorum problem. Yes, santorum with a small s:** Mark Judge, "With Dan Savage, It Doesn't Get Better," *Real Clear Religion,* January 7, 2012, http://www.realclearreligion.org/articles/2012/01/07/with_dan_savage _it_doesnt_get_better.html.

190 **I believe that marriage is the union between a man and a woman:** Barack Obama, Saddleback Presidential Forum, April 17, 2008, http://www.politico .com/news/stories/0512/76109_Page2.html.

191 **The largest defeat by a Republican United States senator seeking election or re-election in modern Pennsylvania history:** Julie Hirschfeld Davis, "Santorum's Electability Pitch Undermined by 2006 Senate Re-Election Loss," Bloomberg News, February 14, 2012, http://www.bloomberg.com/news/2012-02-14 /santorum-pitch-undermined-by-senate-loss.html.

191 **In April of 2003, Santorum, then a senator from Pennsylvania, sat for an interview with:** Andrew Marantz, "Bombs Away," *The New Yorker,* January 16, 2012, http://www.newyorker.com/talk/2012/01/16/120116ta_talk_marantz.

194–95 **Griswold,** Salon's Irin Carmon points out, "struck down a ban on discussing or providing contraception to married couples:** Irin Carmon, "Rick Santorum Is Coming for Your Birth Control," *Salon,* January 4, 2012, http://www .salon.com/2012/01/04/rick_santorum_is_coming_for_your_birth_control/.

198 **It is tough, after all, being a young surrogate for a candidate and father clinging to an older worldview:** Elise Foley, "Rick Santorum Saves Cash, Gains a Surrogate, By Turning to Daughter," *The Huffington Post,* January 2, 2012, http://www .huffingtonpost.com/2012/01/02/rick-santorum-daughter_n_1179470.html.

200 **Sen. Rick Santorum may have lost the presidential primaries in Arizona and**

Michigan: Ian Sherr and Geoffrey A. Fowler, "Rick Santorum's Google Problem Subsides," *The Wall Street Journal,* February 29, 2012, http://blogs.wsj.com /digits/2012/02/29/rick-santorums-google-problem-subsides/.

200 **Rick Santorum's presidential campaign says his 'Google problem' has been solved:** Alex Pappas, "Santorum Campaign Says 'Google Problem' Has Been Solved," *The Daily Caller,* May 23, 2012, http://dailycaller.com/2012/03/23 /santorum-campaign-says-google-problem-has-been-solved/.

15. Still Evil. Less Evil. But Still Evil.

204 *In November of 2010, the pope weighed in on the debate, calling health care an "inalieanable right,":* Sarah Delaney, "Pope, Church Leaders Call for Guaranteed Health Care for All People," Catholic News Service, November 18, 2010, http://www.catholicnews.com/data/stories/cns/1004736.htm.

205 *The United States is the only major nation in the industrialized world that does not guarantee health care as a right to its people:* Senator Bernie Sanders, "Single Payer Health: It's Only Fair," *The Health Care Blog,* May 19, 2011, http:// thehealthcareblog.com/blog/tag/bernie-sanders/.

206 *As a general rule, societies that do the most to support mothers and childbearing have the fewest abortions:* David Frum, "Let's Get Real About Abortions," *CNN Opinion,* CNN, October 29, 2012, http://www.cnn.com/2012/10/29 /opinion/frum-abortion-reality/index.html.

207 *All, and I mean all, the evidence says that public systems like Medicare and Medicaid, which have less bureaucracy than private insurers:* Paul Krugman, "The Medicare Killers," *Opinion, The New York Times,* August 30, 2012, http:// www.nytimes.com/2012/08/31/opinion/Krugman.html?_r=0.

209 *The core drivers of the [PPACA] are market principles formulated by conservative economists:* J. D. Kleinke, "The Conservative Case for Obamacare," *Opinion, The New York Times,* September 29, 2012, http://www.nytimes.com /2012/09/30/opinion/sunday/why-obamacare-is-a-conservatives-dream .html?_r=1&.

209 *[DeMint] is, arguably, the perfect candidate to run a post-thought think tank:* Dana Milbank, "Come to Think of It, Jim DeMint and the Heritage Foundation Make Sense," *Opinions, The Washington Post,* December 7, 2012, http://articles .washingtonpost.com/2012-12-07/opinions/35673422_1_heritage-foundation -education-policy-president-obama.

210 *That's what* Mitt Romney *said in 2006 . . . when he described the individual mandate in his health care bill:* "Individual Health Care Insurance Mandate Has Roots Two Decades Long," Politics, Fox News, June 28, 2012, http://www .foxnews.com/politics/2012/06/28/individual-health-care-insurance -mandate-has-long-checkered-past/.

211 *People have access to health care in America. . . . After all, you just go to an emergency room:* Rachel Weiner, "Romney: Uninsured Have Emergency Rooms," *Post Politics* (blog), *The Washington Post,* September 24, 2012, http:// www.washingtonpost.com/blogs/post-politics/wp/2012/09/24/romney-calls -emergency-room-a-health-care-option-for-uninsured/.

211 *Five years later Mitt Romney would make the same claim: "We do provide care for people who don't have insurance":* Ibid.

211   *An estimated 44,789 Americans were dying* every year *for lack of health insurance:* Physicians for a National Health Program, "Harvard Study Finds Nearly 45,000 Excess Deaths Annually Linked to Lack of Health Coverage," pnhp.org, September 17, 2009, http://www.pnhp.org/news/2009/september/harvard _study_finds_.php.

212   *We don't have a setting across this country where if you don't have insurance:* Avik Roy, "Why Health Insurance Is Not the Same Thing as Health Care," *The Apothecary* (blog), *Forbes,* October 15, 2012, http://www.forbes.com/sites /aroy/2012/10/15/why-health-insurance-is-not-the-same-thing-as-health-care/.

212   *Lack of health insurance might have led or contributed to nearly 17,000 deaths among hospitalized children in the United States:* Ekaterina Pesheva, "Lack of Insurance May Have Figured in Nearly 17,000 Childhood Deaths, Study Shows," press release from Johns Hopkins Children's Center, October 29, 2009, http://www.hopkinschildrens.org/lack-of-insurance-may-have-figured-in -nearly-17000-childhood-deaths.aspx.

213   *Twelve-year-old Deamonte Driver died of a toothache Sunday:* Mary Otto, "For Want of a Dentist," *The Washington Post,* February 28, 2007, http://www .washingtonpost.com/wp-dyn/content/article/2007/02/27/AR2007022702116 .html.

214   *"You guys are evil," Bieber said:* Vanessa Grigoriadis, "The Adventures of Super Boy," *Rolling Stone,* March 3, 2011, http://www.rollingstone.com/music/news /justin-bieber-talks-sex-politics-music-and-puberty-in-new-rolling-stone -cover-story-20110216#ixzz2Ez30Cyh3.

214   *Rather than simply providing health insurance to everyone by extending Medicare to cover the whole population:* Paul Krugman, "The Big Deal," *The New York Times,* January 20, 2013, http://www.nytimes.com/2013/01/21 /opinion/krugman-the-big-deal.html?_r=0.

215   *And we will still be reading headlines like this one from the Associated Press:* Associated Press, "Bartenders Rally to Help Famous Seattle Barman," *The Wenatchee World,* November 1, 2012, http://www.wenatcheeworld.com /news/2012/nov/01/bartenders-rally-to-help-famous-seattle-barman/.

217   *Unless you're a Warren Buffett or Bill Gates, you're one illness away from financial ruin:* Theresa Tamkins, "Medical Bills Prompt More Than 60 Percent of U.S. Bankruptcies," *CNN Health,* June 5, 2009, http://articles.cnn.com/2009 -06-05/health/bankruptcy.medical.bills_1_medical-bills-bankruptcies -health-insurance?_s=PM:HEALTH.

220   *"We have to do that," Liautaud said on Fox News in October of 2012:* Neil Cavuto, "Jimmy John's Founder: Business Owners Unsure of the Future," Fox News, October 15, 2012, http://www.foxnews.com/on-air/your-world -cavuto/2012/10/16/jimmy-johns-founder-business-owners-unsure-future.

221   *Not that you guys don't have a legitimate gripe against this president. If Obama had fought harder for single-payer health care:* Jon Stewart, "Post-Democalyptic World—Whine Country—Employee Benefits: Lacking Good Outsourcing Options, the Pizza and Coal Industries Cut Employee Benefits and Blame Obamacare," *The Daily Show with Jon Stewart,* November 13, 2012, http://www.thedailyshow.com/watch/tue-november-13-2012/post -democalyptic-world—whine-country—employee-benefits.

221   *Caleb Melby of* Forbes *has graciously done the math on Obamacare's cost to*

Papa John's: Jillian Berman, "Papa John's Obamacare Costs Are Far Less Than Price of Free Pizza Giveaway," *The Huffington Post,* November 13, 2012, http://www.huffingtonpost.com/2012/11/13/papa-johns-obamacare_n_2123207.html.

223   *Many, many, many Christians were praying and we really need to address that issue:* James Dobson, "A Battle Cry to Defend America," *Dr. James Dobson's Family Talk,* November 16, 2012, http://www.drjamesdobson.org/Broadcasts/Broadcast?i=3be080bb-977f-475f-962f-9600ea4eb65c.

224   *He later maintained that Obama's reelection is proof that we Americans have "turned our back on God":* Meredith Bennett-Smith, "Evangelist Franklin Graham Claims 'Complete Economic Collapse' May Be Needed to Fix America (video)," *The Huffington Post,* November 19, 2012, http://www.huffingtonpost.com/2012/11/19/evangelist-franklin-graham-complete-economic-collapse-needed_n_2160769.html.

224   *There was the day the letter arrived from the insurance company, saying that our daughter's lifetime cap had been lifted:* Ezra Klein, "The Night Democrats Reclaimed 'Obamacare,'" *The Washington Post,* September 4, 2012, http://www.washingtonpost.com/blogs/wonkblog/wp/2012/09/04/the-night-democrats-reclaimed-obamacare/.

16. It's Happened Again

234   *Most of us in America, including gun owners, agree on things that would stop the kind of carnage:* Cory Booker, *This Week with George Stephanopoulos,* ABC News, December 23, 2012, http://abcnews.go.com/m/blogEntry?id=18050508&sid=77&cid=77.

236   *Historians are often asked what the Founders would think about various aspects of contemporary life:* Jill Lepore, "The Lost Amendment," *The New Yorker,* April 19, 2012, http://www.newyorker.com/online/blogs/newsdesk/2012/04/the-second-amendment.html.

236–37   *If roads were collapsing all across the United States, killing dozens of drivers:* Ezra Klein, "Twelve Facts About Guns and Mass Shootings in the United States," *The Washington Post,* December 14, 2012, http://www.washingtonpost.com/blogs/wonkblog/wp/2012/12/14/nine-facts-about-guns-and-mass-shootings-in-the-united-states/.

237   *Vice President Biden "is seriously considering measures backed by key law enforcement leaders":* Philip Rucker, "White House Weighs Broad Gun-Control Agenda in Wake of Newtown Shootings," *The Washington Post,* January 5, 2013, http://articles.washingtonpost.com/2013-01-05/politics/36208875_1_gun-issue-brady-campaign-assault-weapons-ban.

17. Bigot Christmas

240   *NOM, like the Family Research Council and Americans for Truth About Homosexuality:* Evelyn Schlatter, "18 Anti-Gay Groups and Their Propaganda," Southern Poverty Law Center, http://www.splcenter.org/get-informed/intelligence-report/browse-all-issues/2010/winter/the-hard-liners.

240   *Suppose you were interested in promoting children's well-being, and in particular, in addressing the problem of fatherlessness:* John Corvino and Maggie Gallagher, *Debating Same-Sex Marriage* (New York: Oxford, 2012), 57–58.

241   *In a blowjob in* The Washington Post—*excuse me, in a profile:* Monica Hesse, "Profile of Brian Brown, Executive Director of the National Organization for Marriage," *The Washington Post,* August 28, 2009, http://www.washingtonpost .com/wp-dyn/content/article/2009/08/27/AR2009082704139_2.html.

242   *Under Brown's leadership, NOM has linked—or has attempted to link— marriage rights for same-sex couples to child rape and crafted a plan:* Lila Shapiro, "Same-Sex Marriage Debate: Racially Divisive NOM Memos Stir Controversy," *The Huffington Post,* March 31, 2012, http://www.huffingtonpost .com/2012/03/31/same-sex-marriage-debate_n_1392668.html.

242   *NOM under Brown has skirted campaign finance disclosure laws, misrepresented attendance at their rallies:* Scott Wooledge, "NOM Steals Image from Obama Rally," *Daily Kos,* October 25, 2011, http://www.dailykos.com /story/2011/10/25/1030072/-NOM-Steals-Image-From-Obama-Rally#.

248   *Bullying is the strong picking on the weak, not the other way around:* J.F., "Christians, Gays and Bullying: A Race to Take Umbrage," *The Economist,* May 1, 2012, http://www.economist.com/blogs/democracyinamerica/2012/05 /christians-gays-and-bullying.

249   *The pope recently said that gay marriage is a threat to the survival of the human race:* Posted by AmericansForTruthAH, "Savaging the Pope!," YouTube, May 1, 2012, http://www.youtube.com/watch?v=Chco0JkpL_A.

251   *My friend and colleague Dominic Holden did a story for* The Stranger: Dominic Holden, "'Why Do You Hate Me?': What Happens When a Faggot Asks People Who Gave Time and Money to Support Anti-Gay Referendum 71 the Most Basic Question?," *The Stranger,* September 3, 2009, http://www.thestranger .com/seattle/why-do-you-hate-me/Content?oid=2156227.

255   *It is full of interest. It has noble poetry in it; and some clever fables:* "Mark Twain quotations—Bible," *Twain Quotes,* http://www.twainquotes.com/Bible .html.

257   *Baptist minister Louie Giglio was invited to give the benediction at Barack Obama's second inauguration:* Natalie Jennings, "Louie Giglio Pulls out of Inauguration over Anti-Gay Comments," *The Washington Post,* January 10, 2013, http://www.washingtonpost.com/blogs/post-politics/wp/2013/01/10/louie -giglio-pulls-out-of-inaugural-over-anti-gay-comments/.

258–59   *In December of 2012, the pope granted an audience to Rebecca Kadaga, the Ugandan lawmaker:* Dan Avery, "Pope Blessed Rebecca Kadaga, Who Promises to Pass Uganda's 'Kill The Gays' Bill," *Queerty,* December 14, 2012, http:// www.queerty.com/pope-blessed-rebecca-kadaga-who-promises-to-pass -ugandas-kill-the-gays-b-20121214/.

267   *It is a routine lie of Christian apologetics that slavery in the Roman imperial period:* Don M. Burrows, "Brian Brown's Slavery Lie," *Nota Bene,* August 30, 2012, http://www.donmburrows.com/2012/08/brian-browns-slavery-lie .html.

268   *Slaveholding theologians had little trouble in demonstrating that the Bible did sanction slavery:* Elizabeth Fox-Genovese and Eugene D. Genovese, "The Divine Sanction of Social Order: Religious Foundations of the Southern Slaveholders' World View," *Journal of the American Academy of Religion* 55, no. 2 (1987): 211–34, http://jaar.oxfordjournals.org/content/LV/2/211.full.pdf+html ?sid=1f23355b-9171-40ed-a1d0-46dc063902b2.

271   *An unbroken series of polls showed that a majority of Americans now supported marriage equality:* Sara Gates, "Gay Marriage Support: 51 Percent of Americans Are in Favor of Marriage Equality, Poll Shows," *The Huffington Post,* November 14, 2012, http://www.huffingtonpost.com/2012/11/14/gay-marriage-support -majority-americans-poll_n_2130371.html.

271   *As of this writing, the Supreme Court has taken up two cases challenging bans on gay marriage:* "Editorial: Supreme Court Can't Stop Marriage Equality," *The MetroWest Daily News,* December 16, 2012, http://www.metrowestdailynews .com/opinions/editorials/x719506777/Editorial-Supreme-Court-can-t-stop -marriage-equality.

272   *According to the commenters on YouTube and at* The New York Times, *I won the debate:* Mark Oppenheimer, "After Dinner, the Fireworks," *The New York Times,* August 22, 2012, http://www.nytimes.com/2012/08/23/garden/dan -savage-and-brian-brown-debate-gay-marriage-over-the-dinner-table.html ?_r=0.

274   *A viewer of* The 700 Club *recently put this question to Pat Robertson: "If America was founded as a Christian nation, why did we allow slavery?":* Brian Tashman, "Pat Robertson: Ignore What the Bible Says About Slavery," *Right Wing Watch,* July 9, 2012, http://www.rightwingwatch.org/content/pat -robertson-ignore-what-bible-says-about-slavery.

Permissions

About the Author

Dan Savage is the author of the syndicated column Savage Love, now also an iPhone app, and the editorial director of *The Stranger,* Seattle's weekly newspaper. In addition to his frequent appearances on CNN, MSNBC, *Real Time with Bill Maher,* and *The Colbert Report,* Savage is a regular contributor to public radio's *This American Life.* He is the author of *Savage Love: Straight Answers from America's Most Popular Sex Columnist; The Kid: What Happened After My Boyfriend and I Decided to Go Get Pregnant; Skipping Towards Gomorrah: The Seven Deadly Sins and the Pursuit of Happiness in America*; and *The Commitment: Love, Sex, Marriage, and My Family.* In September 2010, Dan Savage and his husband, Terry Miller, created the It Gets Better Project. Dan and Terry created the first *It Gets Better* video. Savage lives in Seattle, Washington, with his husband, Terry, and their son, D.J.